IMAGES
of America

PEPPERELL

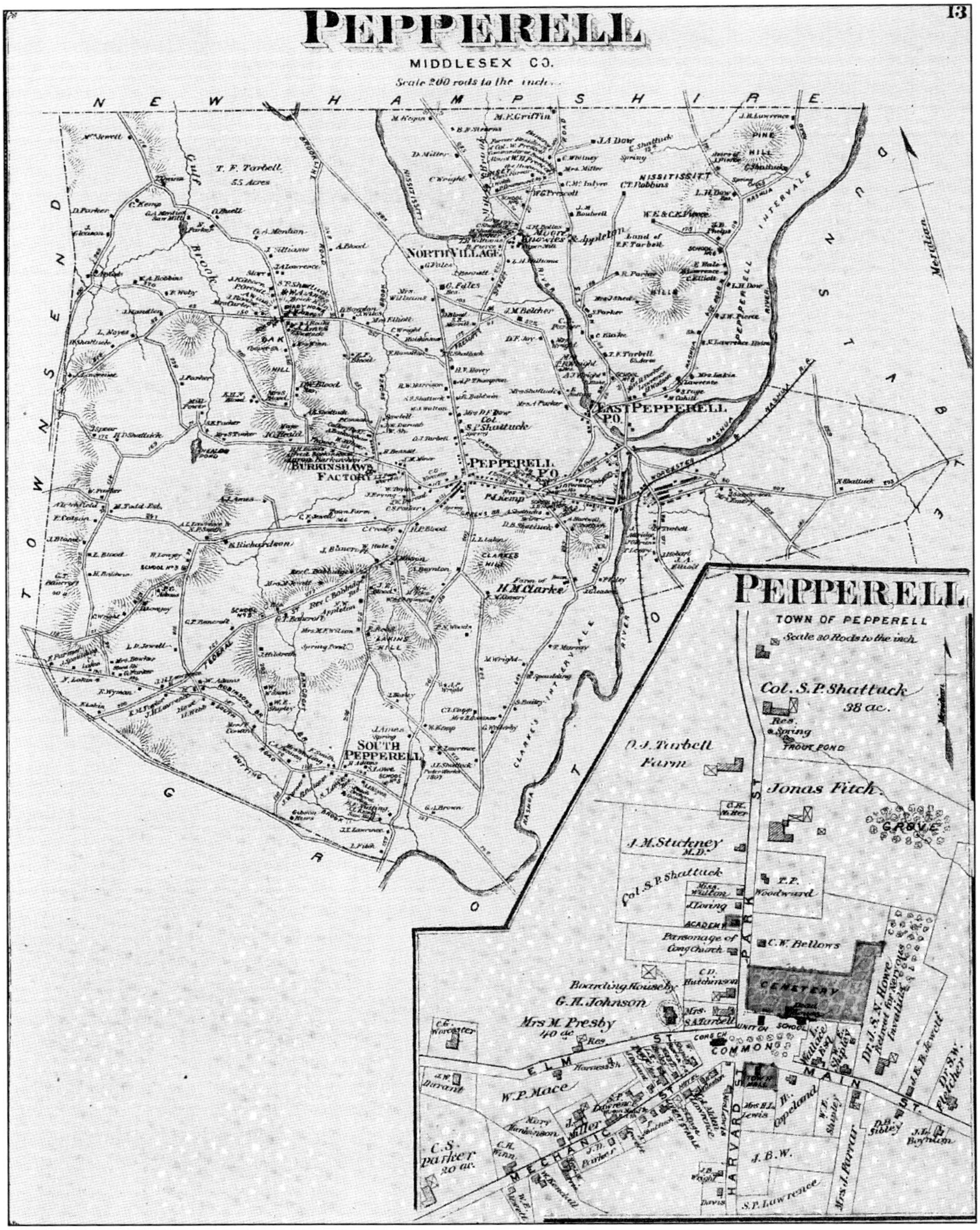

This 1844 map shows Pepperell at a time when industry was building and the town was growing at a steady pace. Stagecoach lines crisscrossed the town, and Pepperell was at its peak agriculturally.

IMAGES
of America

PEPPERELL

Joanne Saunders Foley

ARCADIA
PUBLISHING

ISBN 978-0-7385-8728-8

Published by Arcadia Publishing
Charleston, South Carolina

Printed in the United States of America

Library of Congress Catalog Card Number: Applied for

For all general information contact Arcadia Publishing at:
Telephone 843-853-2070
Fax 843-853-0044
E-mail sales@arcadiapublishing.com
For customer service and orders:
Toll-Free 1-888-313-2665

Visit us on the Internet at www.arcadiapublishing.com

To the people of Pepperell, with the hope that they will enjoy a trip back into the past.

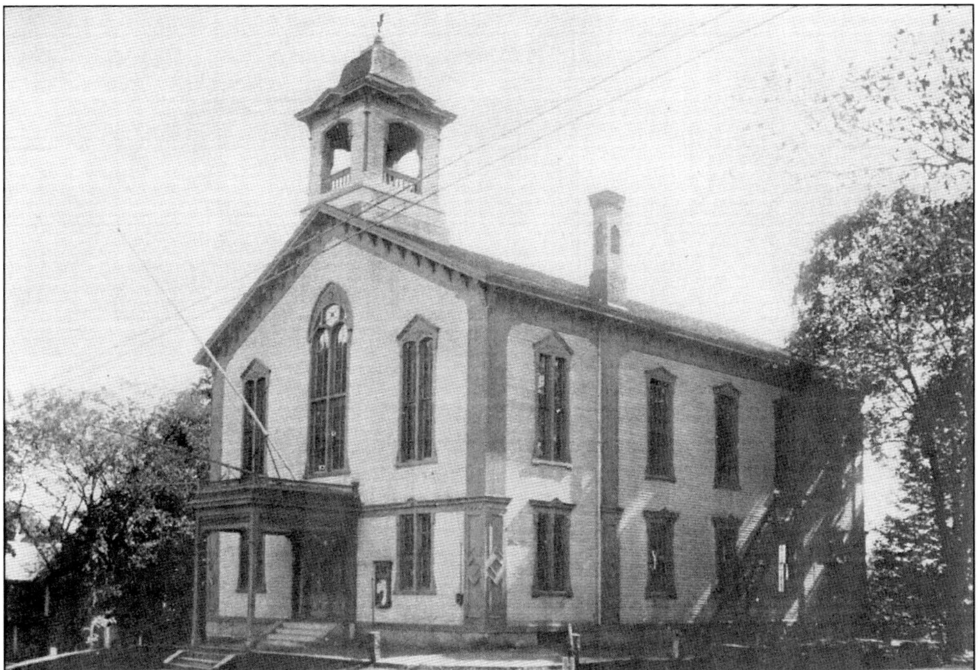

Pepperell's present town hall was erected in 1873 at the corner of Main and Elm Streets and served as a meeting place for many social functions, as well as a center of town business. An earlier town hall had been located on the same spot, as had a general store business and a schoolhouse before it.

Contents

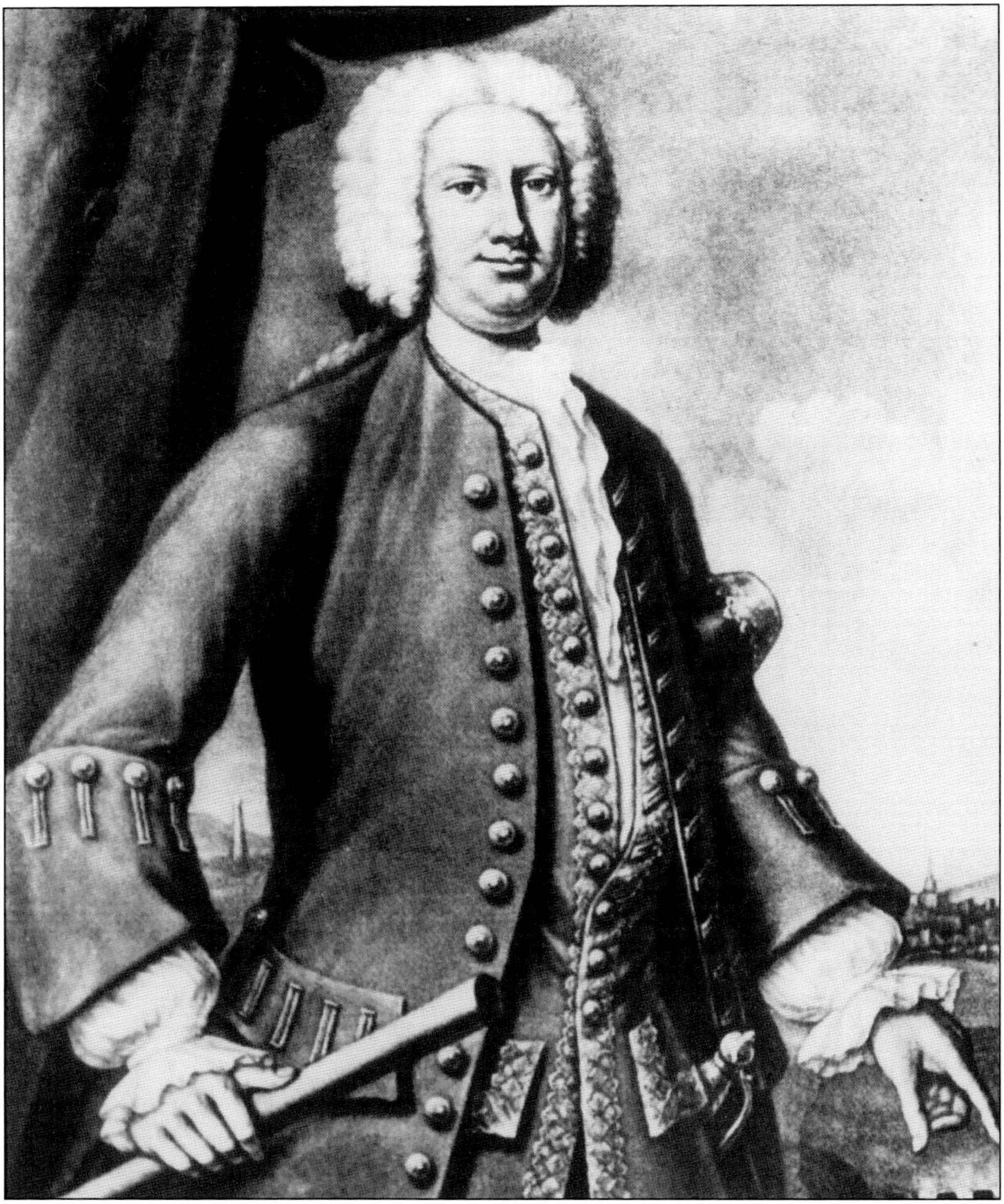

In 1753, when Pepperell became a district, or township, its first minister, Reverend Joseph Emerson, persuaded citizens to name the town after Sir William Pepperrell of Kittery, Maine, who led the colonial forces at the Louisburg Expedition in 1745.

Introduction

As early as 1655 settlers came to Pepperell, attracted by the Nashua River, where they could hunt and fish, and the open land, which was suited to raising crops. The river could be crossed at several fords, and settlers continued to move as far west as Heald Street. An early settler who lived on Park Street was known as "Canada John," as at that time only wilderness stretched between his home and Canada. By 1720 troubles with the Indians were largely over and settlement west of the river grew. People began to feel it was too far for them to attend church in Groton and in a petition granted in 1742 by the general court, the area today recognized as Pepperell became known as Groton West Parish. In April of 1753, Groton West Parish was made a district or township. At the encouragement of its first minister, the town was named for Sir William Pepperrell of Kittery, Maine, hero of the Louisburg Expedition in 1745. Pleased with this honor, Sir William arranged to have a bell cast in England and sent to the town. Although the bell reportedly made it to Boston, for some unknown reason it never arrived in Pepperell.

Pepperell was a patriotic community supplying many brave men to the early wars and contributing more than its share toward the defense of the country. Reportedly tea was burned on the common in 1774, and soon after Pepperell was the first town to fly the nation's "Liberty Flag." From Pepperell came Colonel William Prescott, hero of the Battle of Bunker Hill, and Colonel Edward F. Jones, leader of the 6th Massachusetts Volunteer Militia in the Civil War. The town had the honor of furnishing the first chaplain for the Revolutionary War and the Civil War as well. Prudence Wright and her followers will remain in our memory for their brave capture of treasonous Tories at Jewett's Bridge.

From its earliest beginnings, Pepperell was an industrious town. Its first "industries" were farming, fruit production, and cooperage. Due to the easy access to water power from the Nashua and Nissitissit Rivers, many mills began to spring up along the town's shores. The first mill privilege was granted in 1726 at Babbitassett Falls and from there began a long-lived paper industry which became the lifeblood of the town. The year 1836 marked the beginning of machine paper manufacturing in Pepperell, and as the business grew so did the town. Shoe manufacturing came into its own by the 1870s and flourished for a period of thirty years, at one time providing employment for over five hundred people. However, devastating fires caused financial crises, and the prosperous shoe-making era came to an end.

By 1831 Pepperell had five taverns that served as relay stations for the stagecoach lines that crisscrossed the town. The principal route was over the "Great Road" between Boston and

Keene, with a regular stop at the Artemus Hemenway Tavern. Fifteen thousand passengers were transported via stagecoach on this route in 1831. A second means of transportation became available in the 1890s as the railroad extended its operation through town, allowing people to become more mobile and providing a faster and more effective way to sell perishable farm products in the cities. As Pepperell prospered in the last half of the century, new homes and churches were built, orchards were planted, townspeople celebrated with parades and outings, and the Babbatassett Driving Park became a popular place for many to watch horses race.

There are many fascinating old stories and legends that make up Pepperell's history. The photographs in this book have been selected to illustrate that unique and colorful past, and have been gathered with the hope that they will be a source of enjoyment to all who read the book.

One

Around Town

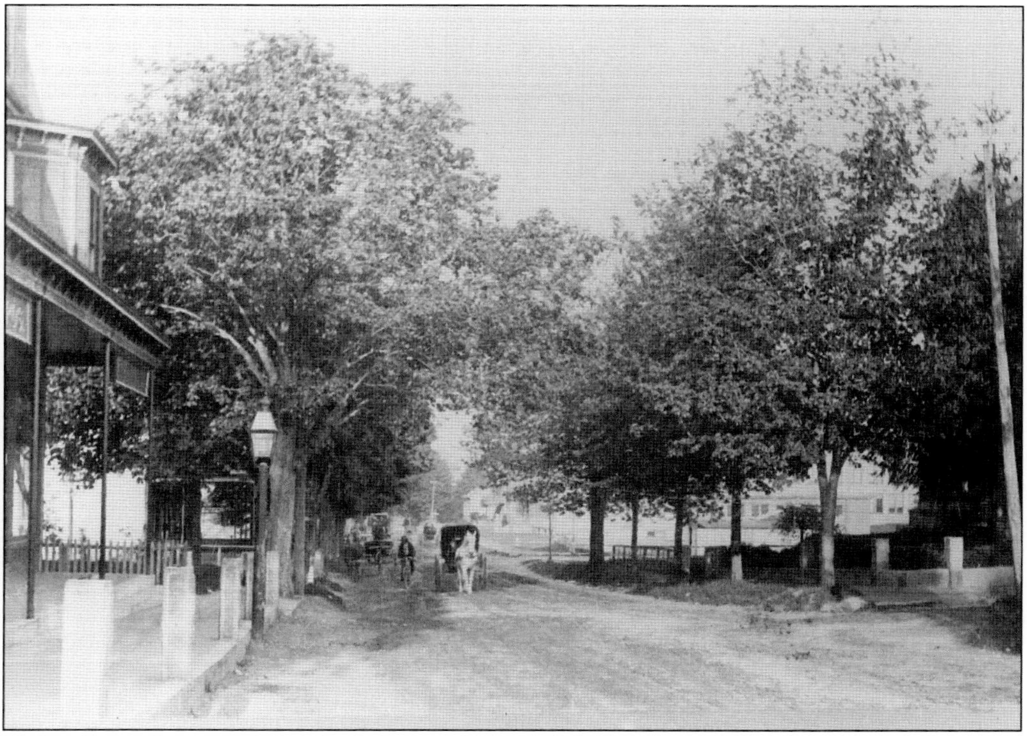

Horse-driven buggies and bicycles travel side by side up Main Street. This image, captured before the advent of telephone poles, was taken from Davis Street looking east. At the right of the photograph you can catch a glimpse of the Leighton Shoe Factory beneath the trees.

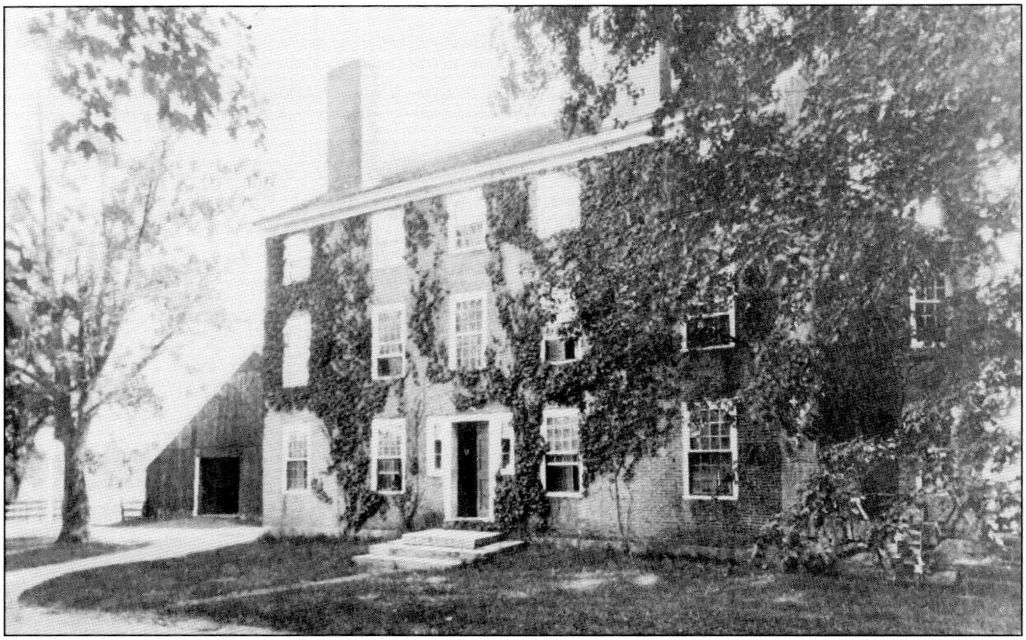

Pepperell was known as a stage route tavern center and had five taverns, each with a public hall and stables from which relays of horses supplied the stages. The old Artemus Hemenway Tavern was located on South Road, or "Great Road," and was perhaps the best-known tavern in town. It was on the principal stagecoach line between Boston and Keene, which reportedly transported fifteen thousand passengers in 1831.

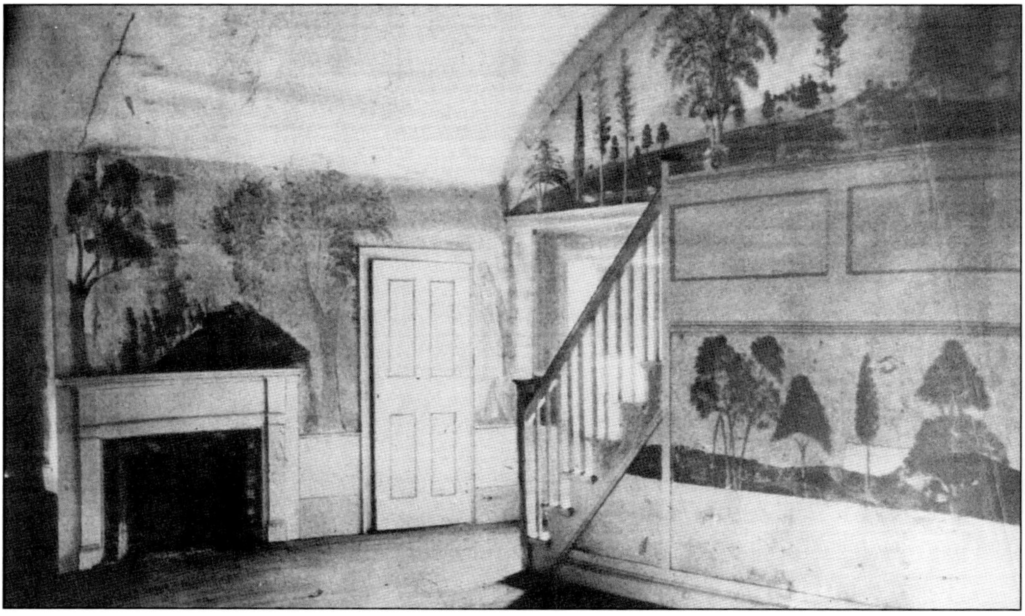

Thought to be built about 1812, the three-story tavern has a ballroom on the third floor that extends the length of the house. To the right of the picture are stairs leading up to a small stage where musicians sat during dances held there. Murals covering the walls have been attributed to a number of different artists, one of whom was Rufus Porter, who reportedly painted Pepperell Common in 1820–24.

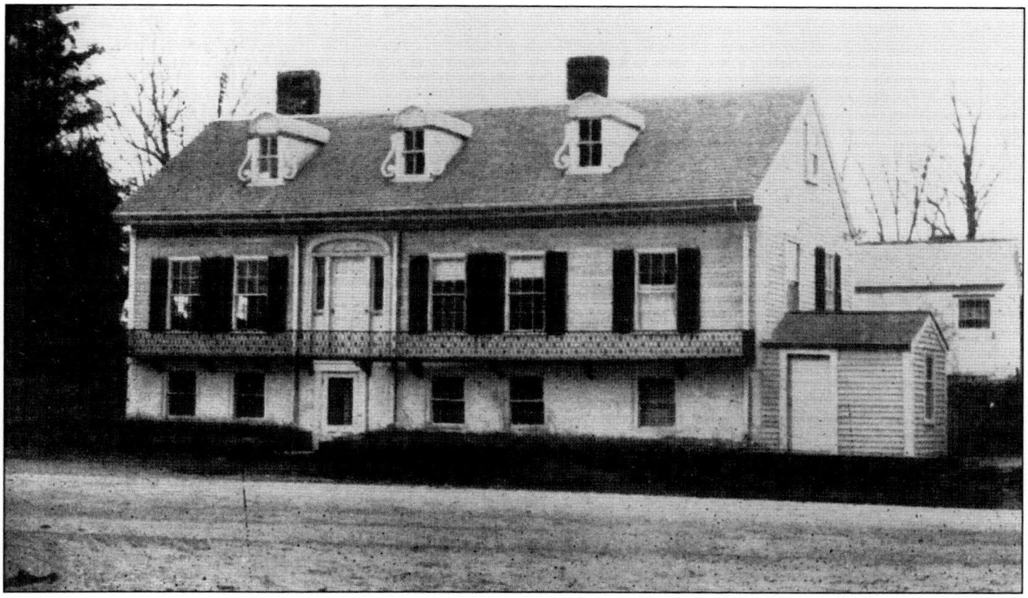

The Harvey Tileston house is located at Pepperell Center and is one of the town's most unusual houses. The structure was built about 1770 as a one-story house, but as the road was changed a basement was added. It was once used as a tavern where many enjoyed refreshment between long sermons at the church next door. The iron balcony and grillwork was added to the house by an early owner in hopes that his Southern-born wife would feel more at home in a house of a more familiar style. Today this is the home of Sarah Bosley.

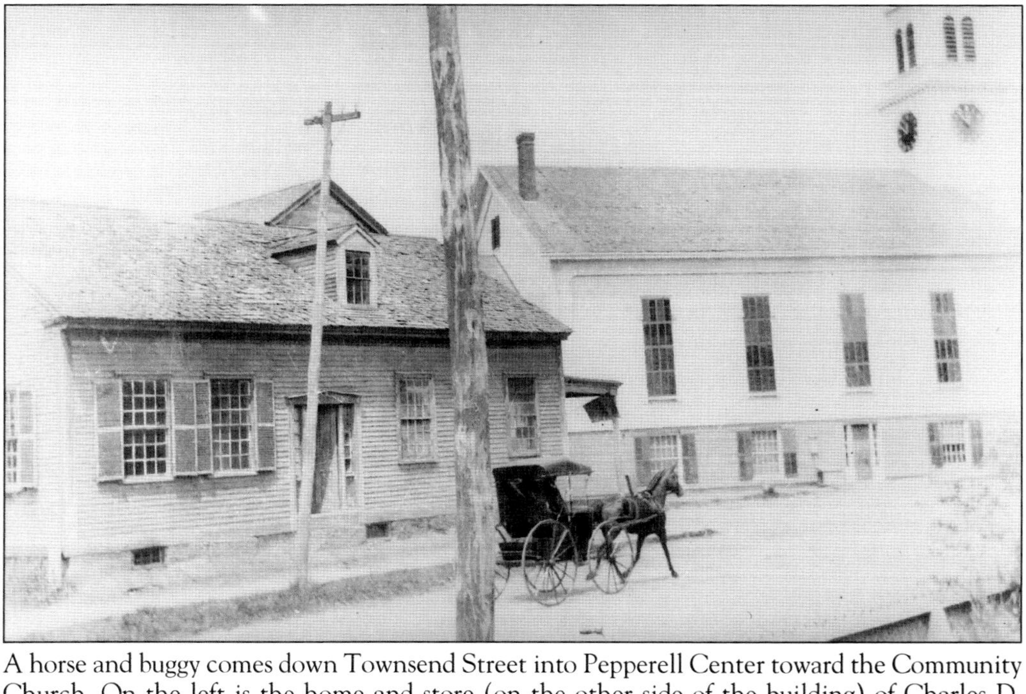

A horse and buggy comes down Townsend Street into Pepperell Center toward the Community Church. On the left is the home and store (on the other side of the building) of Charles D. Hutchinson, who carried on business there for thirty-five years.

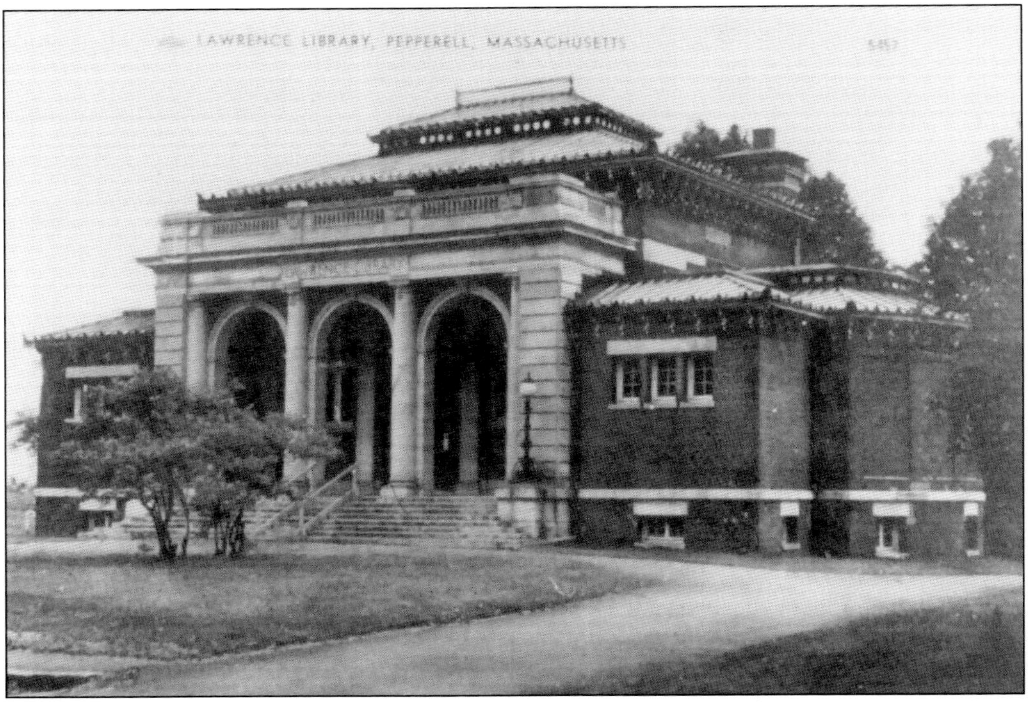

The public library was established in 1877. With the generous gift of $100,000 from Charles F. Lawrence in 1901, the Lawrence Library was built at a total cost of about $75,000, which included land, the building, and furnishings. The gift also included a total of twenty thousand books.

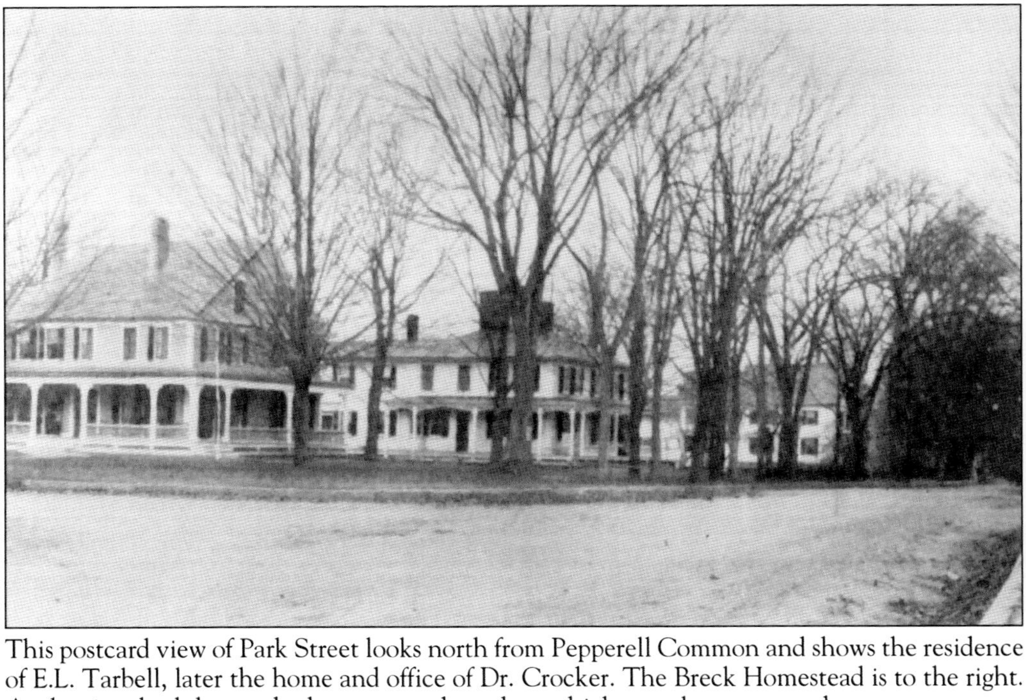

This postcard view of Park Street looks north from Pepperell Common and shows the residence of E.L. Tarbell, later the home and office of Dr. Crocker. The Breck Homestead is to the right. At the time both houses had wraparound porches, which were later removed.

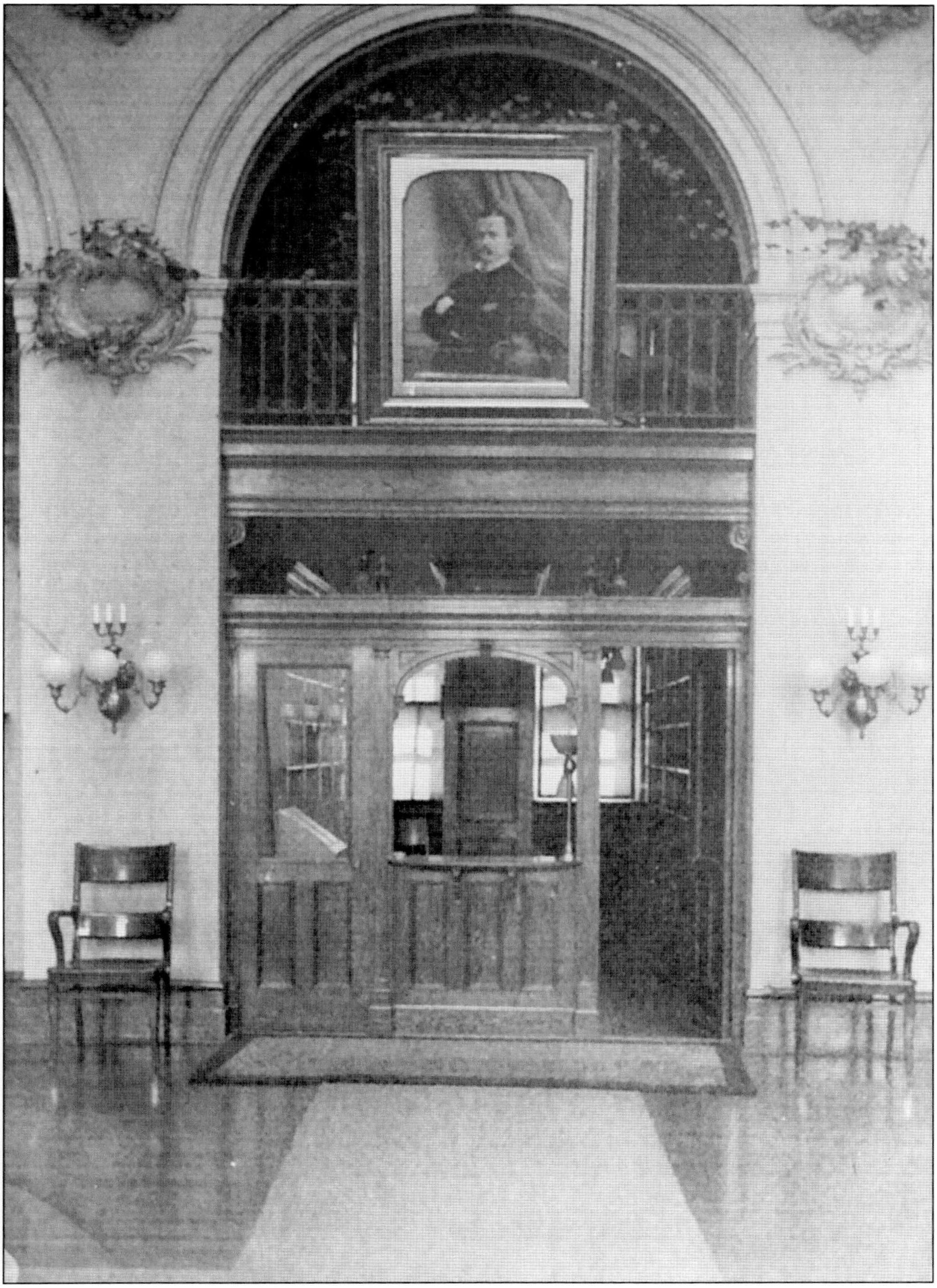

Years ago people coming to the Lawrence Library were greeted by this view as they came in the front door. The librarian sat behind the paneled desk directly ahead with a large painting of the library's benefactor looking down from above.

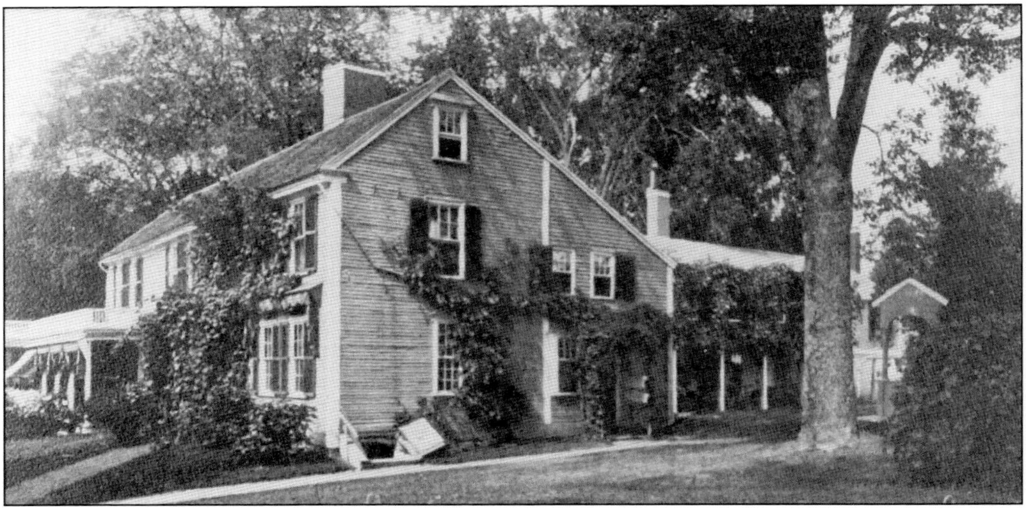

The Colonel William Prescott house was built in North Pepperell about 1749 on land that stretched from the Nissitissit River to the New Hampshire border. It sat at the edge of a once-busy and prosperous village, and was the scene of many social gatherings and visits from distinguished guests. Audubon came to the house to study his birds, and Colonel Prescott's nephew, historian William Hickling Prescott, spent many hours working on his writings here. A secret room in the house was used to hide slaves until they could be transported safely to Canada.

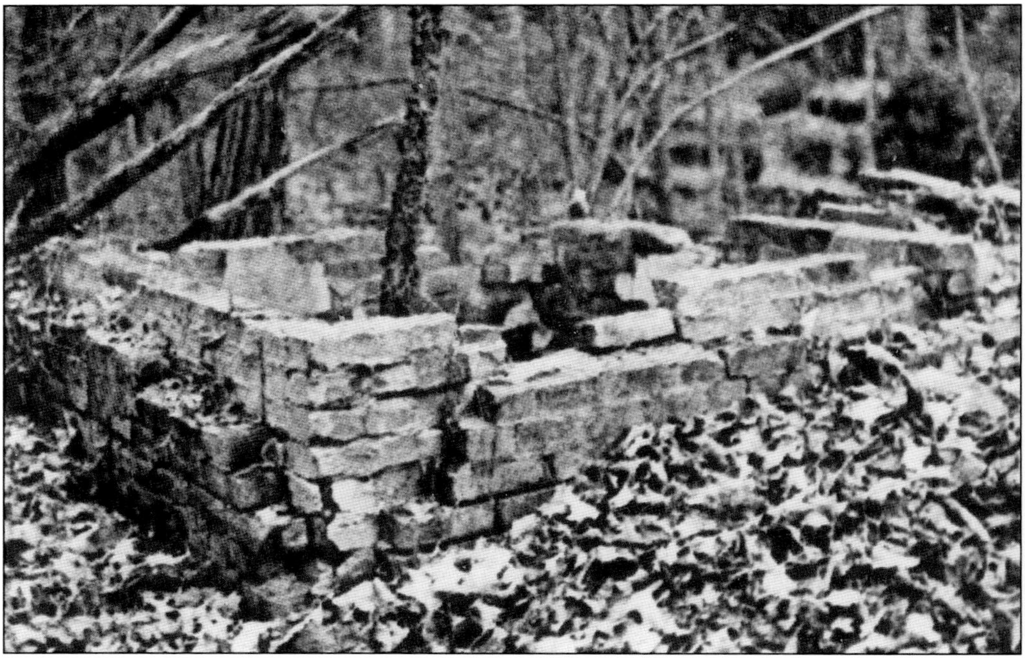

Many years later, cellar holes were all that was left of a village that had been the central business district of North Pepperell. At one time there were two paper mills, a large fulling mill, grist and sawmills, a cigar factory, a casket manufactory, blacksmith and cooper shops, and, in 1834, a shoe shop, all of which relied on water power from the Nissitissit River. Many homes centered around the village, which included a post office, tavern, store, and the old brick schoolhouse that still stands at the corner of Prescott and North Streets.

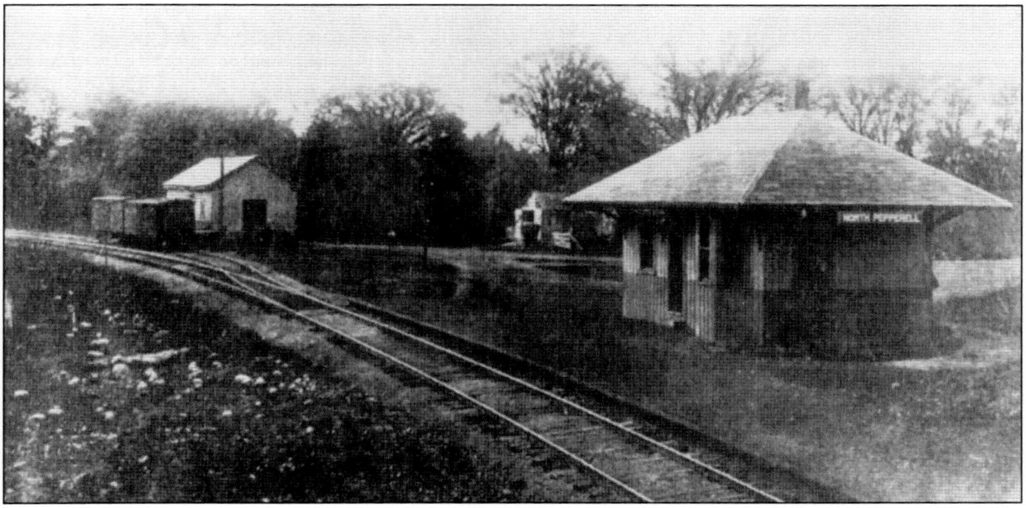

This is a picture of the old North Pepperell Depot taken about 1900. Built after most of the mills had gone, the railroad remained in existence until the early 1930s. It stood one-eighth of a mile behind the old brick schoolhouse and saw six passenger trains stop daily, along with ice and granite trains on Sunday. For many years the railroad bed could still be seen and old railroad spikes and pieces of track could be found, mementos of days past.

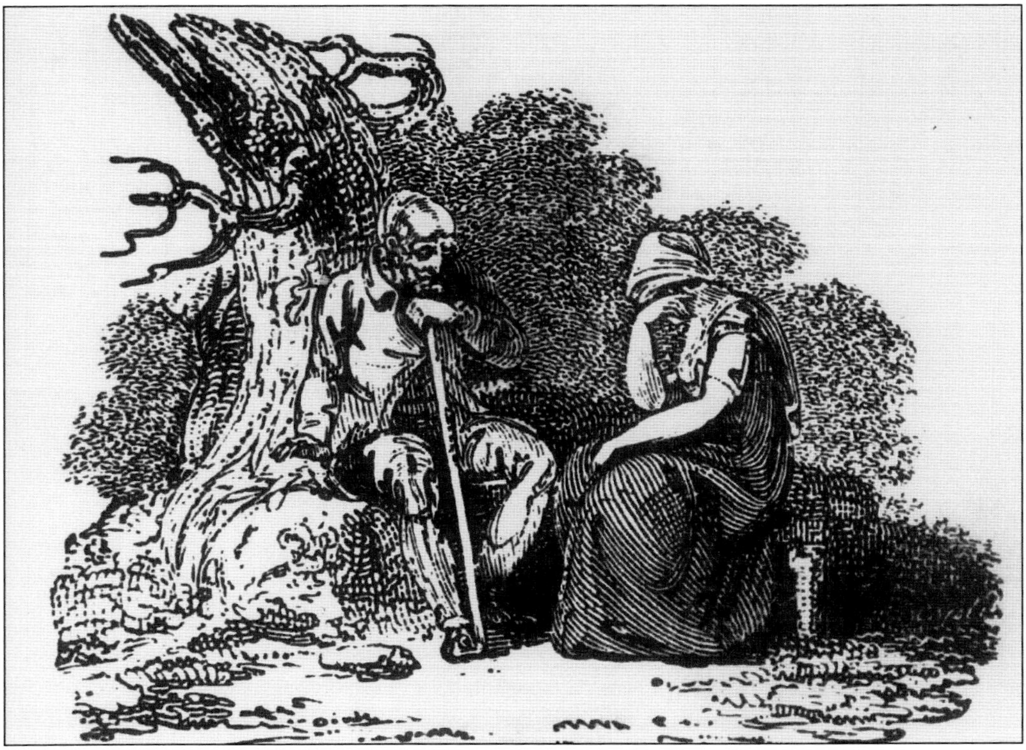

After the War of 1812 an old woman moved to the North Village. Because of her queer looks and actions, the townspeople thought her to be a witch and murderess, and she was branded with a hot iron in the center of her forehead. This etching depicts the suffering experienced by people in the village after a witch's curse threatened that "the river will dry up and run away" and that mills and homes would be consumed by fire.

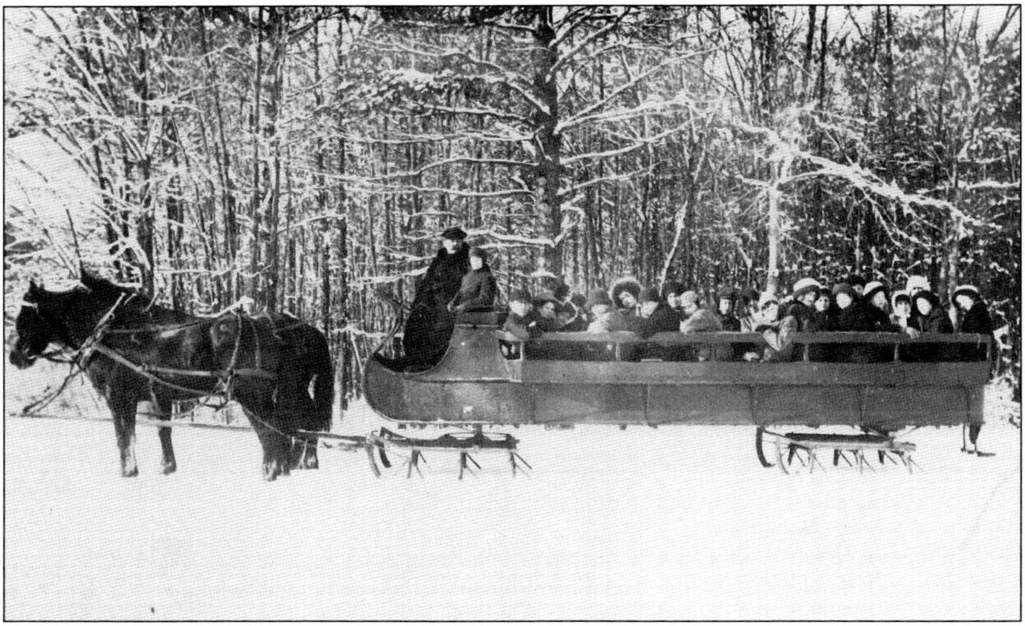

Winter transportation was fun for people who got together for organized social functions or for just an impromptu sleigh ride. In days gone by, the large horse sleds were sometimes seen filled with happy couples skimming over the snow on the way to a ball at the old Brick Tavern, or perhaps to Nashua, Hollis, or Brookline for an evening of dinner and dancing.

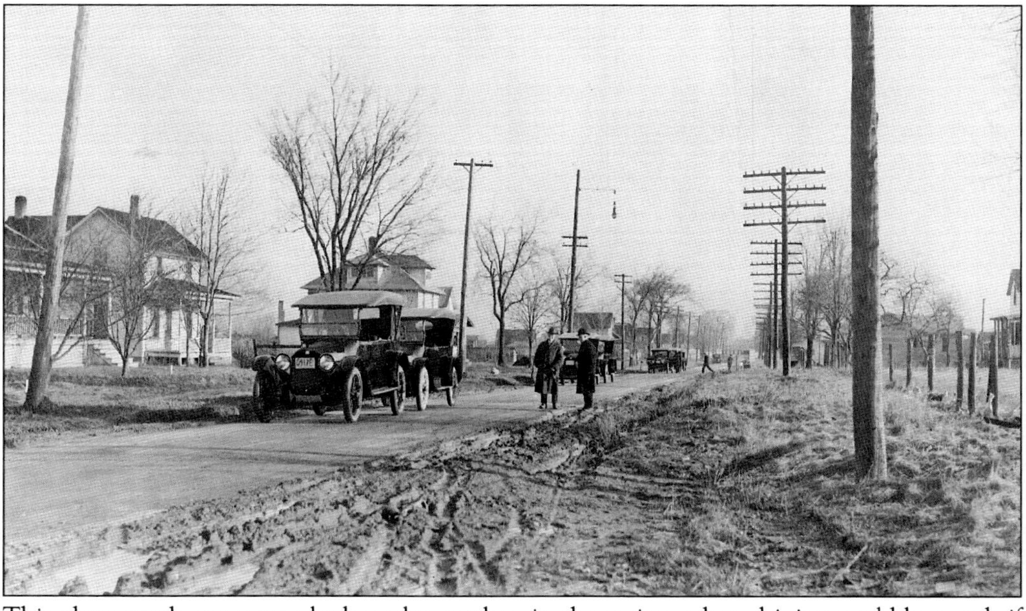

This photograph appears to be have been taken in the spring, when driving could be rough if you got off the beaten tracks and into the muddy ruts at the edge of the road.

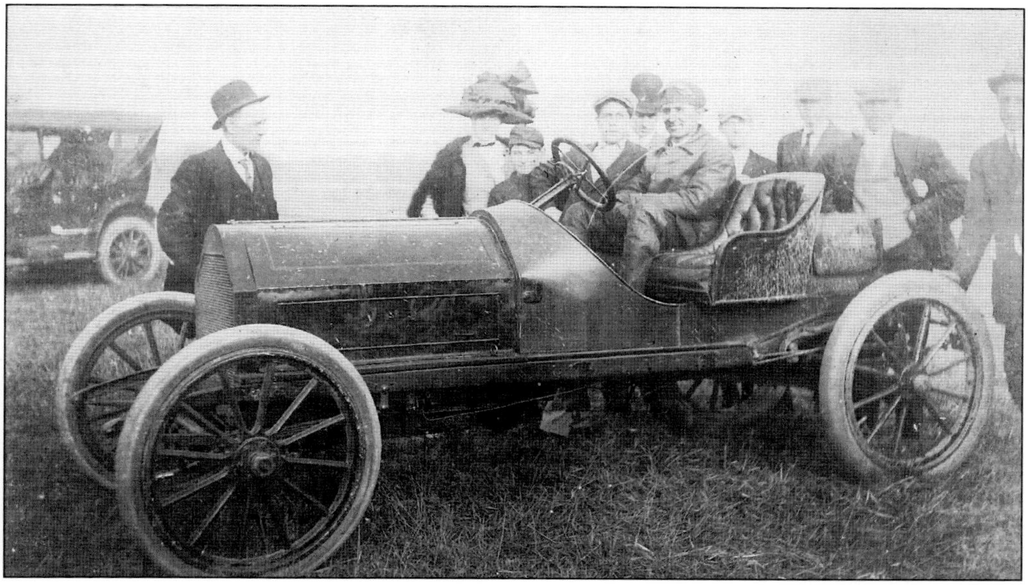

In this early 1900s photograph, a young fellow shows off his racing car to friends and interested onlookers.

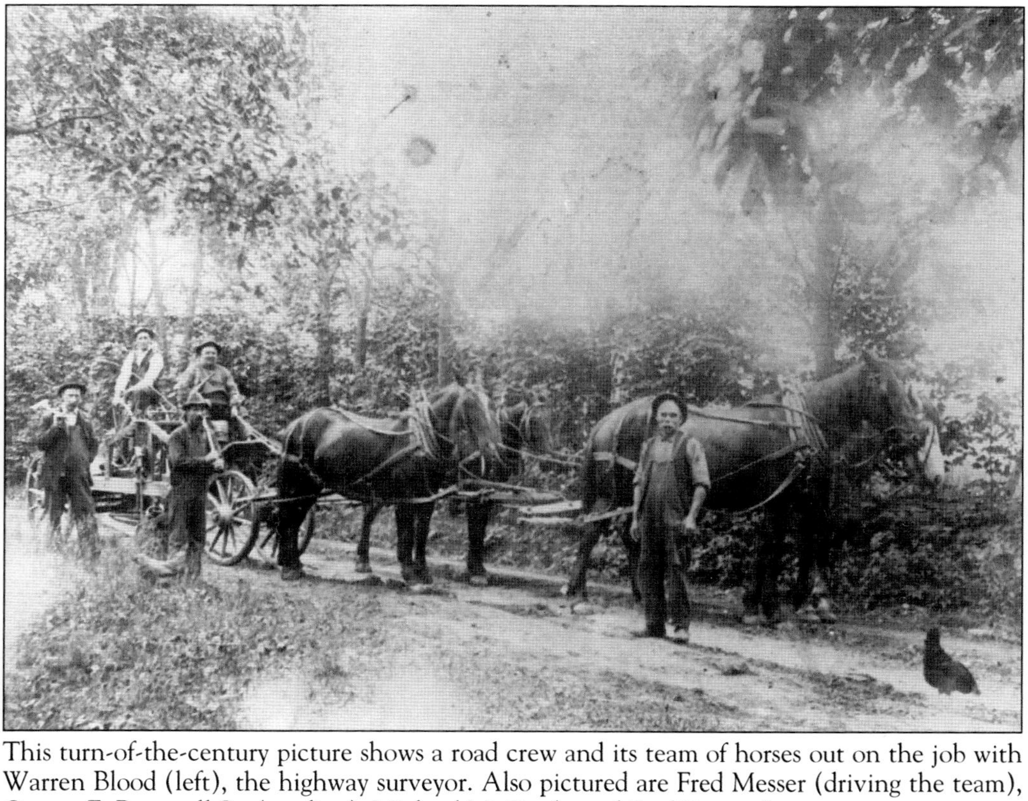

This turn-of-the-century picture shows a road crew and its team of horses out on the job with Warren Blood (left), the highway surveyor. Also pictured are Fred Messer (driving the team), George E. Boutwell Sr. (tending), Michael McGrath, and Fred Bancroft.

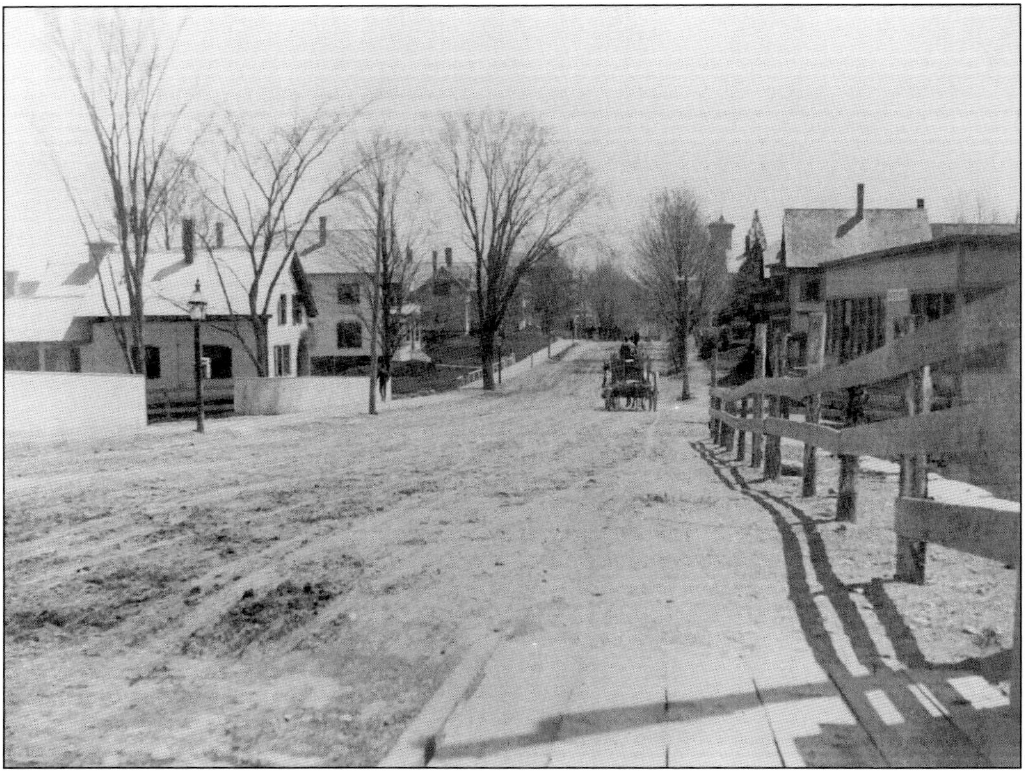

This view of Main Street was photographed about 1900 from the edge of the railroad bridge near the corner of Pleasant and Main Streets. On the right is J.A. Thibeault's furniture store and meat market. Just visible in the distance is the tower of the shoe factory, and on the left is the road to the railroad station.

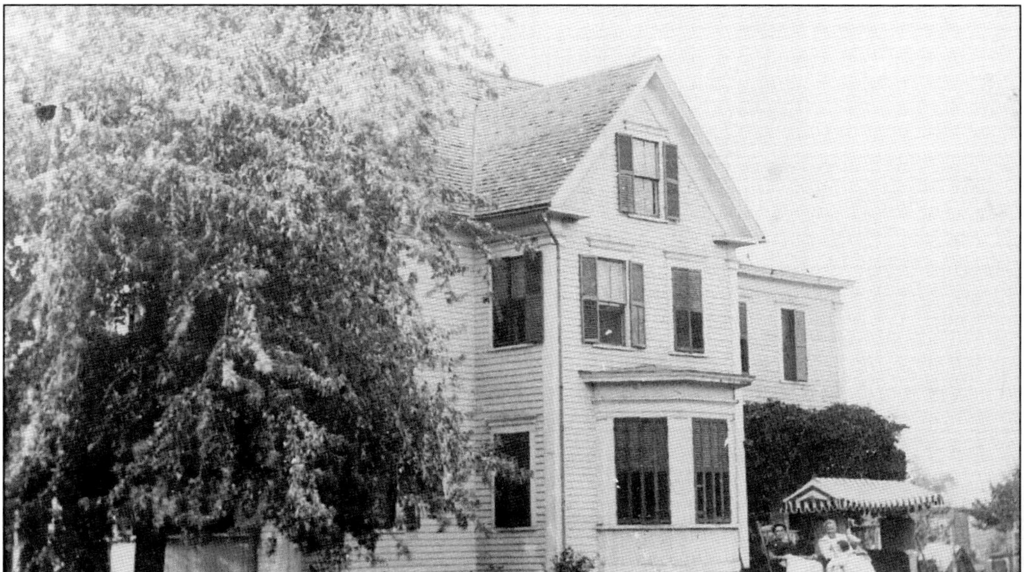

Shown here on a photographic postcard are members of the James Dunn family enjoying a pleasant day outside their home on Cross Street.

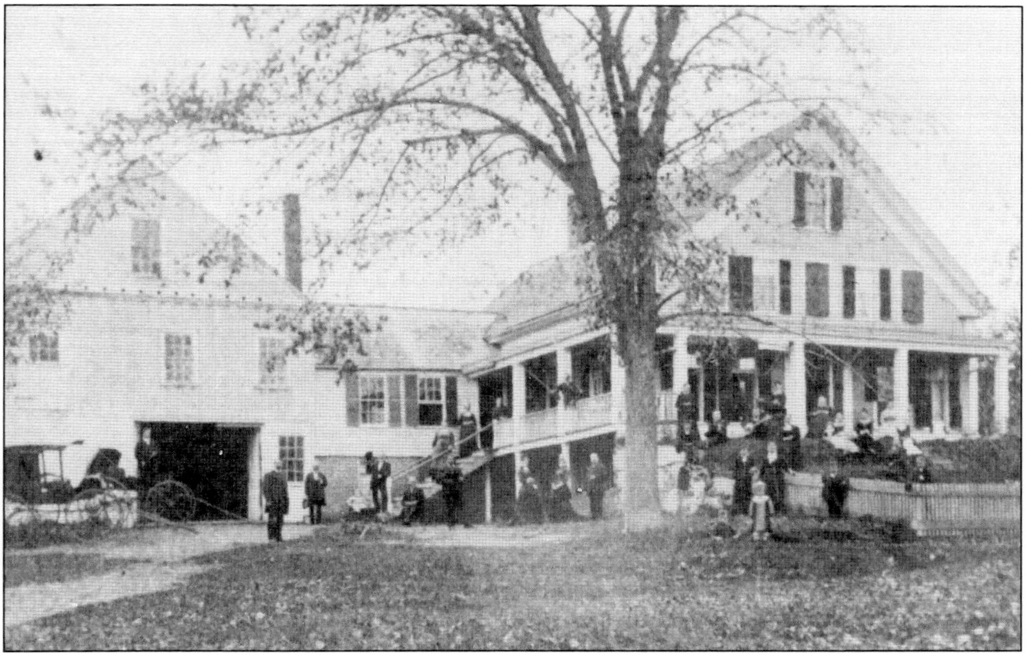

This interesting 1889 photograph of the Cowdrey house on Mill Street shows people gathered to celebrate the 50th wedding anniversary of Mr. and Mrs. Thomas Vinal. The image was taken by Ezra Goss, portrait and landscape artist, who was in business at the corner of Main and Foster Streets for a number of years.

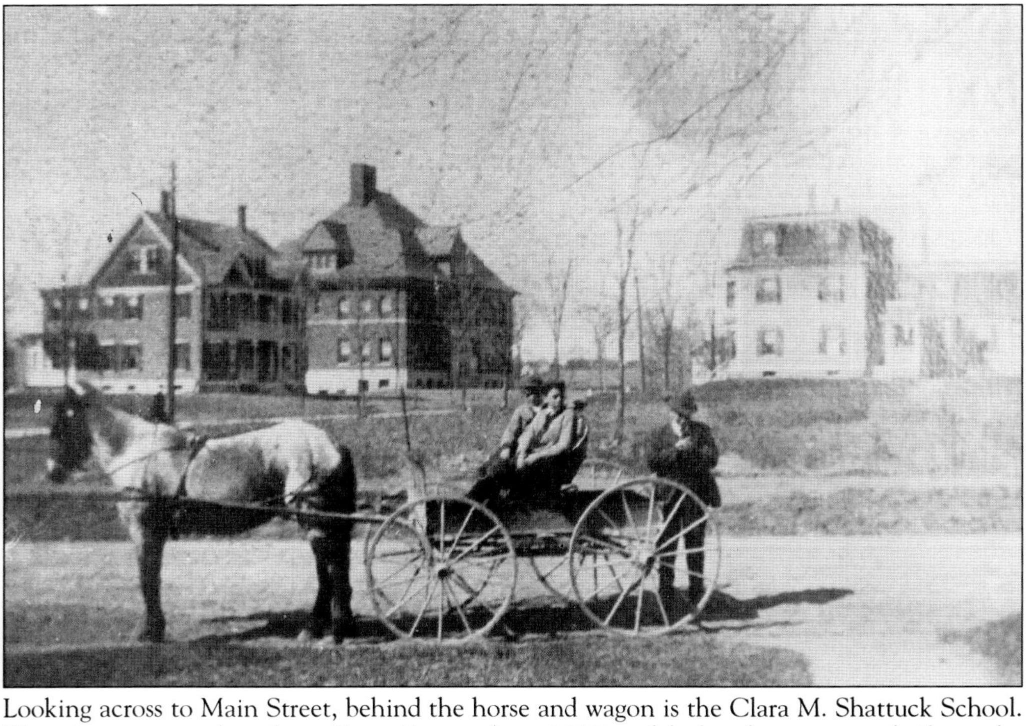

Looking across to Main Street, behind the horse and wagon is the Clara M. Shattuck School. The picture was taken from Cross Street about 1910 and before houses were built at the northwest corner of Main and Cross Streets.

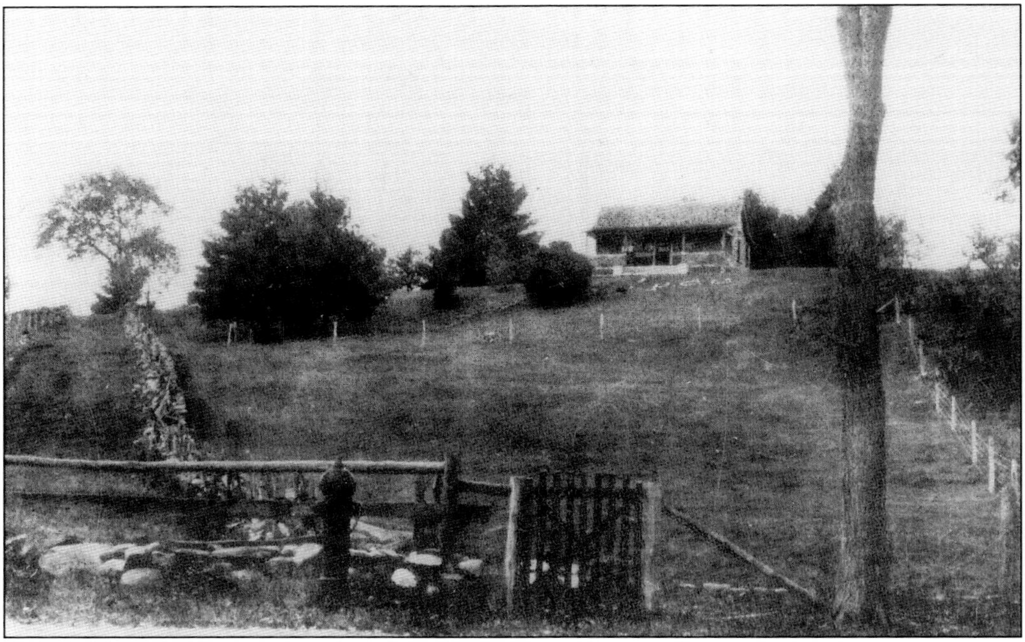

The Pepperell Country Club on Elm Street is shown here from the front gate. The country club was formed in 1897 and was popular for a while, but people had little time for golf and interest in the game waned after a short time.

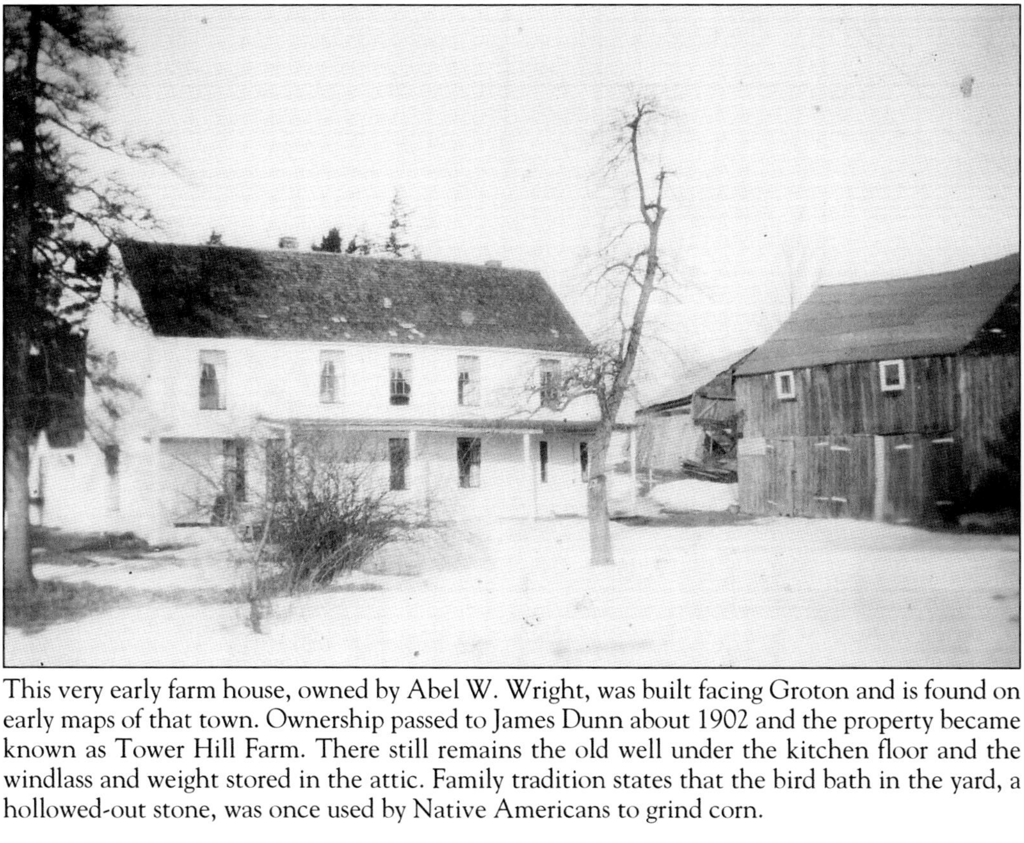

This very early farm house, owned by Abel W. Wright, was built facing Groton and is found on early maps of that town. Ownership passed to James Dunn about 1902 and the property became known as Tower Hill Farm. There still remains the old well under the kitchen floor and the windlass and weight stored in the attic. Family tradition states that the bird bath in the yard, a hollowed-out stone, was once used by Native Americans to grind corn.

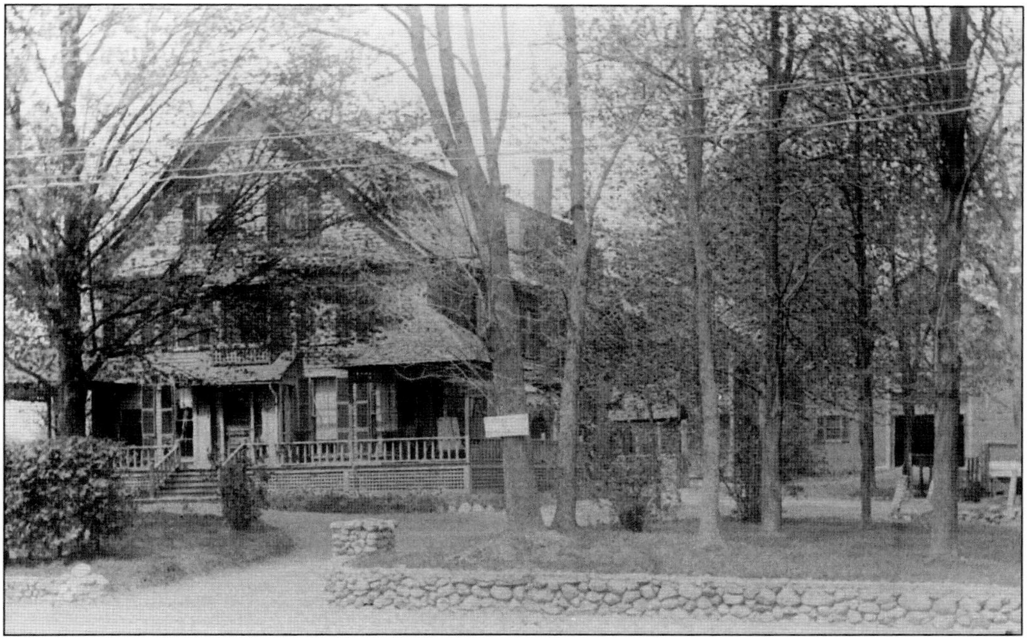

Pepperell was home to the first institution for the mentally ill in the state of Massachusetts. In 1825 Dr. Nehemiah Cutter and his partner, Charles Parker, began the Cutter Retreat on the north side of Main Street, east of the common. After several fires and changes of location, the property was sold to Dr. William F. Heald in 1886, and the institution prospered until his death in 1907. This photograph of the Cutter Retreat was taken in 1909.

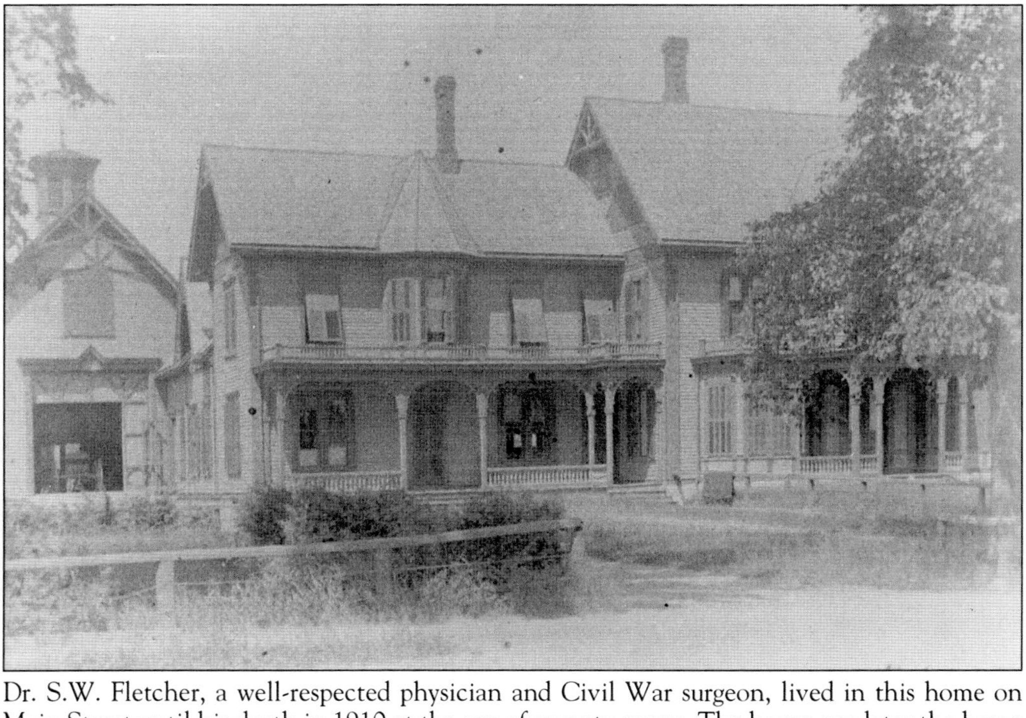

Dr. S.W. Fletcher, a well-respected physician and Civil War surgeon, lived in this home on Main Street until his death in 1910 at the age of seventy-seven. The house was later the home of the Donnelly family for many years.

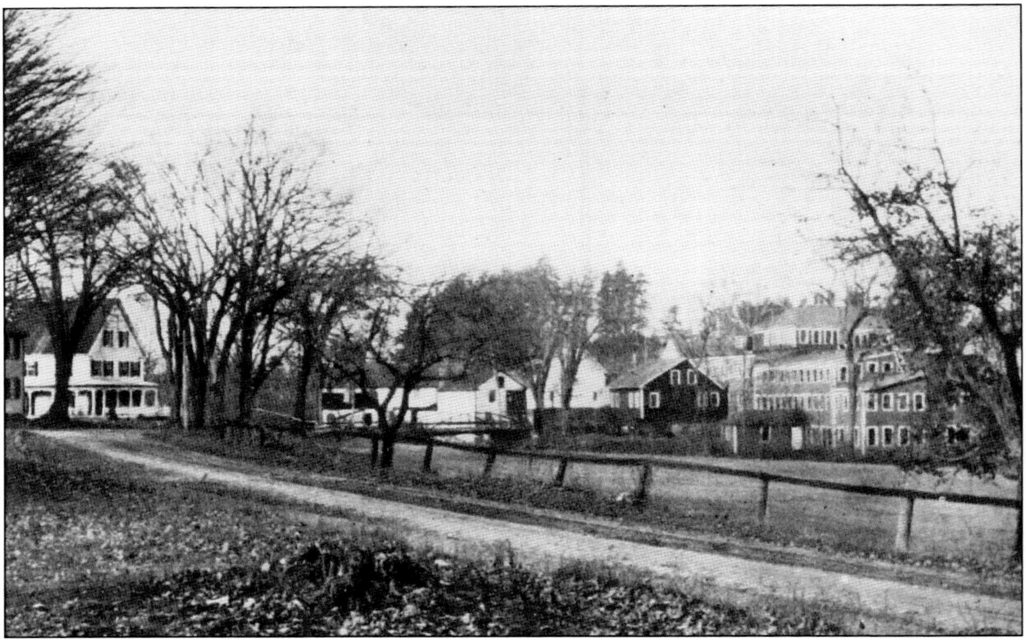

This is a postcard view of the East Village showing the old red mill at the corner of Hollis and Nashua Streets by the bridge over the Nissitissit River. In 1890 there was a gristmill on the corner next to Boynton's planing mill. Much later, the building was used as a plastics plant.

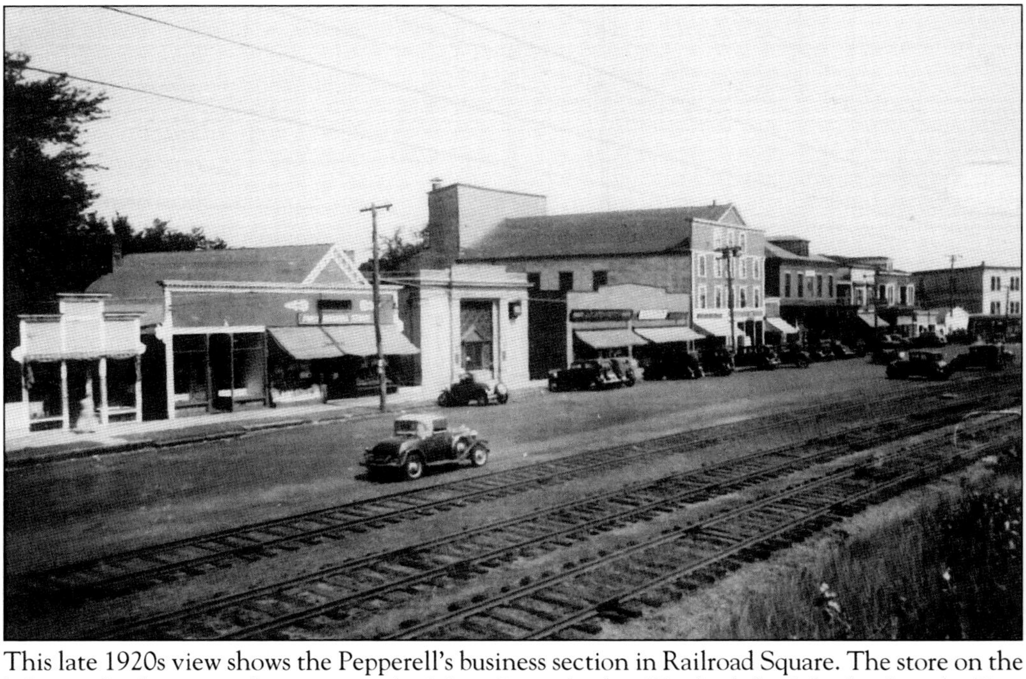

This late 1920s view shows the Pepperell's business section in Railroad Square. The store on the left was the first one after crossing the Main Street bridge. To the left of the bank is the First National store.

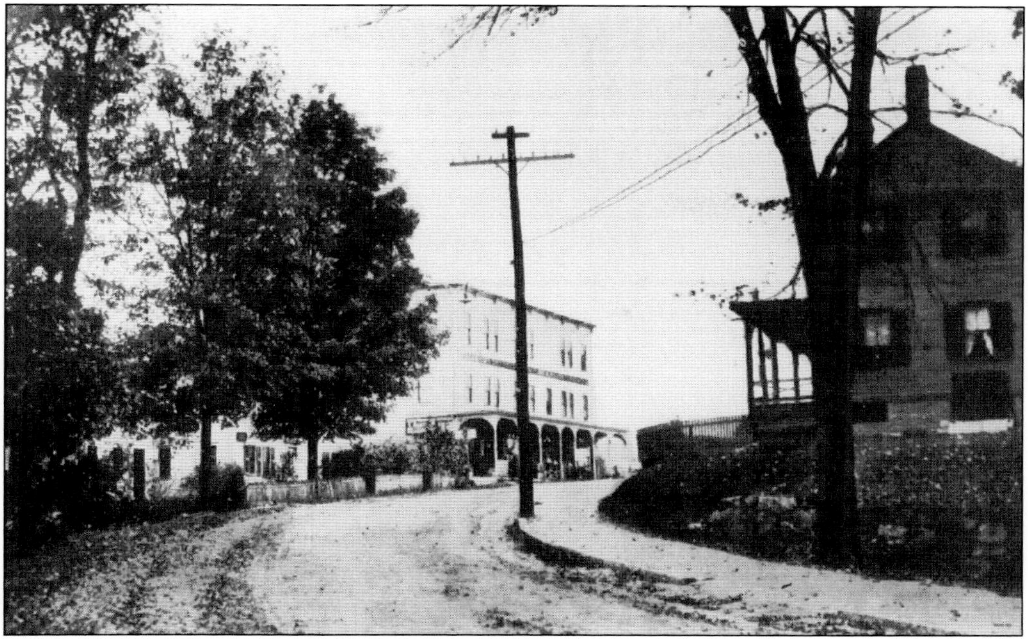

Coming up Main Street to the bend in the road just past the mill, this view approaches the intersection of Canal, Mill, and Main Streets. Directly ahead is Saunders Corner, now the Odd Fellows Building, whose neighbor to the left is a private residence. The house on the right was usually lived in by the employees of the mill.

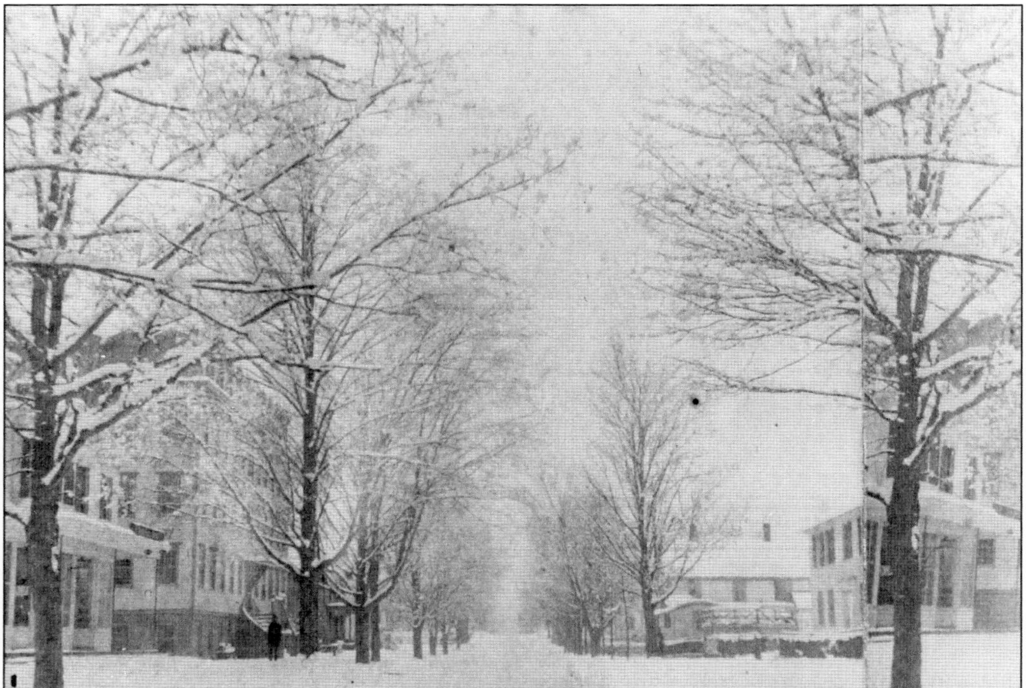

This snowy scene a little further up Main Street was taken in the 1890s. Partially obscured from view on the left is the second Leighton Shoe Factory, next to a general store and residence.

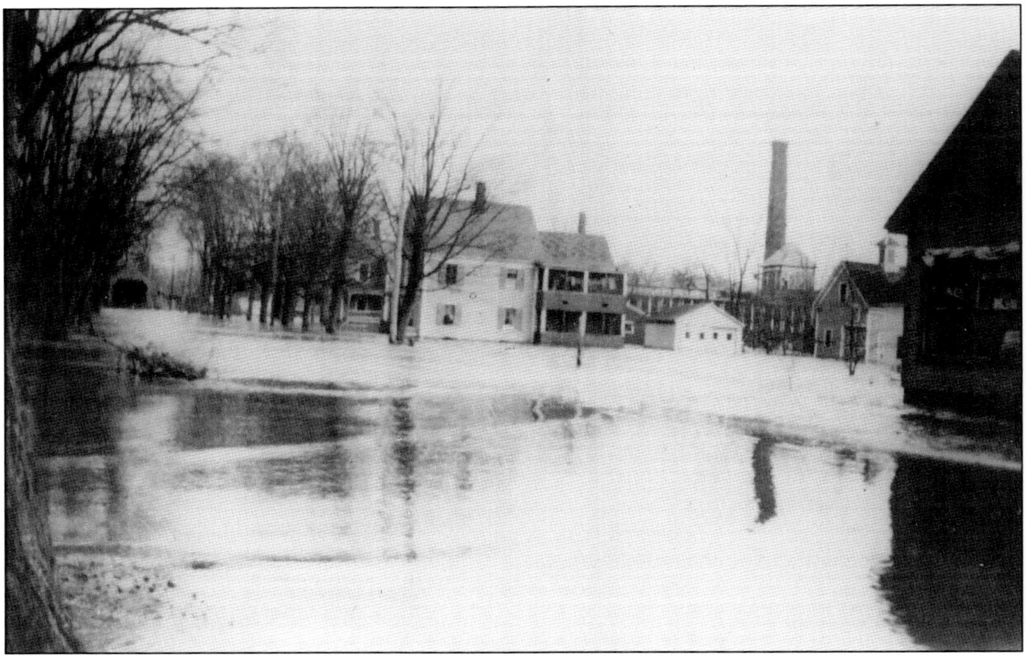

It was not uncommon for the river to overflow its banks in the springtime and submerge parts of Canal, Main, and Mill Streets. In this picture, flood waters cover Mill Street down to the covered bridge. On the right can be seen part of the Champion Card and Paper Company.

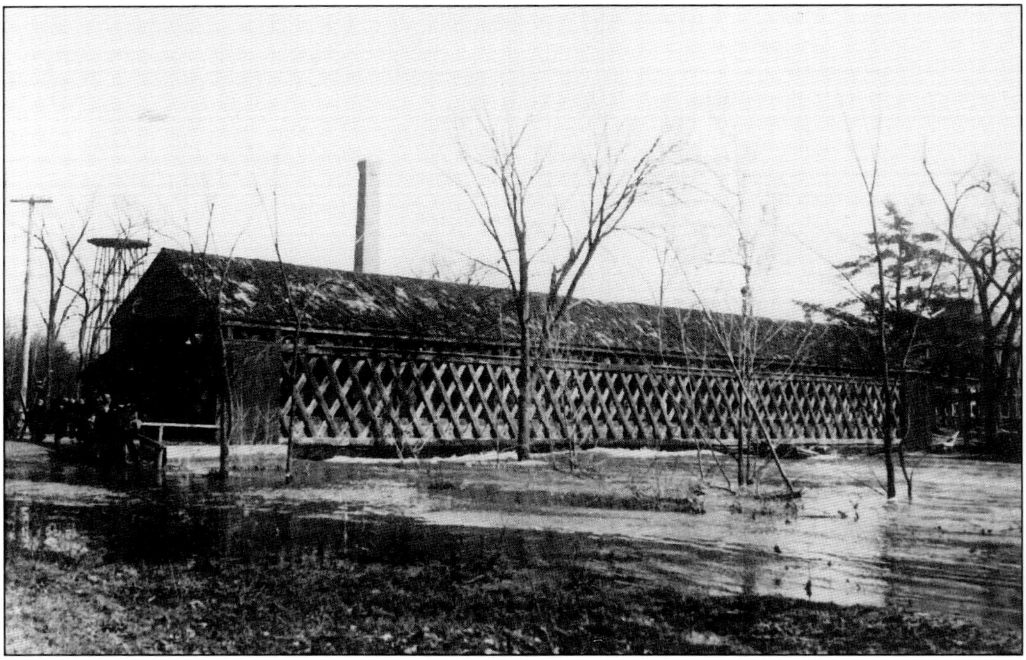

Water laps at the bottom of the "Old Covered Bridge" as the Nissitissit River overflows its banks. To the left, curious onlookers lean over the railings and watch the flood waters rise. The bridge was originally built in 1726 and known as Jewett's Bridge; only later did it become known as the "Old Covered Bridge." A second covered bridge was built in 1846 and the current bridge was officially opened November 4, 1963, after being under construction for nearly a year.

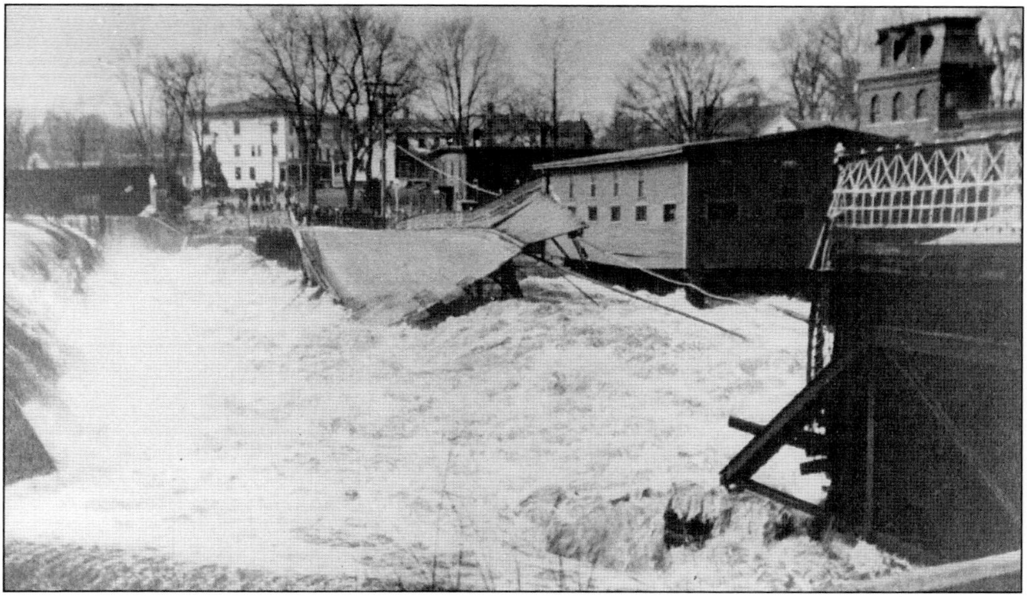

During the flood of 1936, raging torrents of water came crashing over the mill dam and destroyed the Main Street bridge. Groton Street was flooded with water 4 feet deep in some areas, and the railroad tracks were covered with a foot of water. Damage was estimated at $200,000. Many months went by before another bridge was built, forcing people to take the long way around through the covered bridge to get downtown.

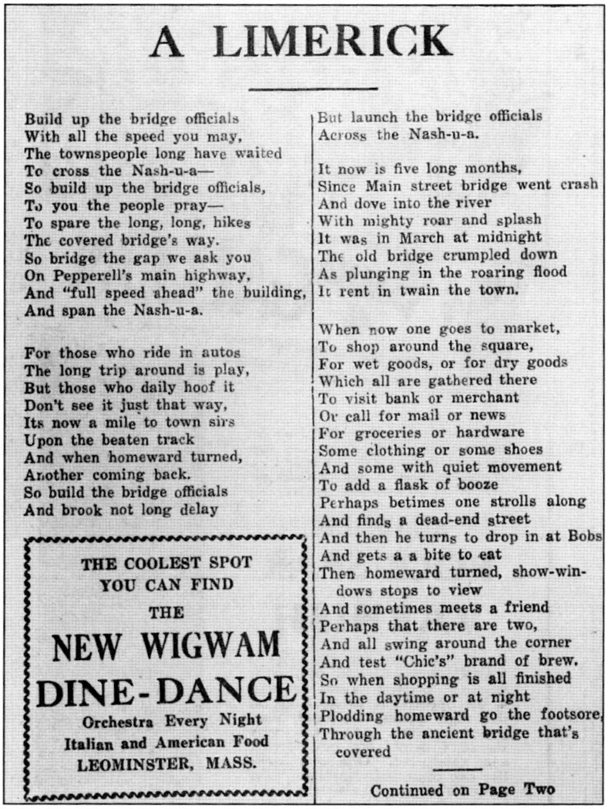

A LIMERICK

Build up the bridge officials
With all the speed you may,
The townspeople long have waited
To cross the Nash-u-a—
So build up the bridge officials,
To you the people pray—
To spare the long, long, hikes
The covered bridge's way.
So bridge the gap we ask you
On Pepperell's main highway,
And "full speed ahead" the building,
And span the Nash-u-a.

For those who ride in autos
The long trip around is play,
But those who daily hoof it
Don't see it just that way,
Its now a mile to town sirs
Upon the beaten track
And when homeward turned,
Another coming back.
So build the bridge officials
And brook not long delay
But launch the bridge officials
Across the Nash-u-a.

It now is five long months,
Since Main street bridge went crash
And dove into the river
With mighty roar and splash
It was in March at midnight
The old bridge crumpled down
As plunging in the roaring flood
It rent in twain the town.

When now one goes to market,
To shop around the square,
For wet goods, or for dry goods
Which all are gathered there
To visit bank or merchant
Or call for mail or news
For groceries or hardware
Some clothing or some shoes
And some with quiet movement
To add a flask of booze
Perhaps betimes one strolls along
And finds a dead-end street
And then he turns to drop in at Bobs
And gets a a bite to eat
Then homeward turned, show-windows stops to view
And sometimes meets a friend
Perhaps that there are two,
And all swing around the corner
And test "Chic's" brand of brew.
So when shopping is all finished
In the daytime or at night
Plodding homeward go the footsore
Through the ancient bridge that's covered

Continued on Page Two

This poem appeared in the *Pepperell Free Press* on September 17, 1936, after the town had been without a bridge over the "Nash-u-a" for five long months.

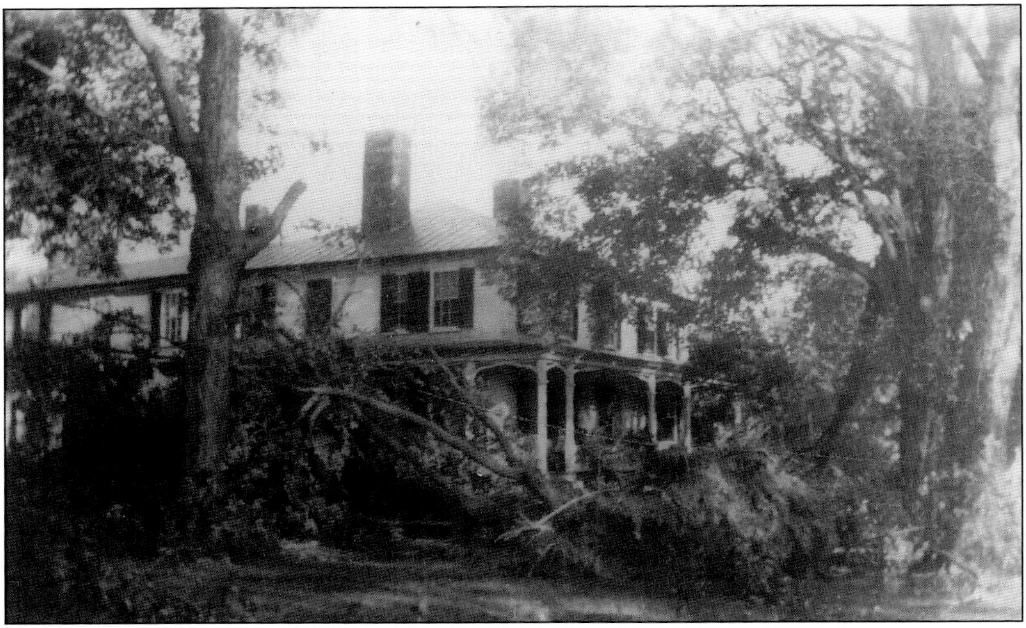

The Breck Homestead on Park Street suffered the wrath of the 1938 hurricane as did many other homes in town. By the time Joseph Breck had moved into his Federal-style home in the summer of 1819, he had already established the Breck Chaise Manufactory and founded the Breck Seed Company. In 1852 Adelia E. Conant opened a boarding school for young ladies at the homestead. Owned for many years by the Hutchinson family, the school was sold to Mr. and Mrs. Willard Cousins in 1940.

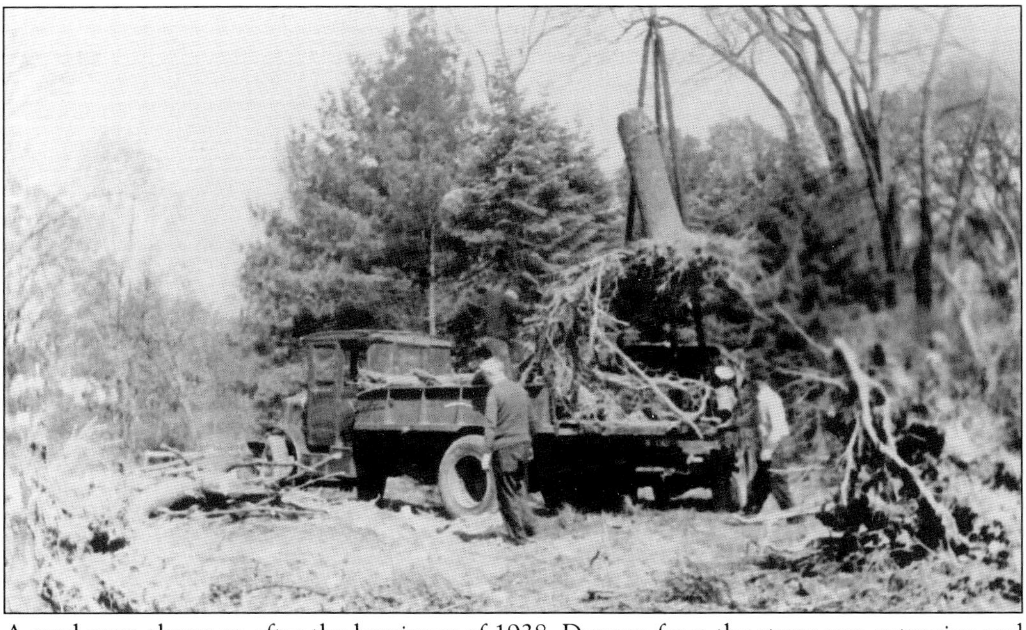

A road crew cleans up after the hurricane of 1938. Damage from the storm was extensive and Pepperell lost many of its lovely old trees.

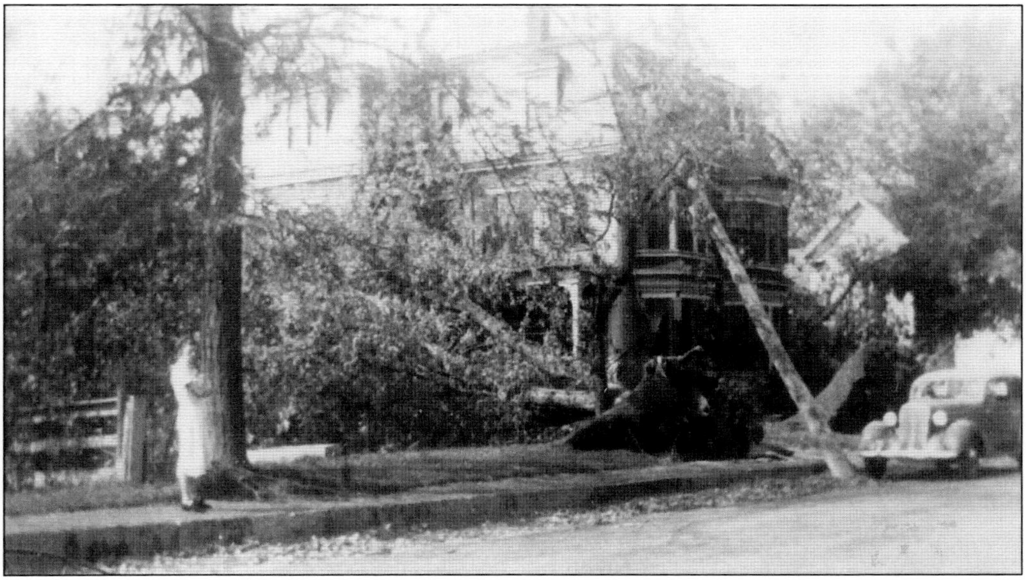

Laura Saunders stands outside her home at 21 High Street sadly surveying the damage caused by falling trees and a telephone pole during the hurricane.

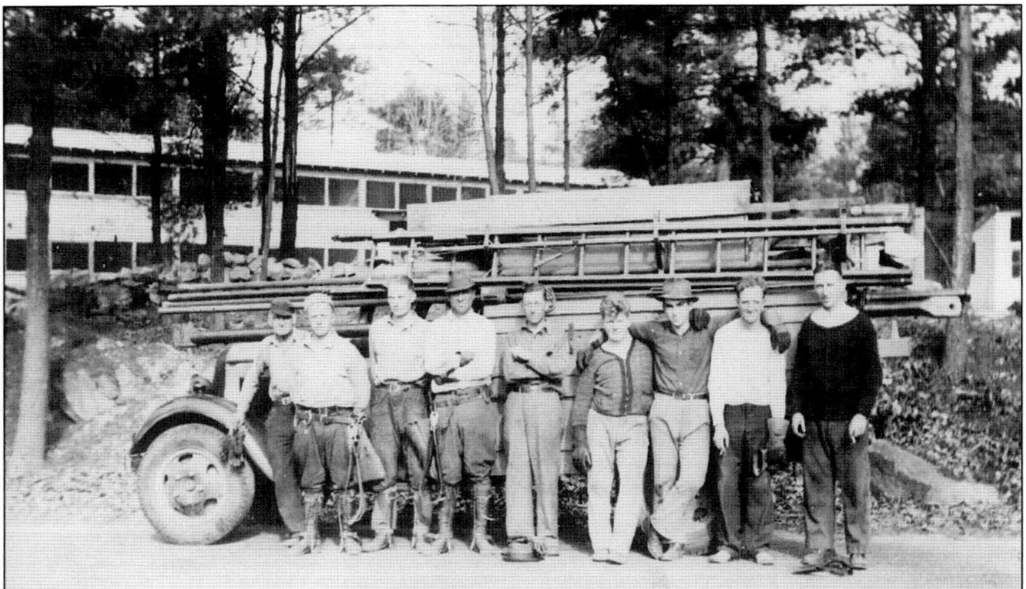

The electric company was on the job during the course of the storm, working day and night for some time to restore electric service. Pictured here from left to right are four unidentified workers followed by Amos Saunders, "Butch" Scheaffer, Len Davis, "Red Treadin," and "Bowse" Crowley.

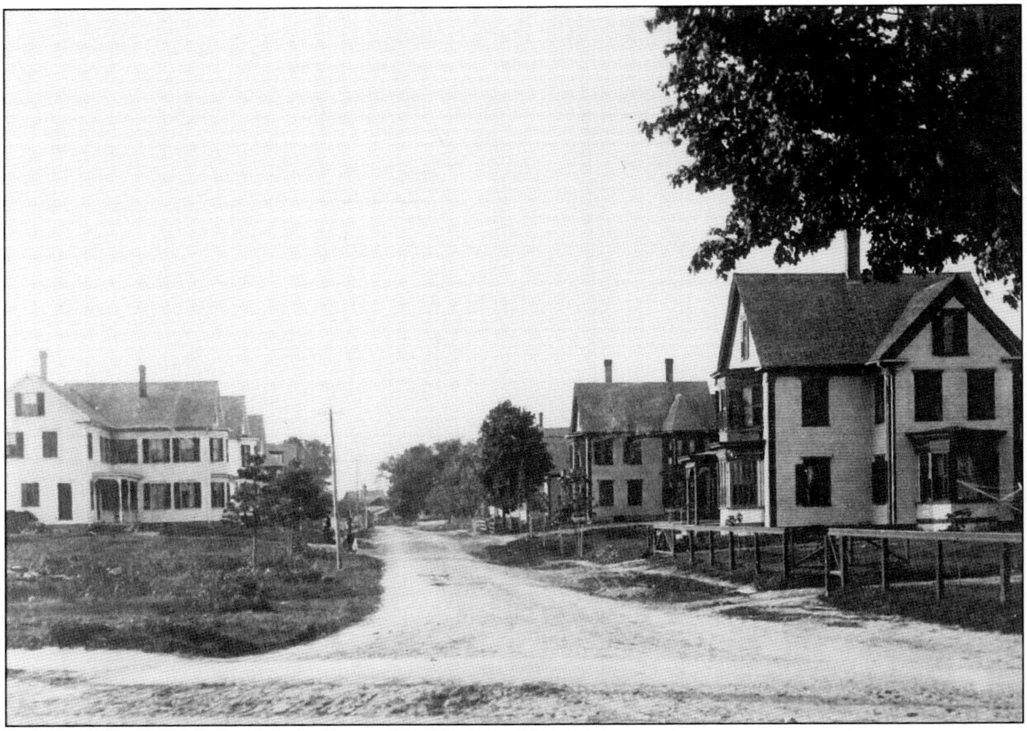

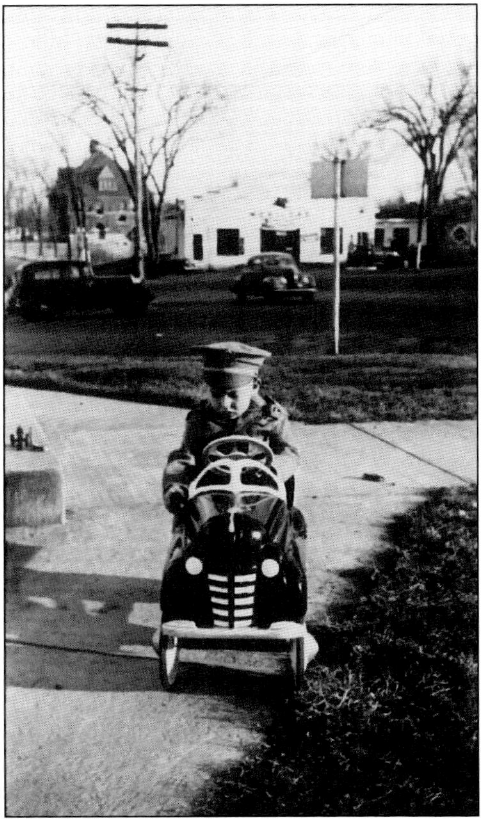

This early 1900s picture was taken from the south side of Main Street looking down Cross Street. On the right are the Dunn and Bartlett houses. At the time of the photograph, N.S. Pike ran a blacksmith and carriage shop and a livery stable opposite Cross Street. These businesses were located just a short distance from the train station and were available to anyone needing their transportation services.

Donnie Gagnon rides in his new little car on the sidewalk in front of his house. The photograph, taken in 1941, shows the intersection and Mobil gas station before the advent of the rotary. Also in the background is the Clara M. Shattuck School.

Two

Railroad Square and Beyond

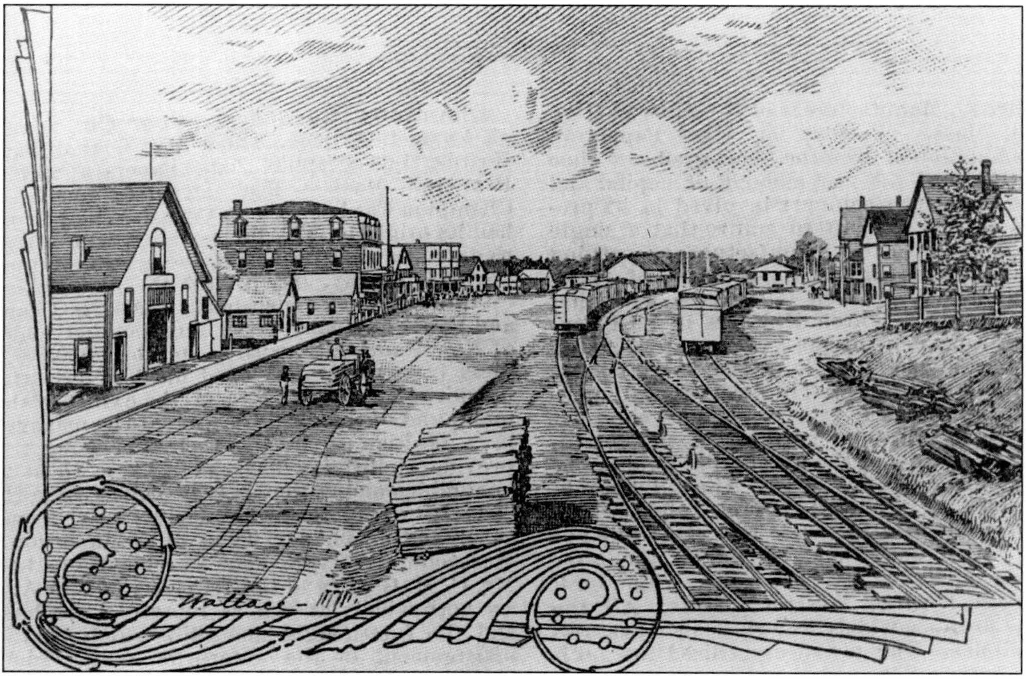

This pen-and-ink drawing of Railroad Square was done by Wallace in 1890.

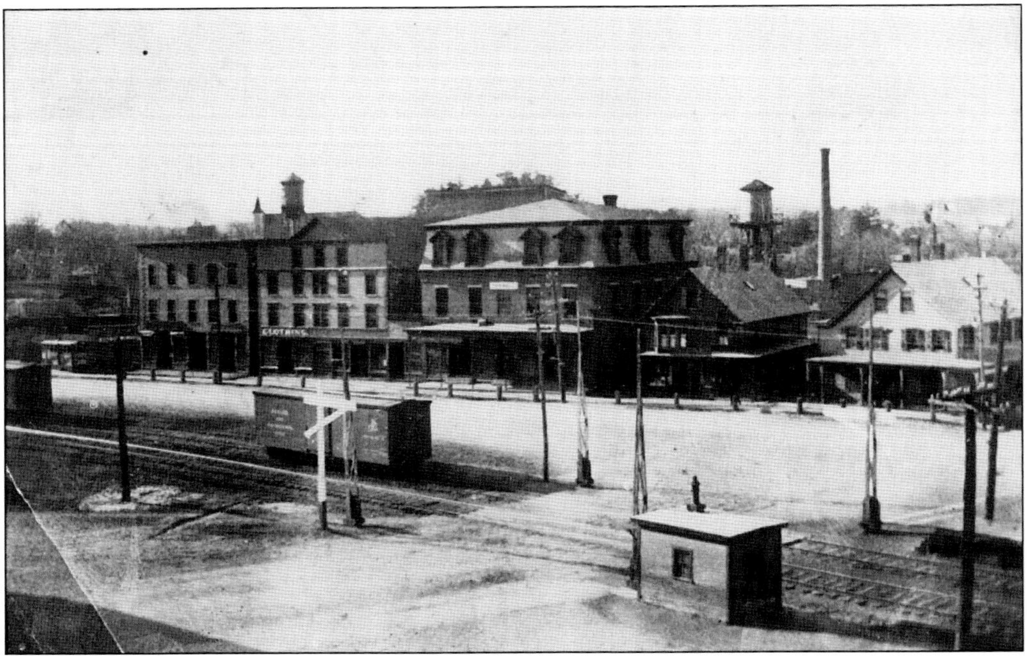

An early photograph showing the business district in Railroad Square from across the tracks on Groton Street.

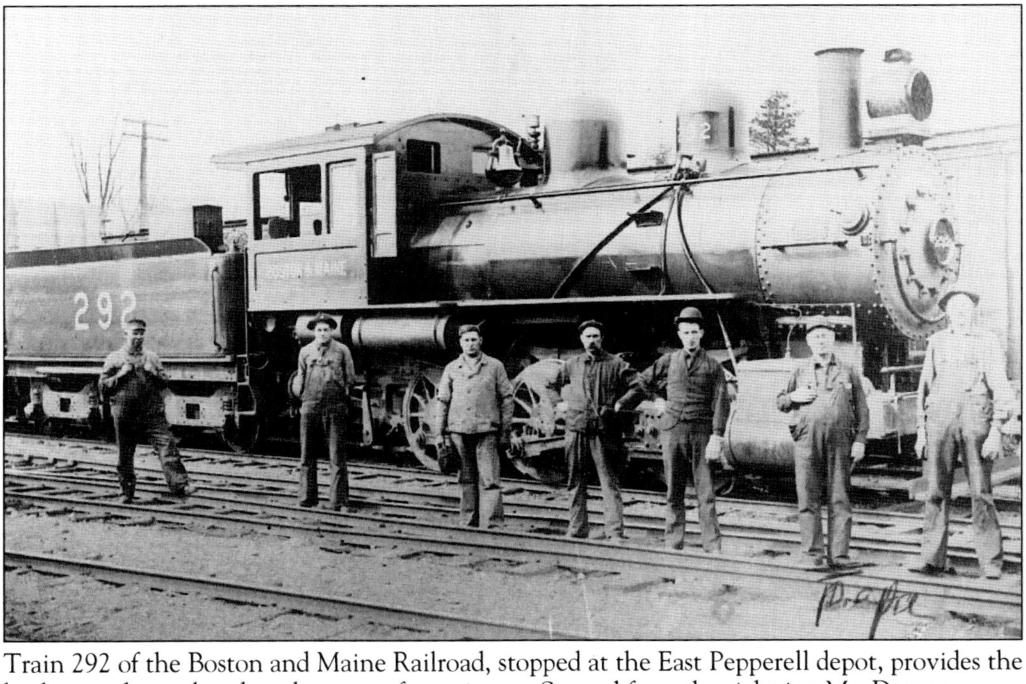

Train 292 of the Boston and Maine Railroad, stopped at the East Pepperell depot, provides the background as railroad workers pose for a picture. Second from the right is a Mr. Draper.

The *Pepperell Advertiser* was published every Friday night and regularly printed the Boston & Maine and the Fitchburg Railroad train schedules. This winter schedule for October 1901 was still in effect in the newspaper of February 8, 1902.

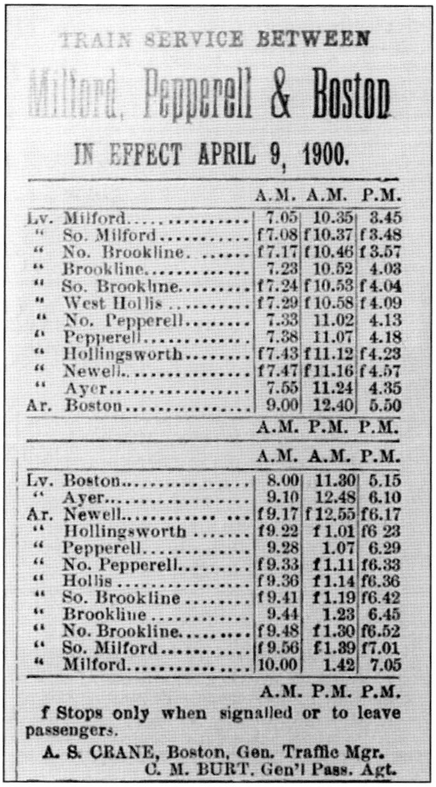

TRAIN SERVICE BETWEEN

Milford, Pepperell & Boston

IN EFFECT APRIL 9, 1900.

		A.M.	A.M.	P.M.
Lv.	Milford	7.05	10.35	3.45
"	So. Milford	f7.08	f10.37	f3.48
"	No. Brookline	f7.17	f10.46	f3.57
"	Brookline	7.23	10.52	4.03
"	So. Brookline	f7.24	f10.53	f4.04
"	West Hollis	f7.29	f10.58	f4.09
"	No. Pepperell	7.33	11.02	4.13
"	Pepperell	7.38	11.07	4.18
"	Hollingsworth	f7.43	f11.12	f4.23
"	Newell	f7.47	f11.16	f4.57
"	Ayer	7.55	11.24	4.35
Ar.	Boston	9.00	12.40	5.50
		A.M.	P.M.	P.M.

		A.M.	A.M.	P.M.
Lv.	Boston	8.00	11.30	5.15
"	Ayer	9.10	12.48	6.10
Ar.	Newell	f9.17	f12.55	f6.17
"	Hollingsworth	f9.22	f1.01	f6 23
"	Pepperell	9.28	1.07	6.29
"	No. Pepperell	f9.33	f1.11	f6.33
"	Hollis	f9.36	f1.14	f6.36
"	So. Brookline	f9.41	f1.19	f6.42
"	Brookline	9.44	1.23	6.45
"	No. Brookline	f9.48	f1.30	f6.52
"	So. Milford	f9.56	f1.39	f7.01
"	Milford	10.00	1.42	7.05
		A.M.	P.M.	P.M.

f Stops only when signalled or to leave passengers.

A. S. CRANE, Boston, Gen. Traffic Mgr.
C. M. BURT, Gen'l Pass. Agt.

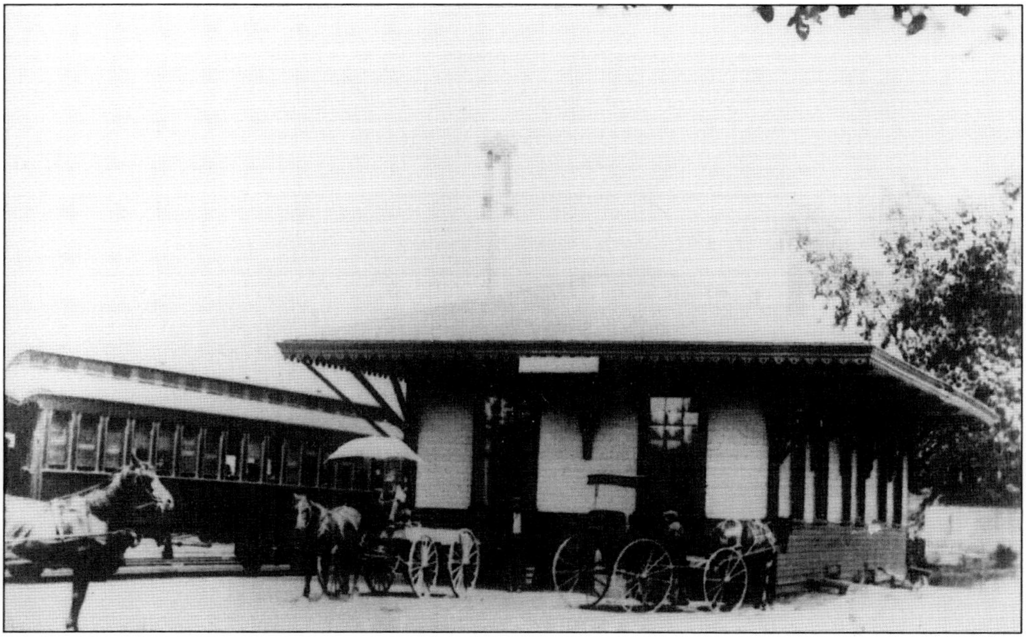

A passenger train sits at the East Pepperell depot while horses and wagons stand ready to transport people or goods to their destinations.

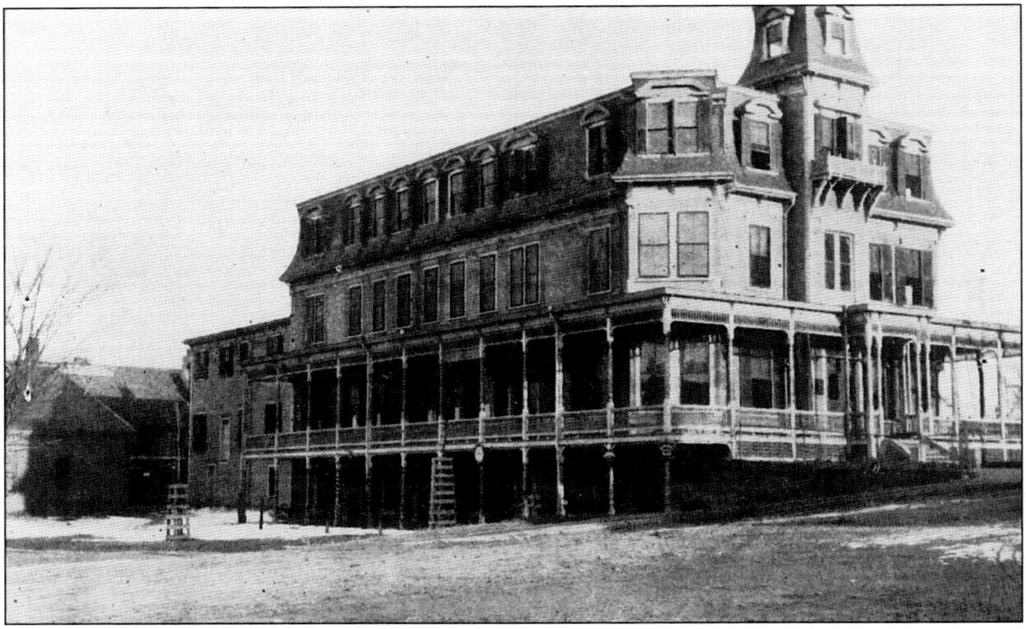

The New Prescott House was built by George H. Johnson in 1895 at the edge of Depot Square. It was three stories high with a basement and had a balcony around the first floor. Each of the twenty-three guest rooms had a fireplace and a call bell. The hotel had a fine reputation and, being the "only show in town," was popular with visiting businessmen and horsemen alike.

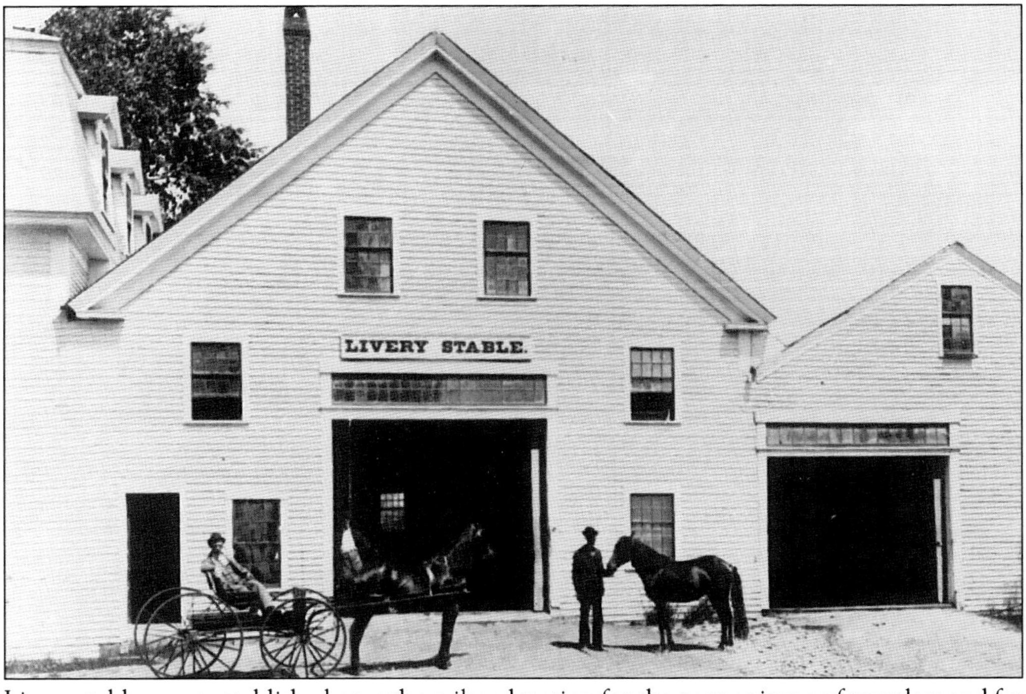

Livery stables were established near the railroad station for the convenience of travelers and for the purpose of transporting goods to and from the station. This stable was attached to the back of the Prescott Hotel (seen to the left), making transportation available to all who stayed there. Riding in the wagon is George Tenney and standing next to the horse is Anson Nutting.

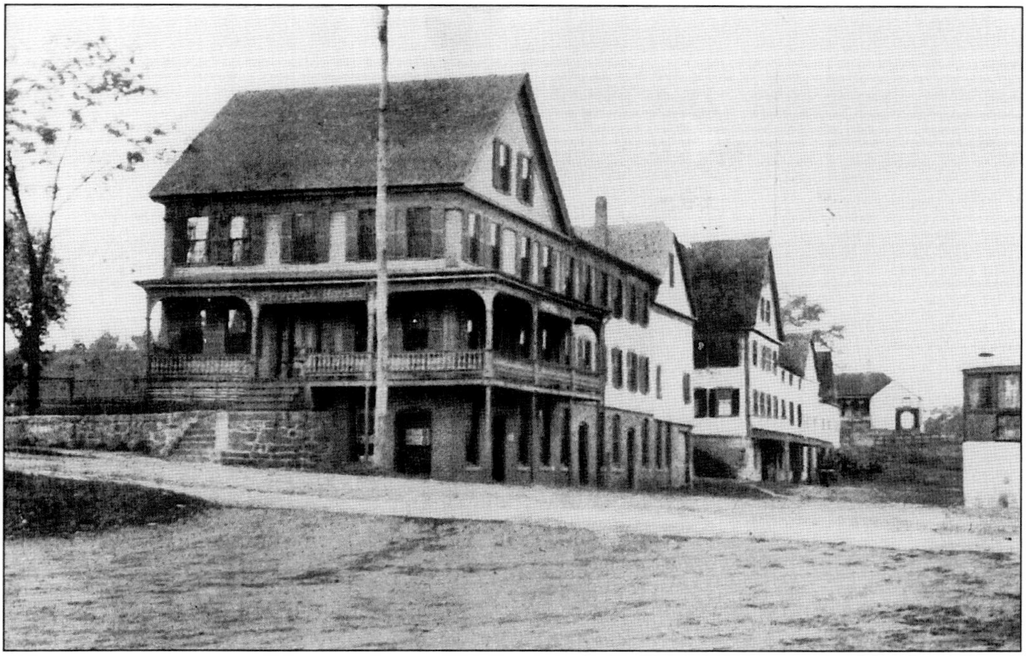

The Ideal sits on the edge of Pepperell's business district. In the early 1900s it was operated by John F. Reagan, who rented rooms and ran a restaurant. At one time Joseph Thibault gave music lessons here. Mr. Timberlake had his plumbing business in the building and Steve West also ran an antique and second-hand business here.

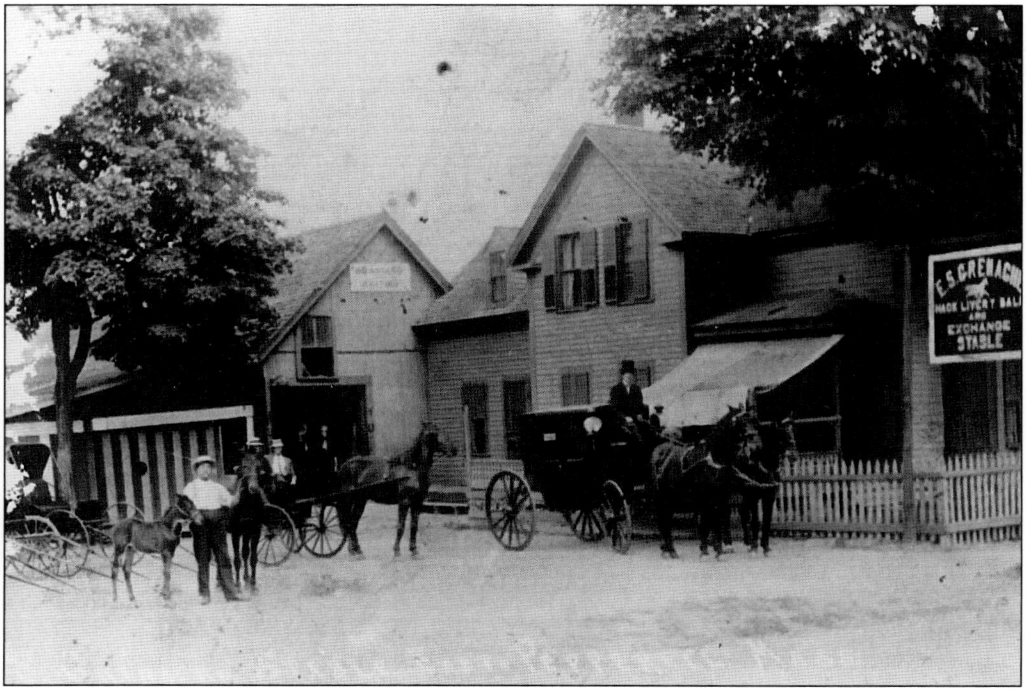

This photograph of the Elgin S. Greenache livery stable was taken about 1912. The livery stable was located on Railroad Street, close to the railroad station, and was previously owned by George L. Lakin.

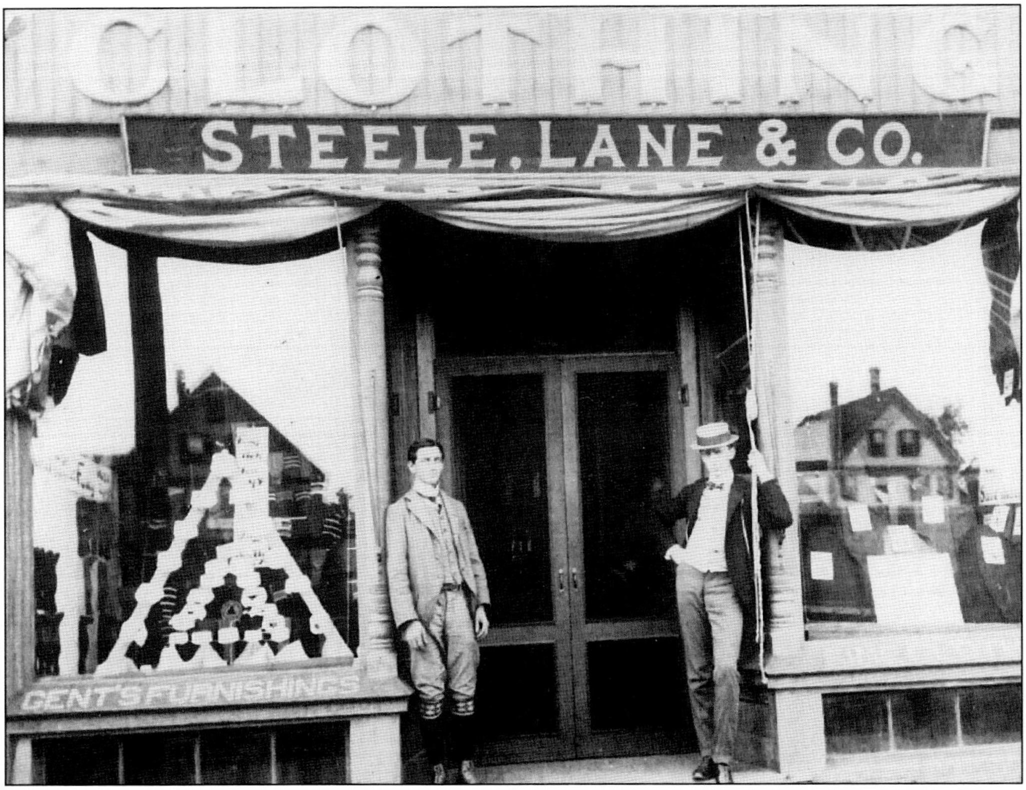

Owner Matthew C. Lane (right) and Verne Willson (a clerk) stand outside the Steele, Lane & Company clothing store for a picture in 1899. The store was located on the first floor of the Tarbell Building, and was one of the first clothing stores in Pepperell. It later became Lane Brothers and eventually Parker & Lane. In 1902 the store advertised a new line of shirts with two detachable collars and cuffs for 48¢.

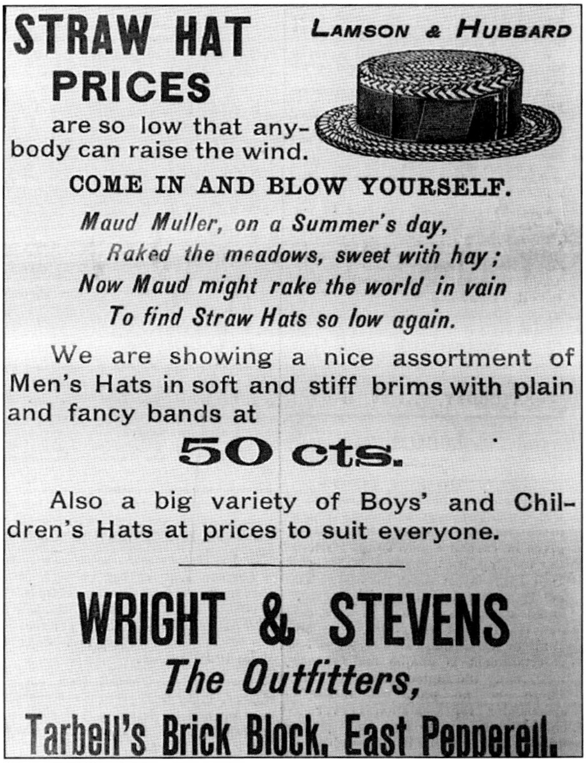

This advertisement for straw hats appeared on the front page of the *Pepperell Advertiser* on May 26, 1900.

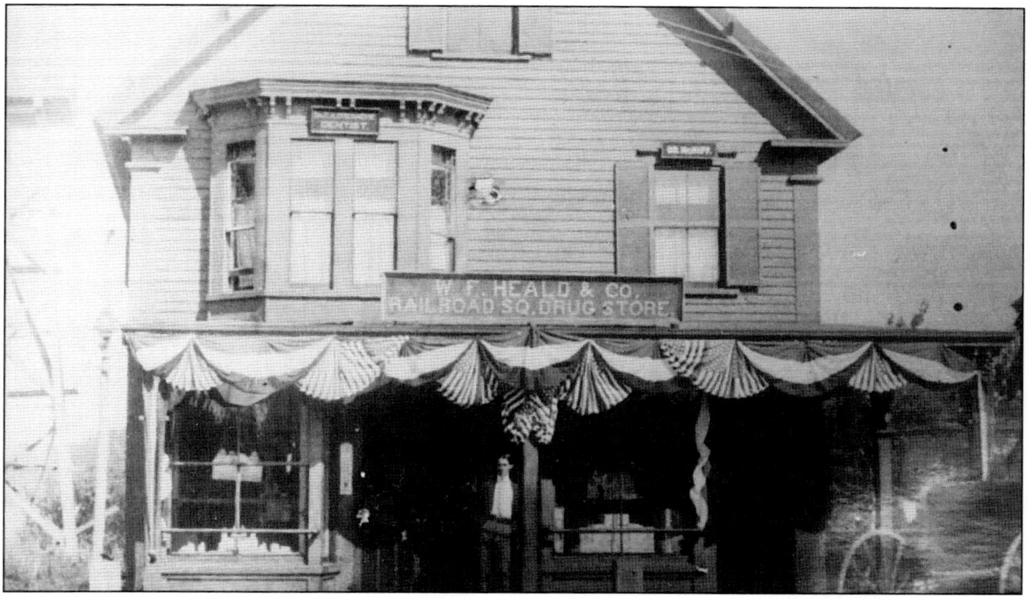

William F. Heald's drug store in Railroad Square is decorated for one of the many celebrations in town around the turn of the century. This building provided many of the medical services in Pepperell; over the years it housed numerous pharmacies, doctors, and dentists. Chester Babineau had his pharmacy here, following the McDermott and Dupaw pharmacies. Doctors' offices on the second floor included those of Dr. Charles Heald and Dr. Charles Porter.

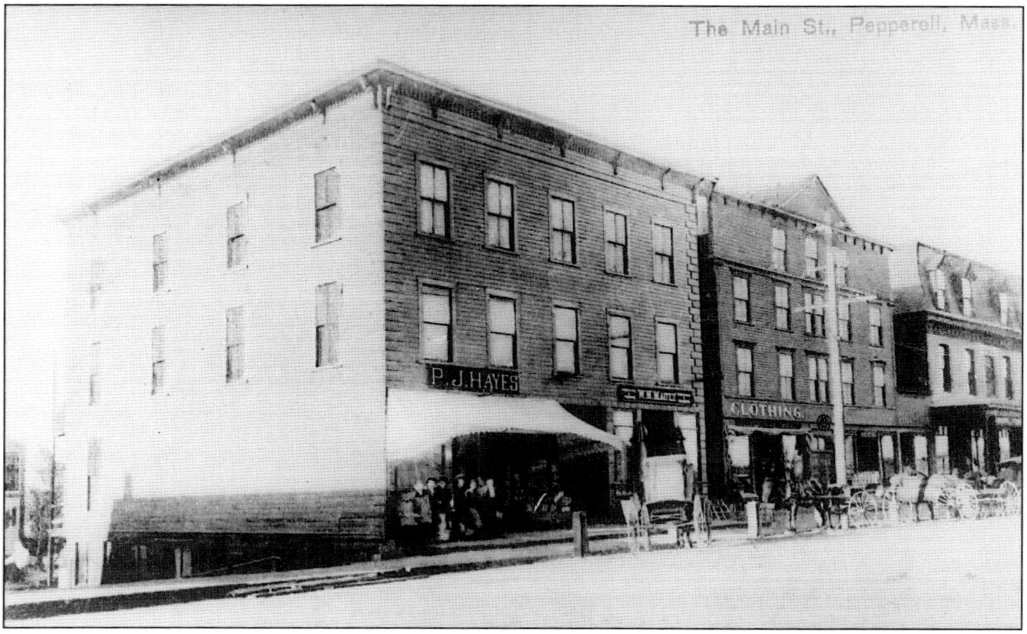

Patrick J. Hayes ran a grocery, meat, and provision business in Railroad Square about the turn of the century. In the same block was Mault's hardware store, years later owned by Arthur W. Bartlett. Adjacent was the Opera House, occupied on the first floor by Steele, Lane & Company and the U.S. Post Office. On the second floor was a large hall, used originally for stock and traveling shows. It was later the site of dances and sporting events, and was finally occupied by a movie theater.

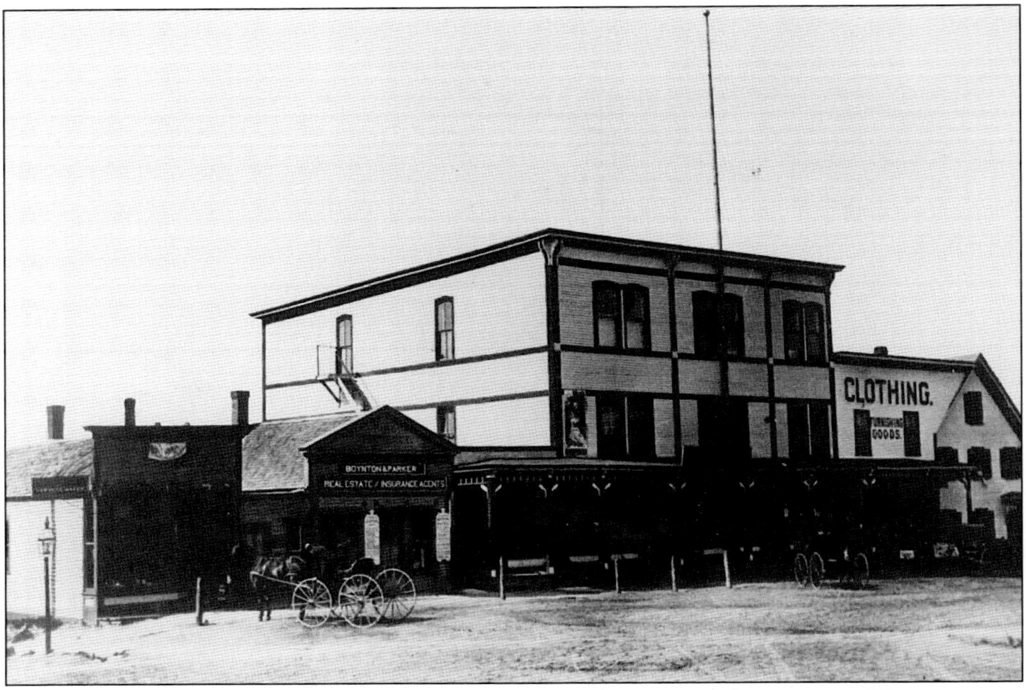

Shown here is the lower end of Railroad Square at the turn of the century. The one-story lunchroom and ice cream parlor on the left would later become a fruit store. Lewis Green also operated a clothing and shoe store there for a number of years.

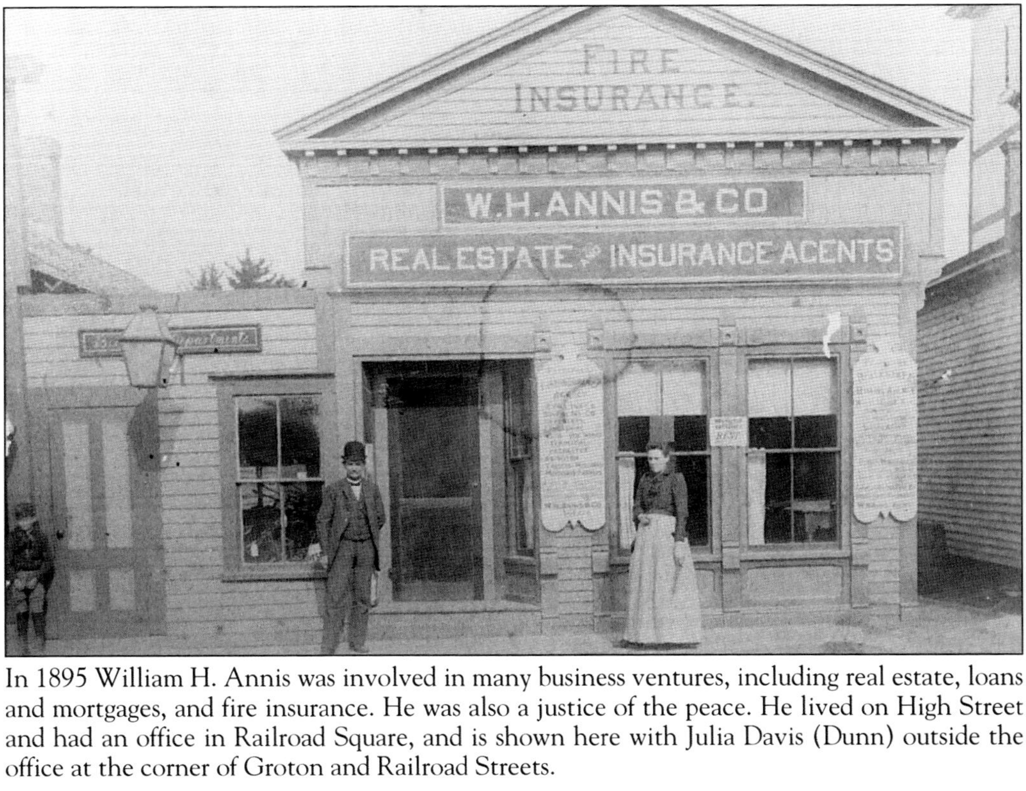

In 1895 William H. Annis was involved in many business ventures, including real estate, loans and mortgages, and fire insurance. He was also a justice of the peace. He lived on High Street and had an office in Railroad Square, and is shown here with Julia Davis (Dunn) outside the office at the corner of Groton and Railroad Streets.

This picture of the "telephone girls" was taken about 1924. The telephone operators are, from left to right: (front row) Agnes West and Dora Deware; (back row) Gertrude McCormack, Bessie Wright, and Elizabeth Reagan. The telephone office at that time was located on the second floor of the Odd Fellows Building.

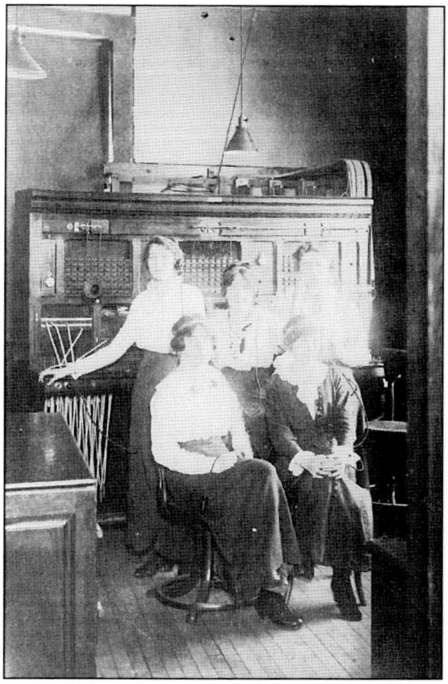

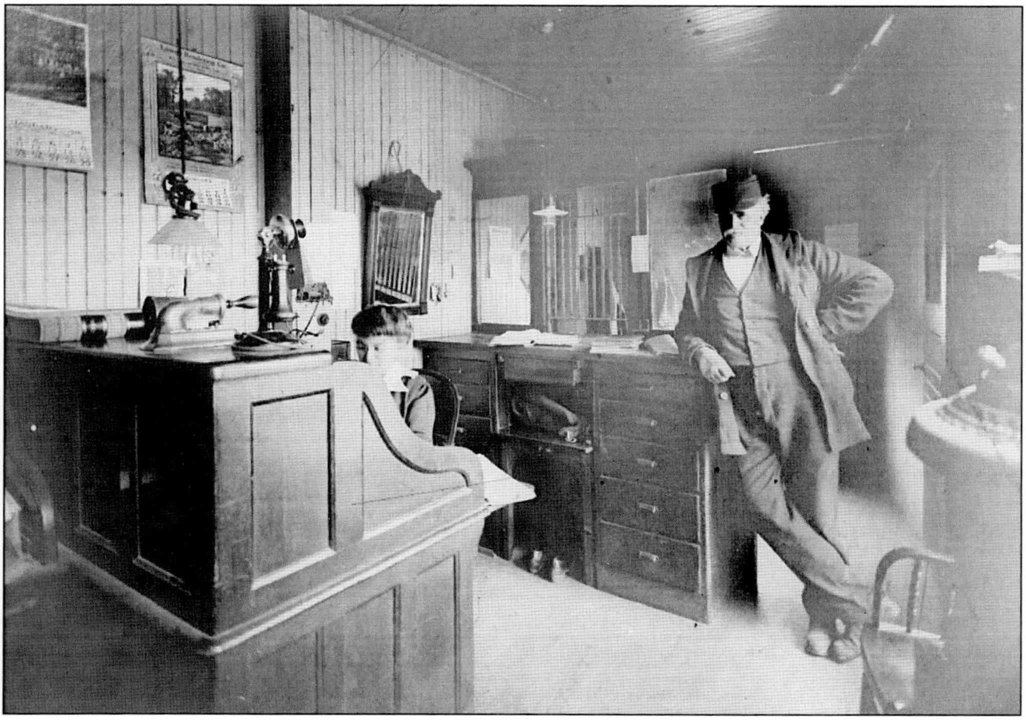

Irving J. Rowells had a coal, wood, and grain office on Railroad Street about 1916 across from the residence of Albert Prince. Previous to 1910, the office was in a small building on the site of Wyman Kemp's garage and gas station; according to tradition the office also housed the first telephone switchboard in Pepperell. Pictured here with Mr. Rowells is his secretary, Edna Kittredge (later Edna Clement).

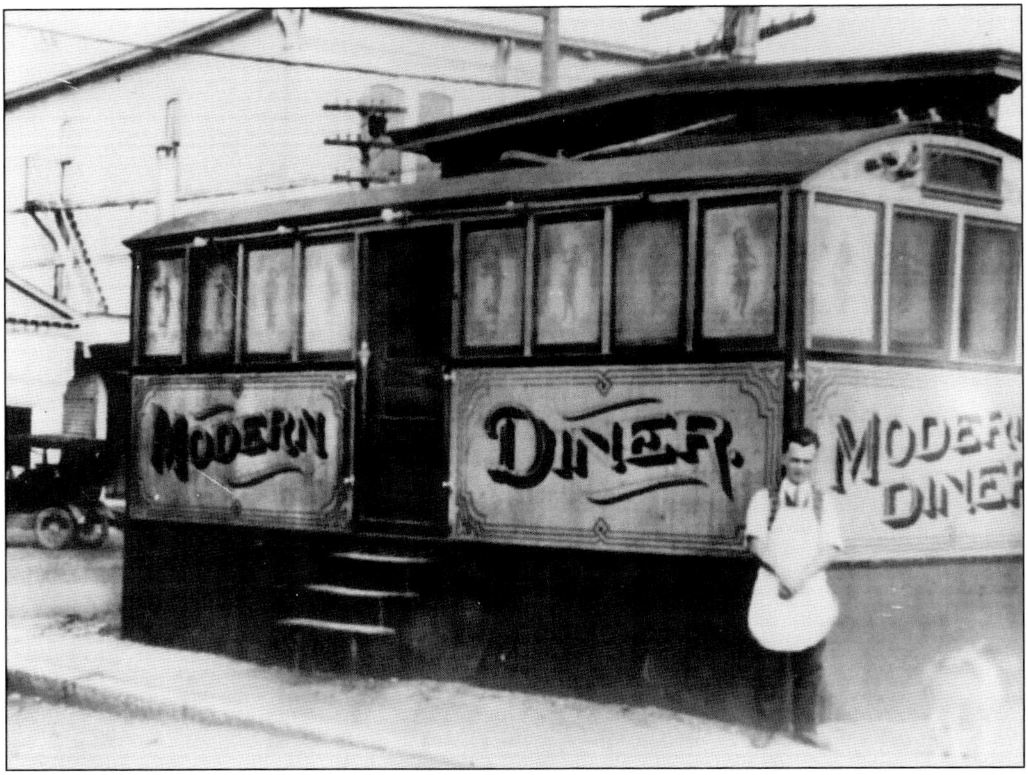

The Modern Diner was moved several times in its lifetime. In this photograph it is located at the intersection of Main, Mill, and Canal Streets, but it was also situated in Railroad Square at one time.

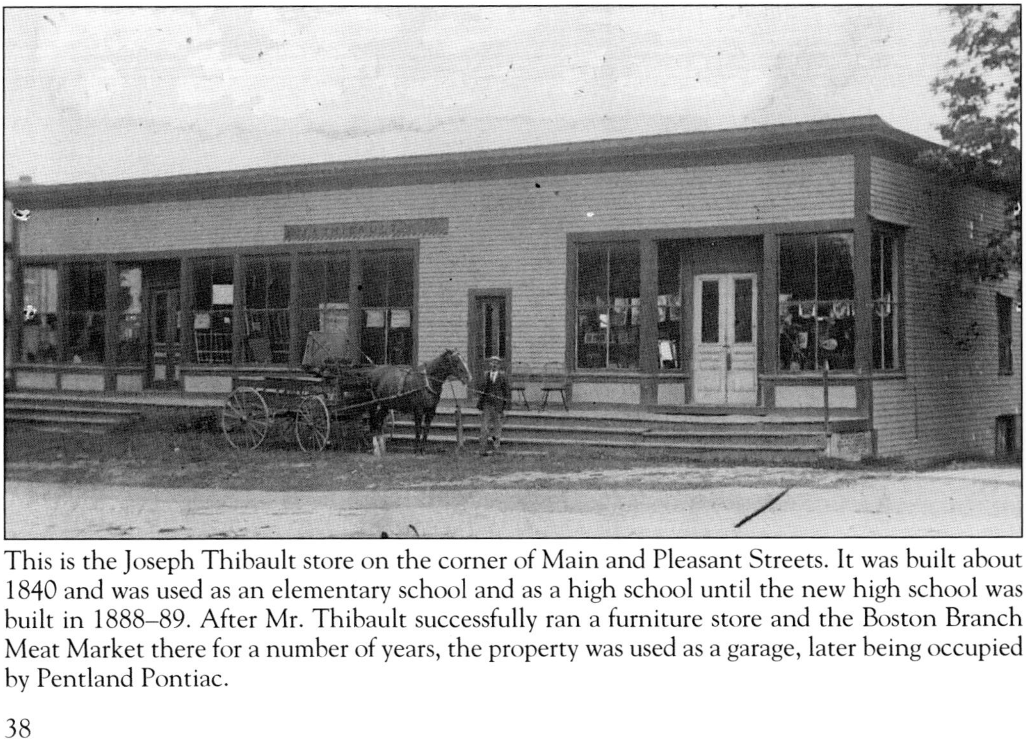
This is the Joseph Thibault store on the corner of Main and Pleasant Streets. It was built about 1840 and was used as an elementary school and as a high school until the new high school was built in 1888–89. After Mr. Thibault successfully ran a furniture store and the Boston Branch Meat Market there for a number of years, the property was used as a garage, later being occupied by Pentland Pontiac.

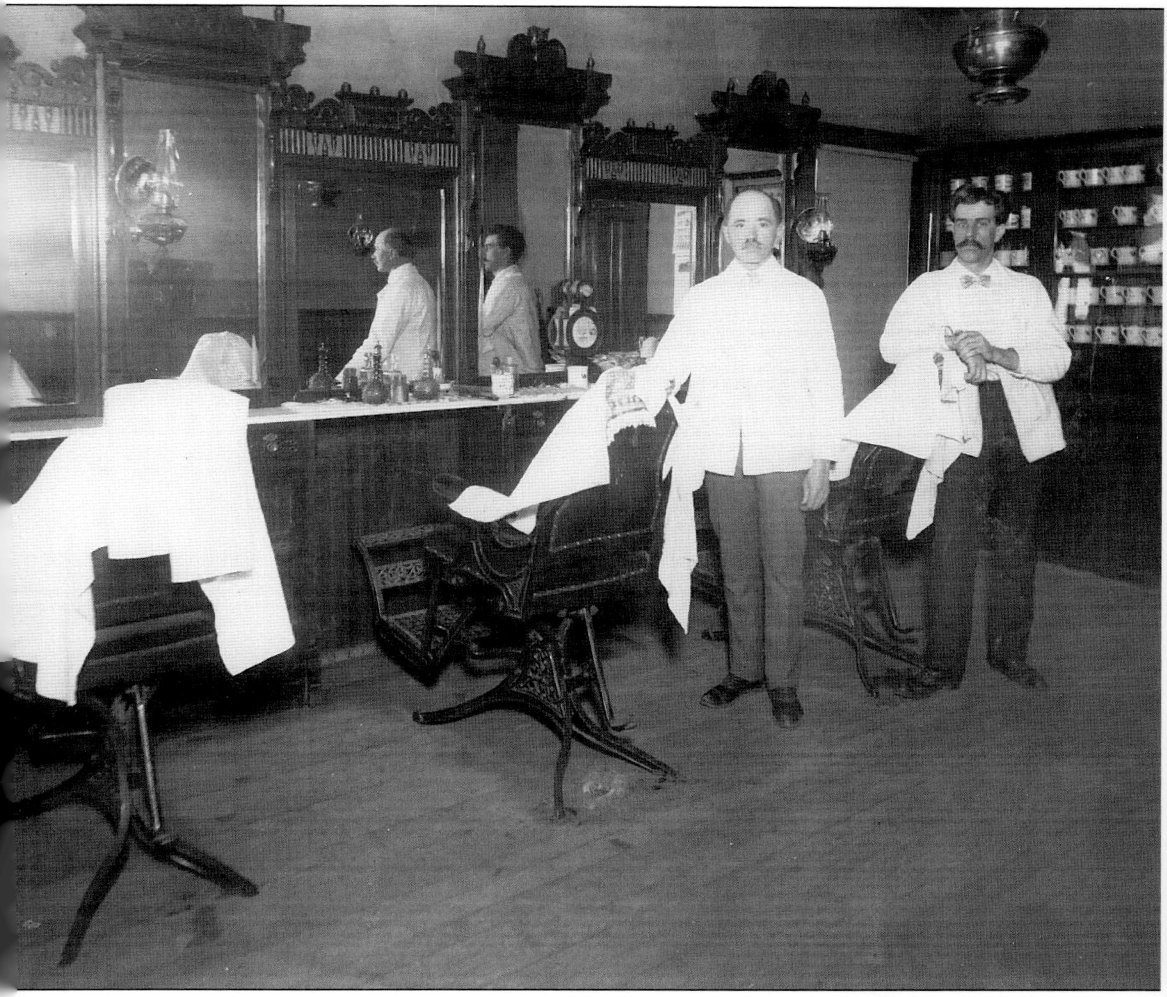

Amos Grenier (left) ran a barbershop on Main Street across from the Odd Fellows Hall. After the fire of 1903, the barbershop was quickly rebuilt as the western end of the Tarbell Block.

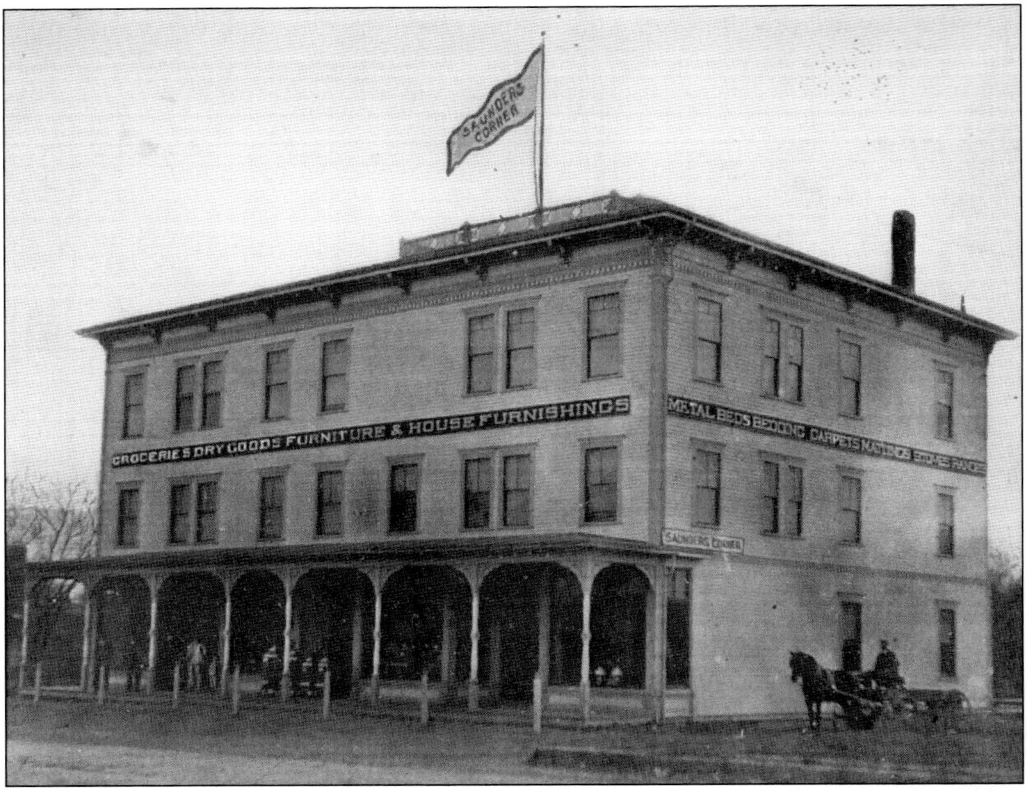

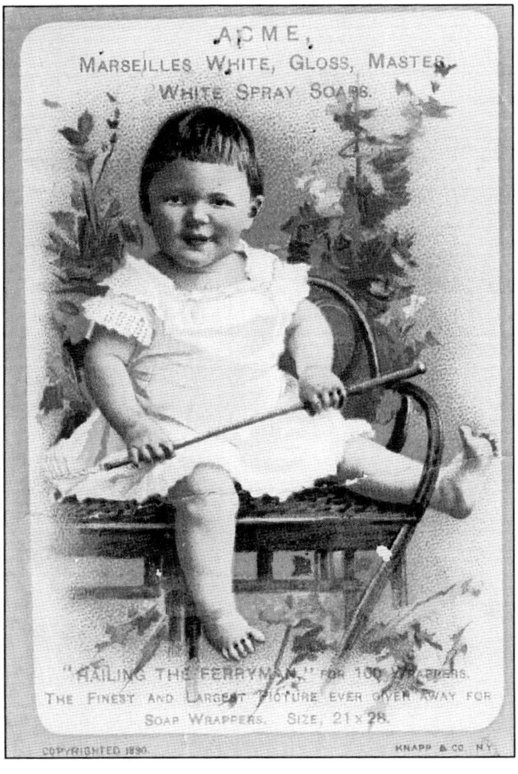

Saunders Corner, now known as the Odd Fellows Building, was built following the fire of 1903, which destroyed the original store at the same location. The new store was dedicated on February 8, 1904, and continued in business until the early 1930s, when it was sold to Frank Tule, who ran a pharmacy there. The current owner, John McNabb, has run McNabb Pharmacy at this location for a number of years.

Merchants' advertising cards were popular in the 1880s and 1890s. This card advertising Acme Soap was given out to customers at Saunders Corner in 1890; it had the proprietor's name, address, and merchandise printed on the back.

This catchy little "Miss Muffet" poem advertises chocolates on sale at Saunders Corner in the early 1900s, and was sent out to customers on a postcard.

Miss Muffet and Chocolates

Little Miss Muffet sat on a tuffet
Eating of curds and whey,
Along came Jack Horner from **Saunders' Corner**
And unto Miss Muffet did say,
"Try these **Chocolates** of mine they really are fine
And are fresh **from the Corner** today."

Then little Miss Muffet hopped up from the tuffet
And again was happy and gay
"Jack you dear boy, my heart's filled with joy,
I'll be your best girl from today.
I like little Boy Blue but I surely love you,
We'll marry whenever you say."

Then Jack and Miss Muffet sat down on the tuffet
And made plans for a very long life.
Jack said "We'll wed in September. I'll always remember
These **Chocolates** that brought me a wife."

Twenty varieties of heavy chocolate-coated creams included in our chocolate sale this week. Regular 60 and 70 cent chocolates for

49 Cents the Pound

Fresh every Saturday.

SAUNDERS' CORNER,

East Pepperell, Mass.

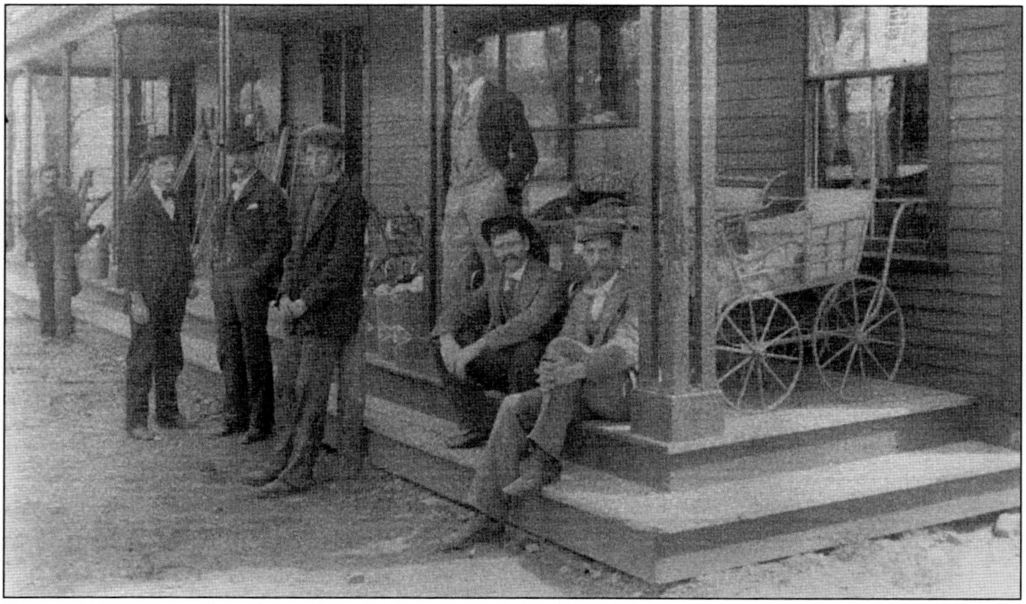

Young gents pose for their picture on the steps of Saunders Corner in 1897. The store was a convenient place for paper makers and horse traders to meet and discuss the affairs of the day. People came here to pay town taxes and rents, and to finalize deals. The store's long piazza was an assembly place for local delegations and was often crowded with sightseers on public occasions.

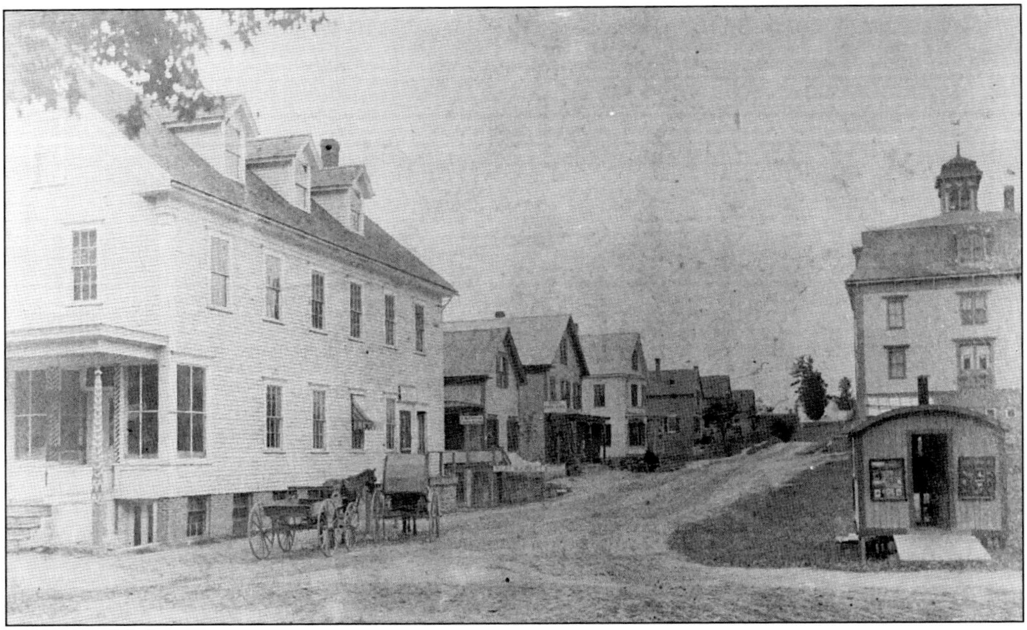

On the right in this view looking up Foster Street is Lovejoy's barn with its fancy cupola, and on the corner is the little photography studio of Ezra Goss. At the end of the street on the left are the three brick houses built by William Ames about 1874. The large building on the left corner is Pepperell Hall, which burned in the fire of 1890.

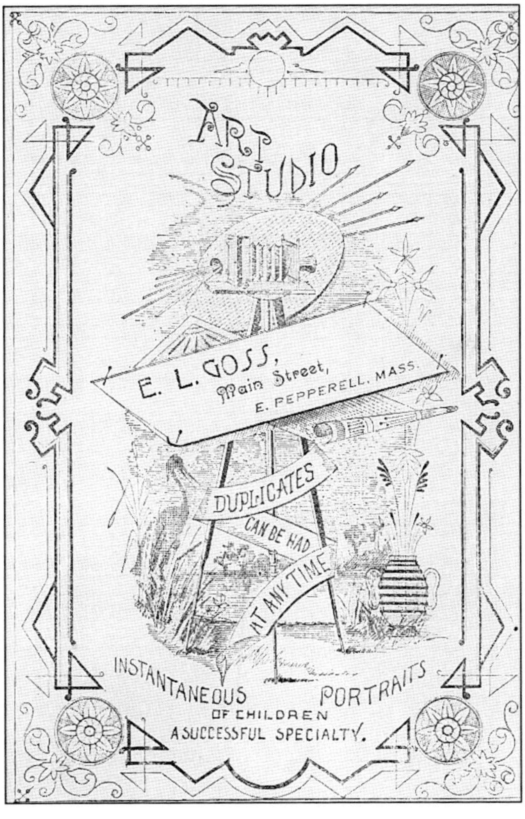

Photographs taken by Ezra Goss generally had fancy backings such as this one, which were common in the late 1800s. Mr. Goss is responsible for many of the photographs of Pepperell taken during this time period.

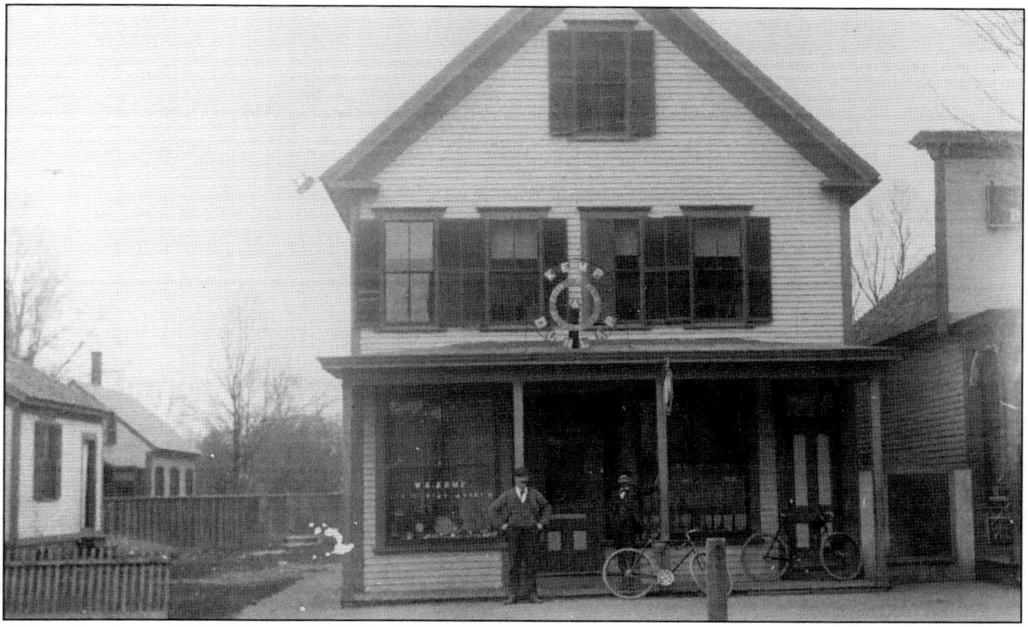

After the fire of 1890 burned their store, Kemp and Dunlap occupied a building on the north side of Main Street, next to Arthur Grenier's barber shop and opposite the site of Leighton's shoe factory. William A. Kemp continued his jewelry business and Fred Dunlap his bicycle shop there.

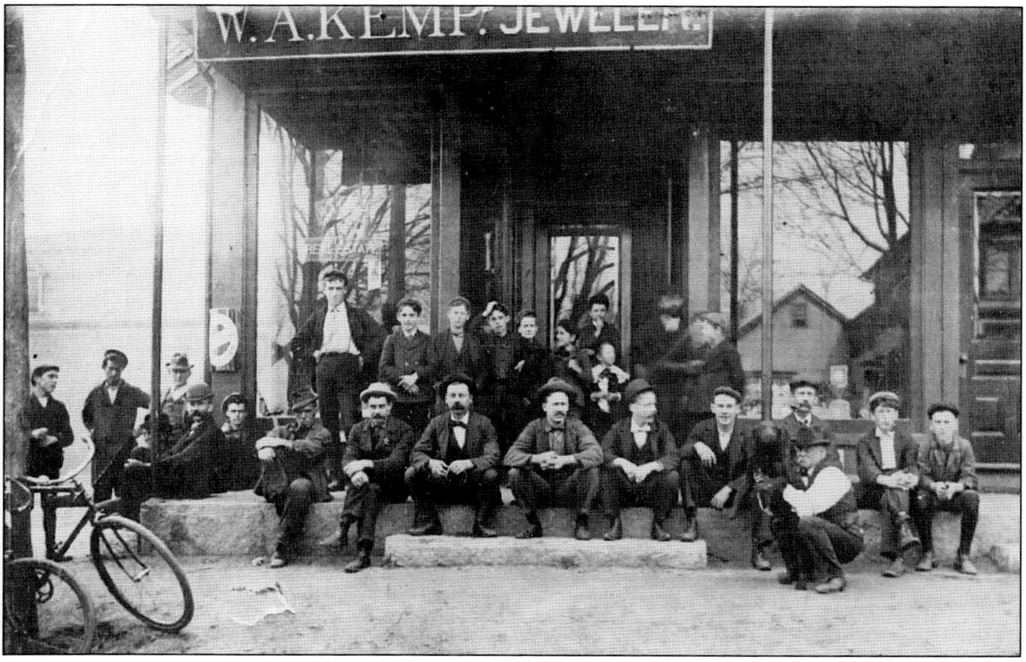

Quite a group, including the dog, gathered on the steps of Kemp's store to have their picture taken. About 1900 Mr. Kemp built this three-story building at the corner of Main and Foster Streets for his jewelry and sporting goods business. Ingalls Kittredge was a clock and watch repairman who worked in the jewelry store and carried on an insurance business there as well. Fred Dunlap ran his bicycle sales and repair shop in the basement.

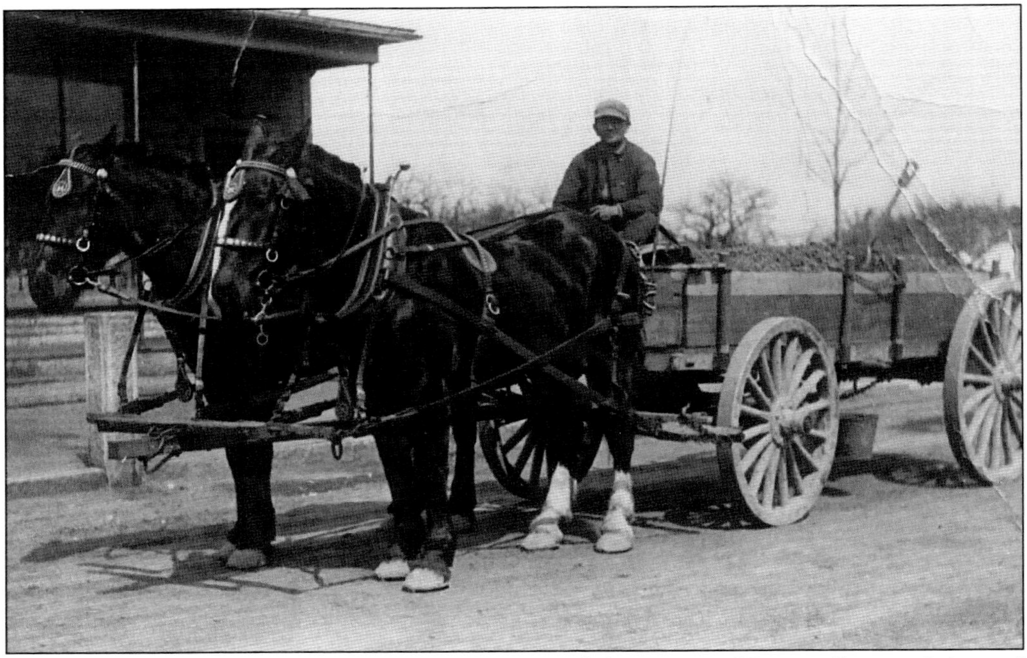

Coal and wood wagons were a common sight around the streets of Pepperell toward the end of summer before cold weather set in. Although the identity of the person driving the team of horses is unclear, Andrew Pillsbury was known to drive a two-horse coal team. Charlie Messer also delivered grain in Pepperell and the surrounding towns.

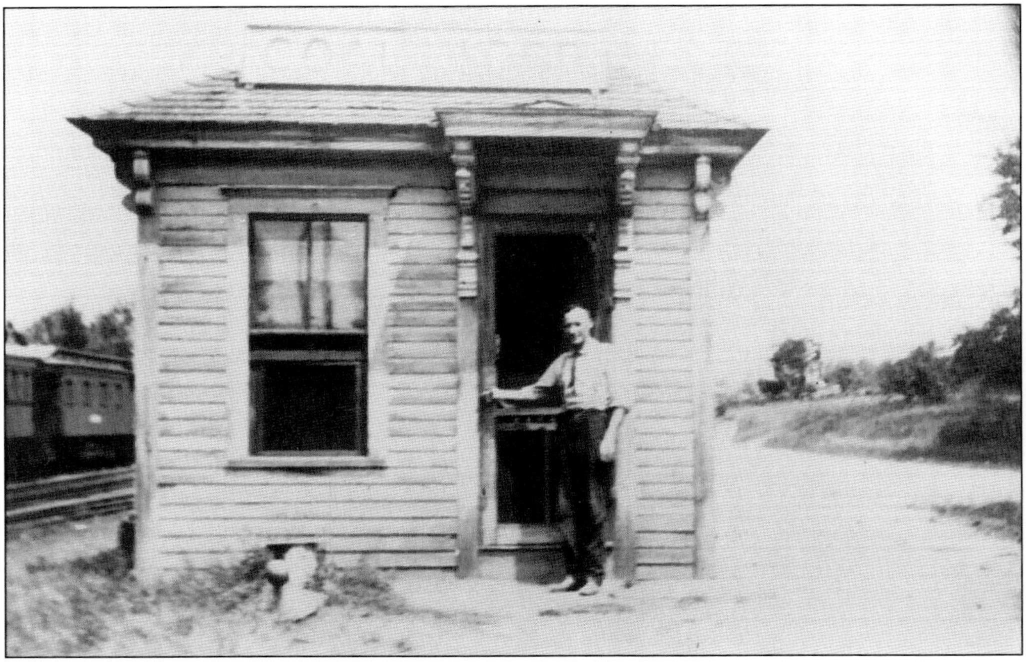

James E. Dunn is standing outside his coal and wood office, which stood conveniently next to the railroad station. Although the station is hidden by the office, the train can be seen to the far left. The coal office was moved some years ago to the Dunn farm, where it remains in its original condition.

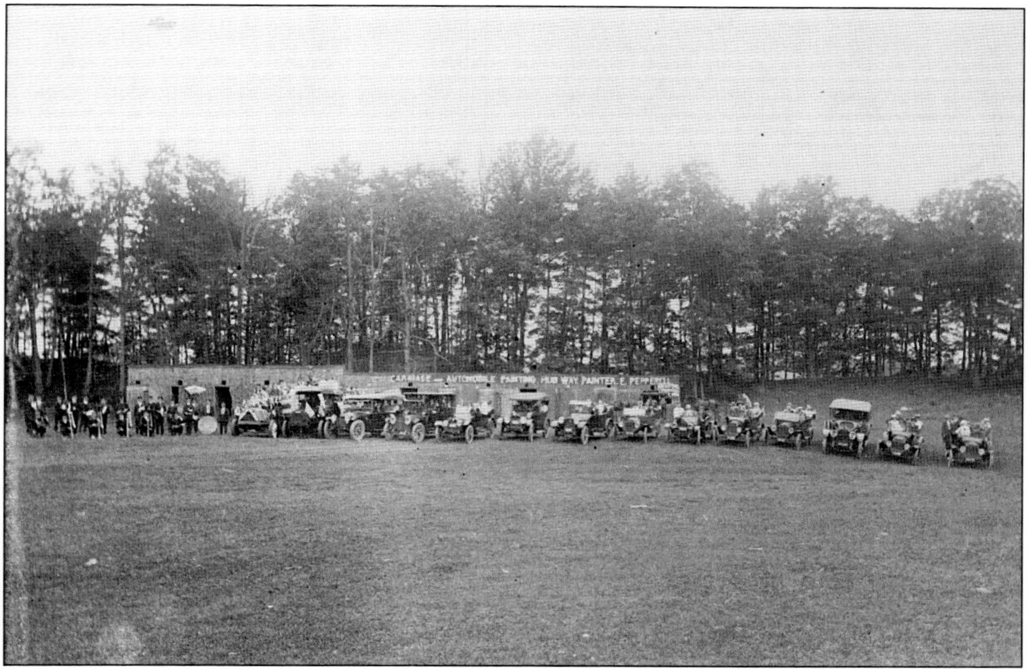

This photograph shows a gathering of cars at the Hub Way Painter, which advertises carriage and automobile painting. Bill Chapman ran the business on Shirley Street in the 1920s and '30s.The occasion is unknown, but the band standing at left indicates that perhaps a meet or parade was about to take place.

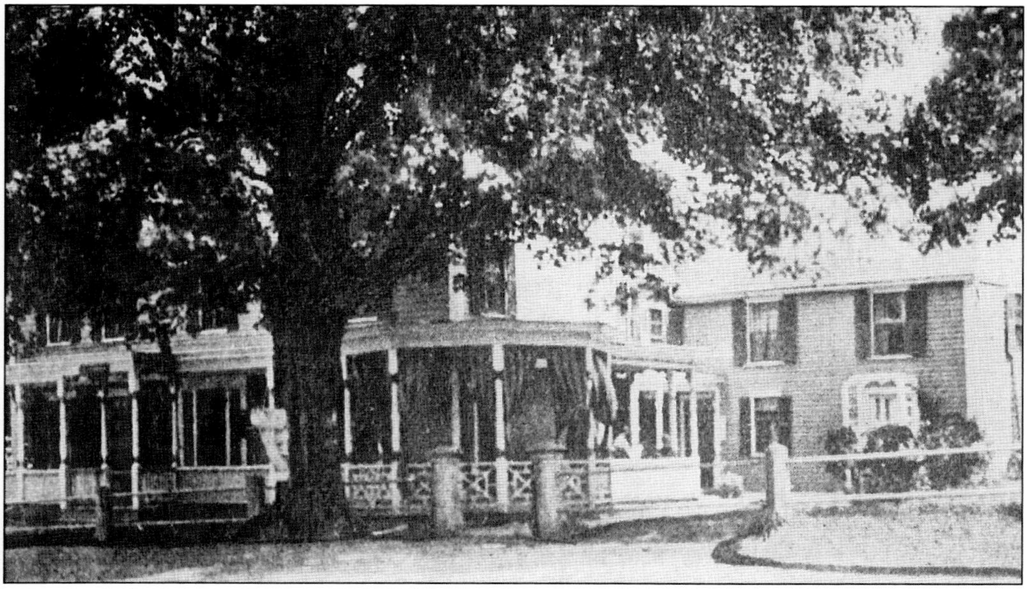

Many people may remember this building as the Villa Lorraine, a restaurant run by Victor Geiger in the 1920s and '30s at the corner of Maple and Oak Hill Streets. This was originally the home of Charles F. Lawrence, who was born here in 1842. Mr. Lawrence is remembered for his generous donation to the town of Pepperell, which paid for the construction of the Lawrence Library. The house was later owned by the Olsens and for many years after that by the Bosquet family.

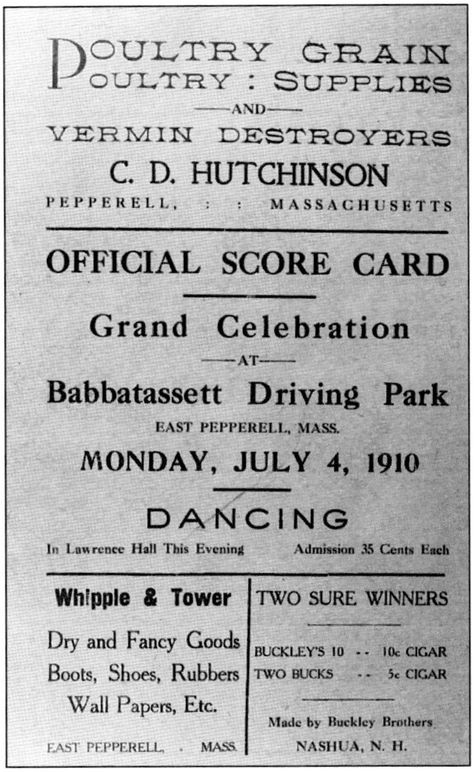

The official scorecard for the races at the Babbatassett Driving Park during this Fourth of July celebration included many advertisements for area businesses. C.D. Hutchinson's advertises poultry, grain, and "vermin destroyers."

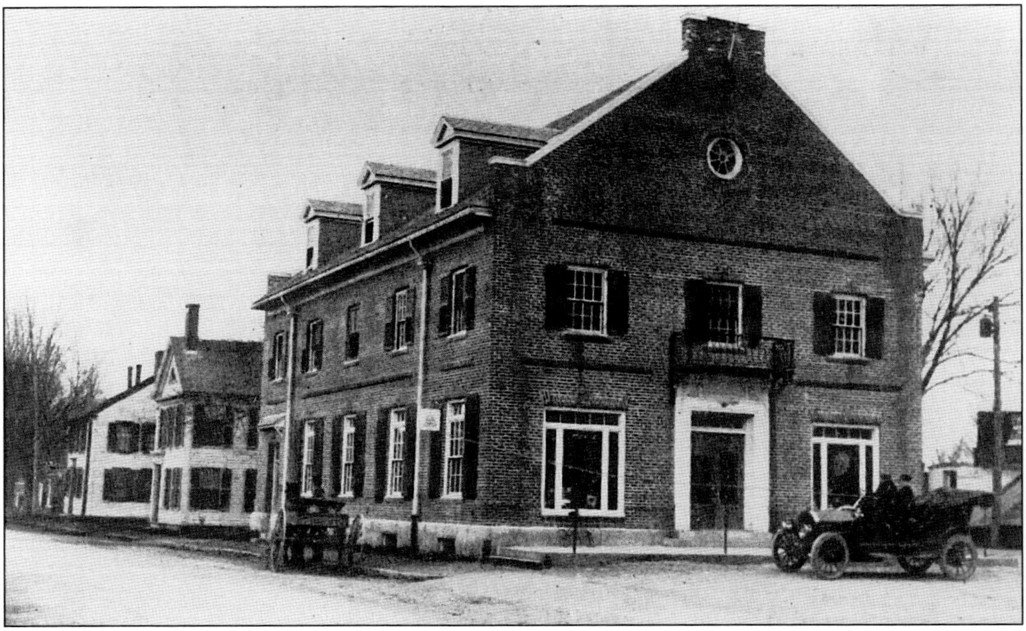

Charles D. Hutchinson replaced his earlier store in Pepperell Center with this brick building in 1906. After his death in 1914, the store passed on to his son, Harry D. Hutchinson, who continued business there for some time. Charles Maynard had a store there in the 1940s, and afterward the building was occupied by the Stewart family, who ran a store and snack bar. This photograph was taken c. 1910.

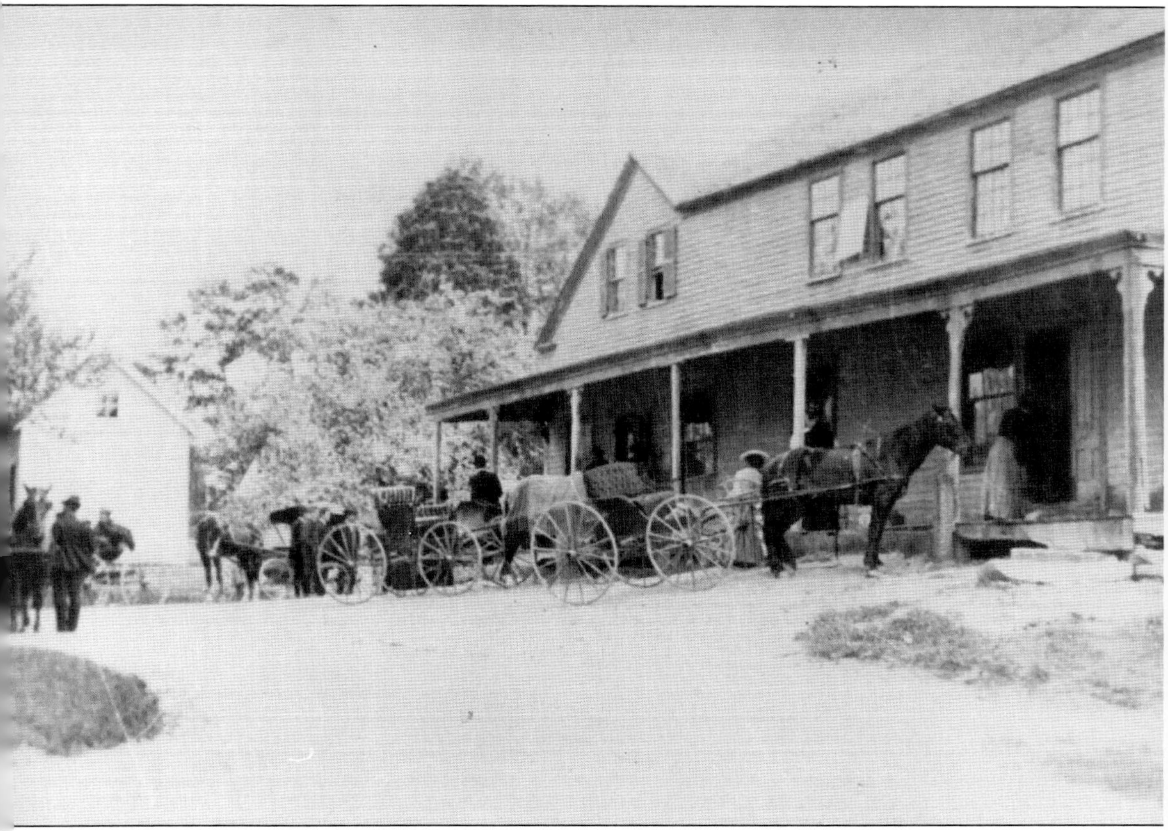

A two-story ell added to a story-and-a-half "cottage" fronting on Townsend Street was at one time a busy business site at Pepperell Center. A Mr. Mace lived here and used the ell as a harness shop; he also rented space to other businesses. Thomas M. Thompson had a law office here, and later Moses Greenlaw's picture and glazing shop, a shoe store, and a tailor shop were also located in the ell. The post office was also always located in this building. About 1862 William Shipley bought the property and the business was run by his brother-in-law, John Loring. Mr. Loring's nephew, Charles D. Hutchinson, became associated with him in 1872, and at the time of Mr. Loring's death in 1878, Hutchinson bought the store contents and became postmaster in the winter of 1879. The building was torn down in 1905 and a new brick building was erected in its place in 1906.

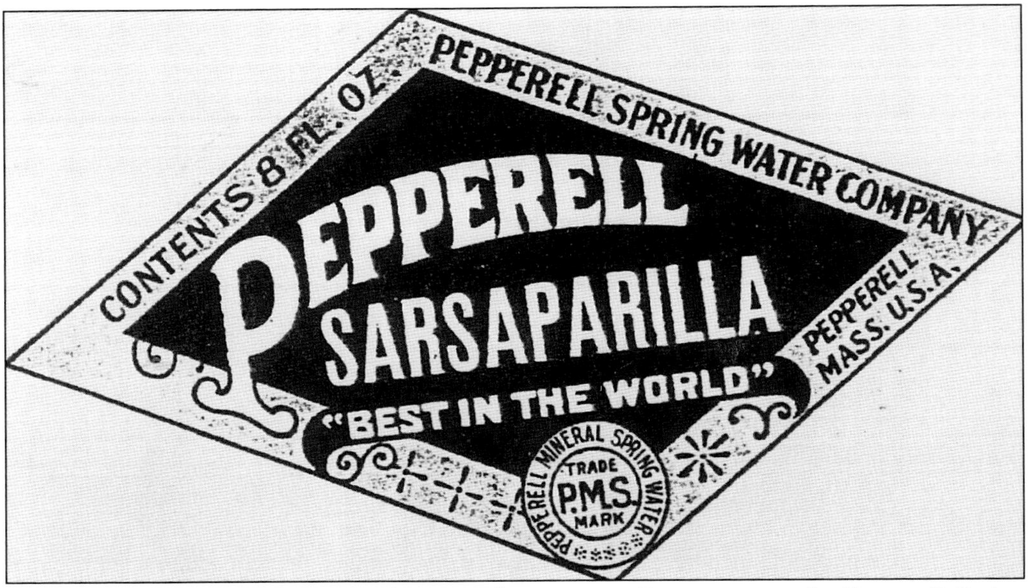

Pepperell was blessed with a natural spring of pure water. For some time the Pepperell Spring Water Company operated here, making a variety of bottled drinks touted as the "Best in the World." At the Saint Louis World's Fair in 1904, Pepperell Spring Water won a silver medal for its product. Pictured below are two young ladies posing at the old spring house at Pepperell Springs. The above image is a copy of a label on a bottle of sarsaparilla.

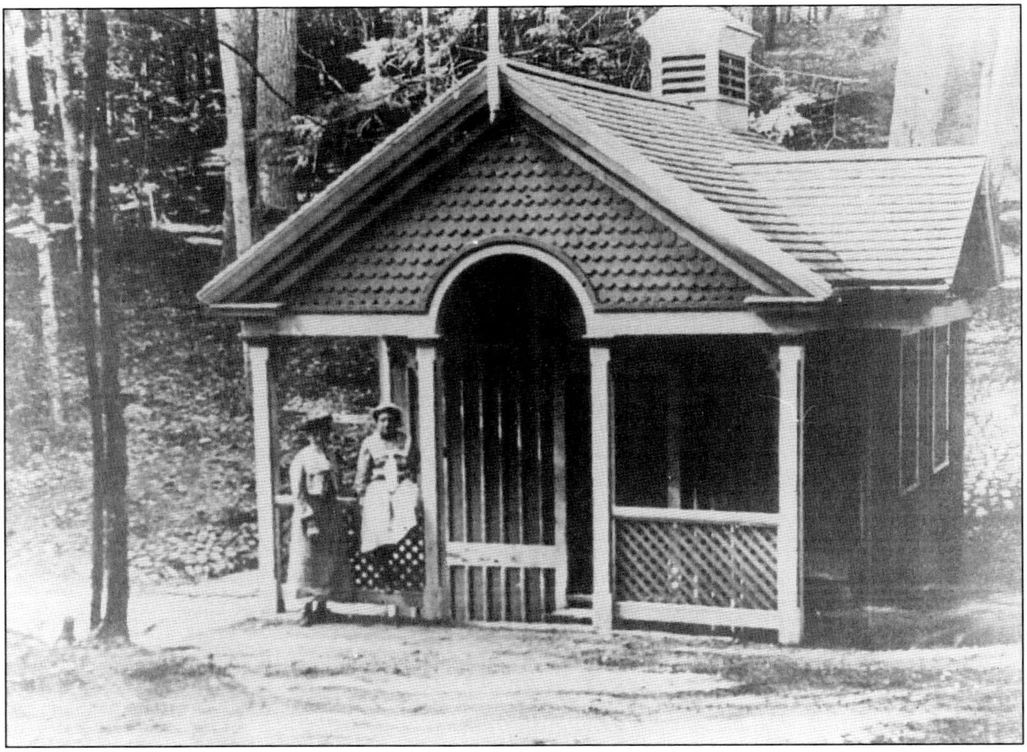

Three

INDUSTRY

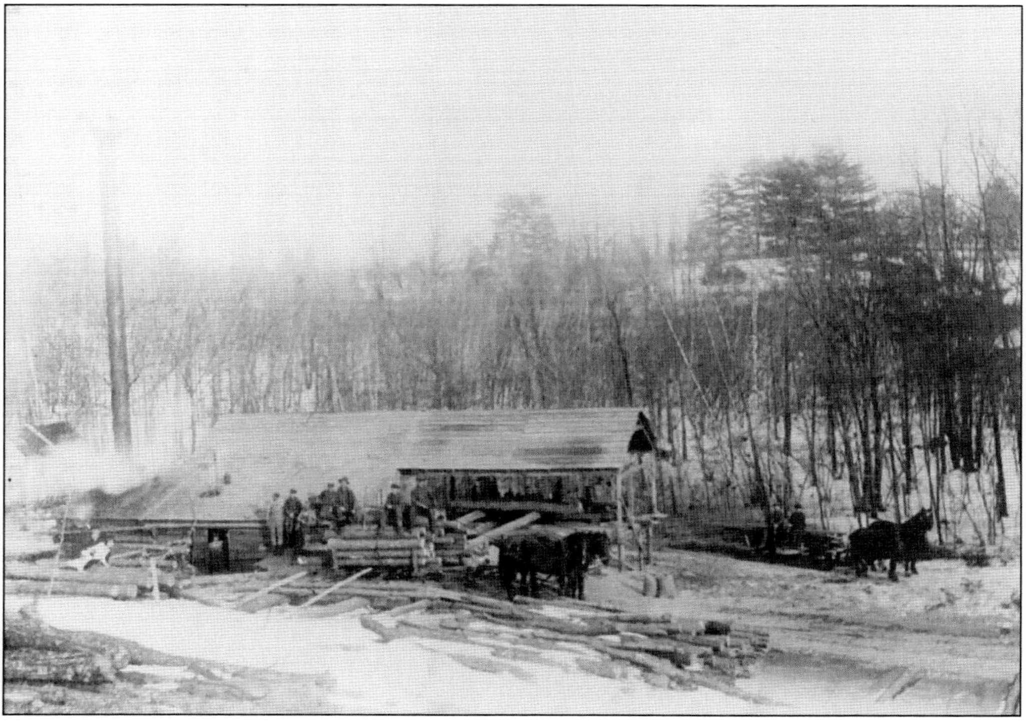

This is a picture of one of the portable sawmills that operated around town. These unique businesses had the advantage of being able to pack up and move to another location in pursuit of more work.

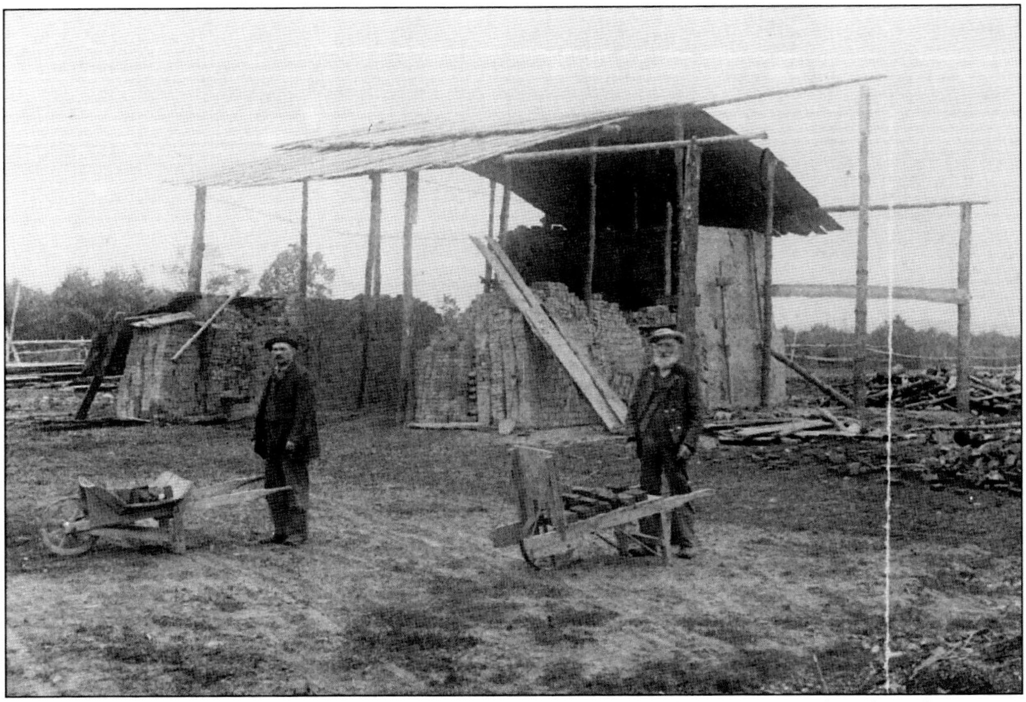

The oldest brickyard in Pepperell was located at the corner of Boynton and Oak Hill Streets. About 1874, William Ames built the three brick houses on Foster Street with brick manufactured by him at this brickyard. Bricks made here were used in the building of the Town House that same year. A Mr. Woodworth burned brick here as late as 1892, when he fired about 175,000 at each burning.

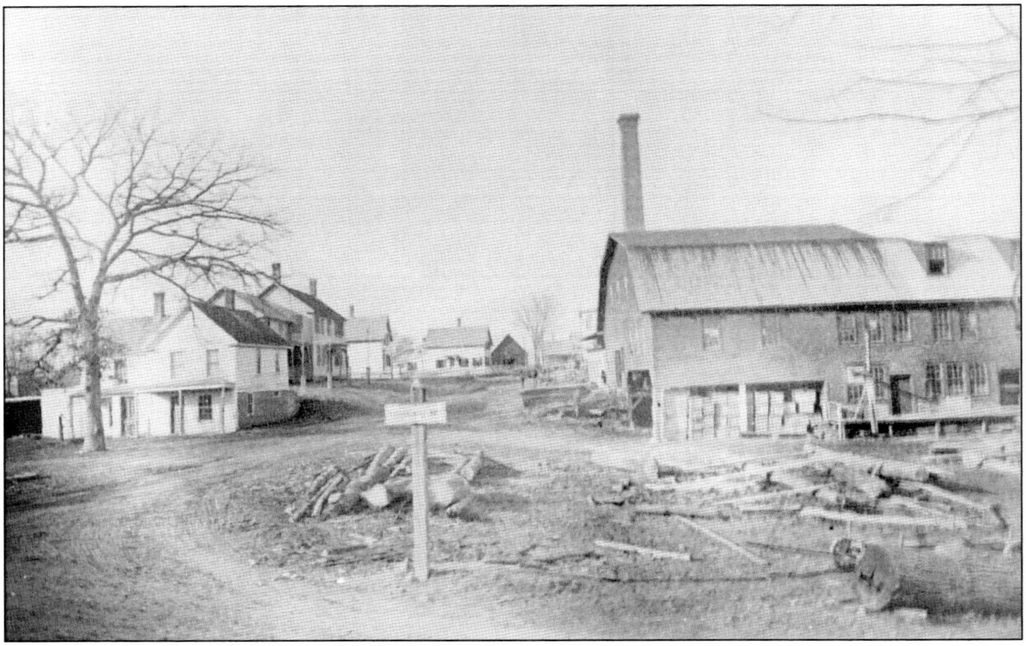

By 1875 Henry A. Parker had a sawmill and a gristmill at the corner of Mill and Groton Streets. On the other side of the river were Parkers Paper Mills, which were operated by steam power.

Blake's Improved Turbine Water Wheel was invented and manufactured by the Blake Brothers. Blake's complex of mills, machine shops, and a gristmill was located on the Nissitissit River near the corner of Hollis and Nashua Streets.

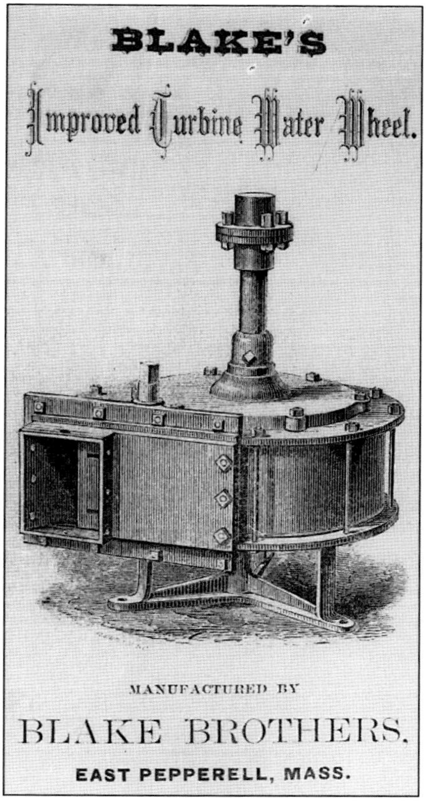

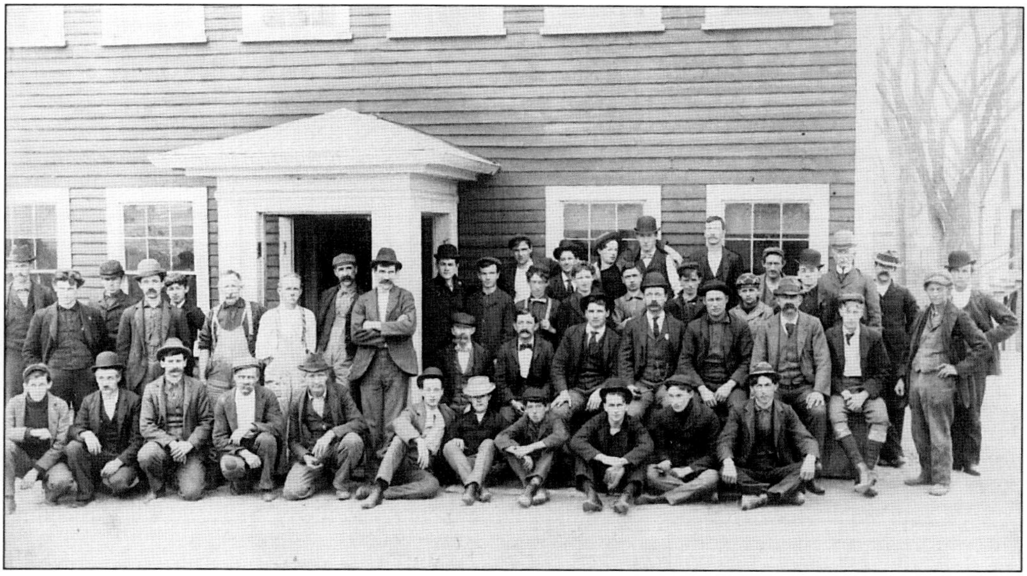

Workers pose for a picture about 1900 outside the old red mill at the corner of Nashua and Hollis Streets. At this time harps and zithers were made there by the Flag Manufacturing Company. Previously the mill was owned by John Pierce, who ran a gristmill from 1880 to 1898. Later ventures included the manufacture of rubber heels, shoes, paper cups, caskets, and bicycles. A new bridge was built next to the site of the building, which was taken down in the 1950s.

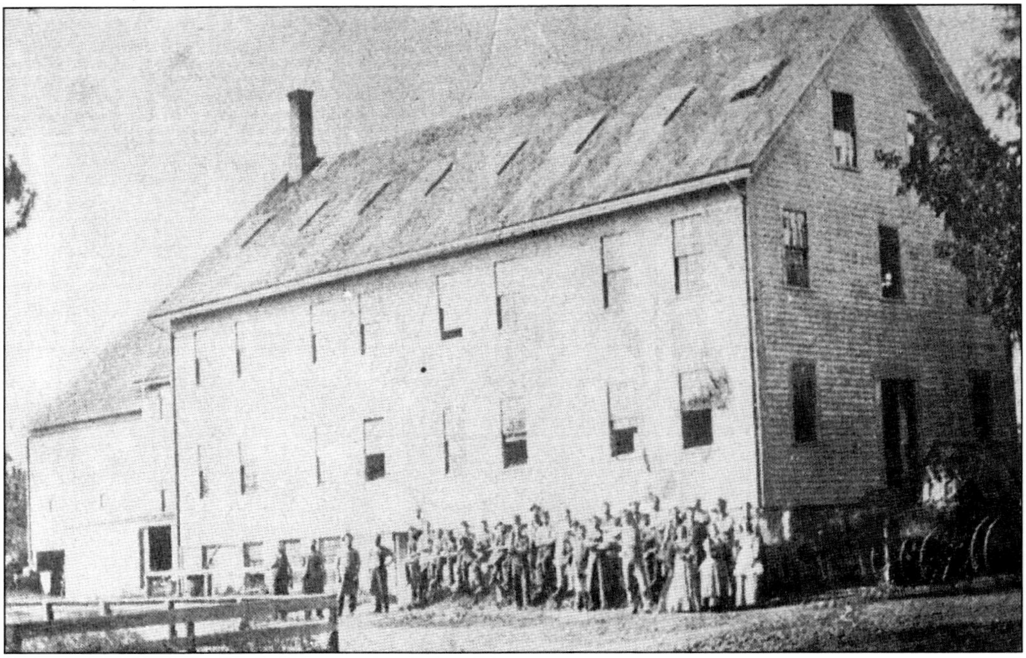

With the building of the first Leighton Shoe Factory in 1868, the shoe industry in Pepperell was boosted into the machine age. The factory, built by Albert Leighton at a cost of $50,000, was located on Main Street at the southwest corner of Foster Street, and employed seventy men and women. A decade later, Mr. Leighton sold his interest to his three sons, Frank, Charles, and Elbert, and they continued the business as Leighton Brothers.

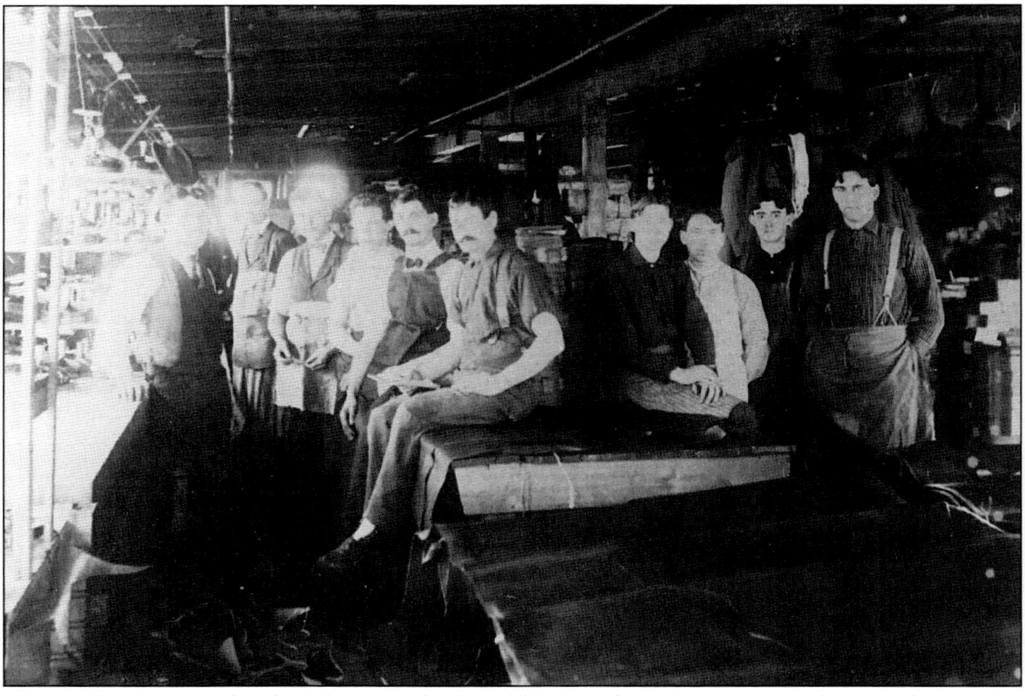

This early photograph of workers inside the old Lane Shoe Factory was taken in the cutting room. In the foreground is leather that is spread out and waiting to be cut.

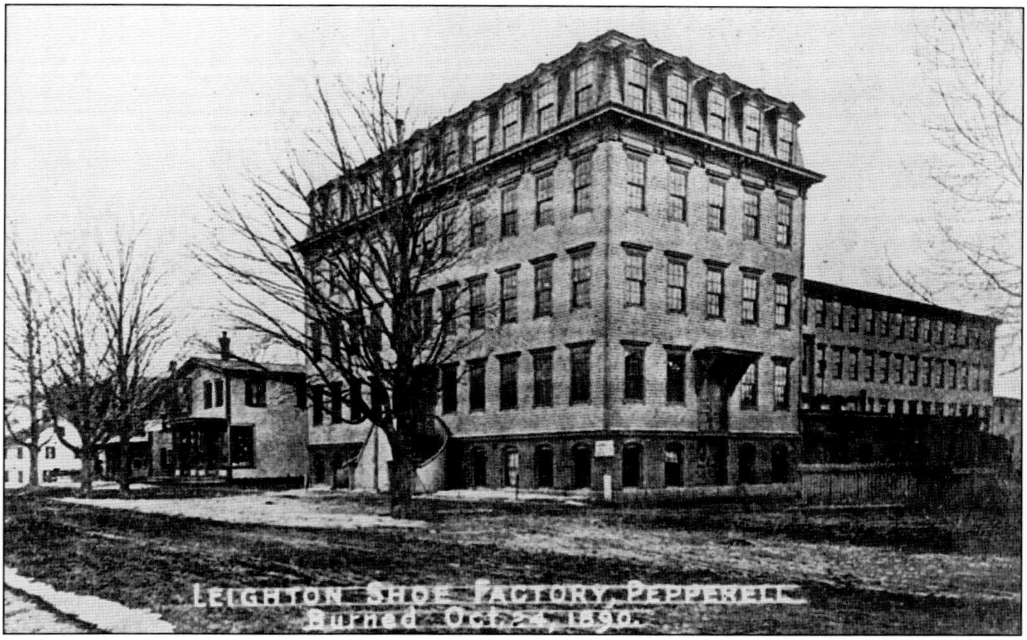

The second Leighton Shoe Factory was built on Main Street between Foster and Canal Streets after fire destroyed the first factory in 1879. With the new factory, shoe production increased to over $300,000 per year, and the factory provided employment for about three hundred men and women.

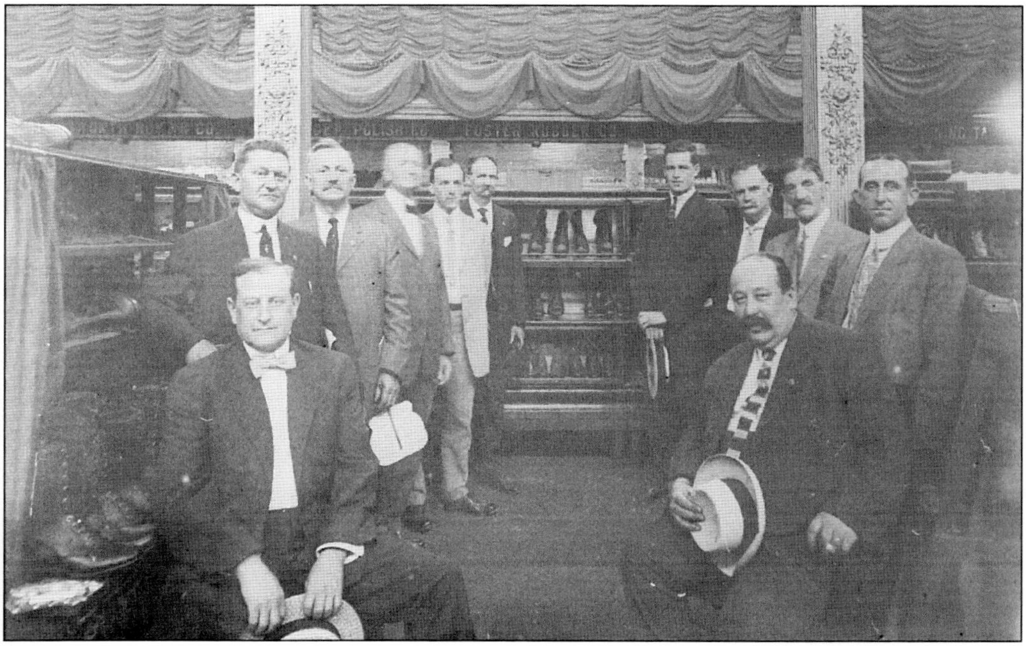

This picture was taken at a convention in the main office of the Buffalo/Larkin Shoe Company. The first person on the left is Mr. Gilmore of the Larkin Soap Company, and sixth on the left is Jonas Andrews (Forrest Andrews's father). The Larkin Shoe Company was a subsidiary of the Larkin Soap Company that began its business on Lowell Street after the great fire of 1903. Shoe production continued there until 1917, when it became the Pepperell Braiding Company.

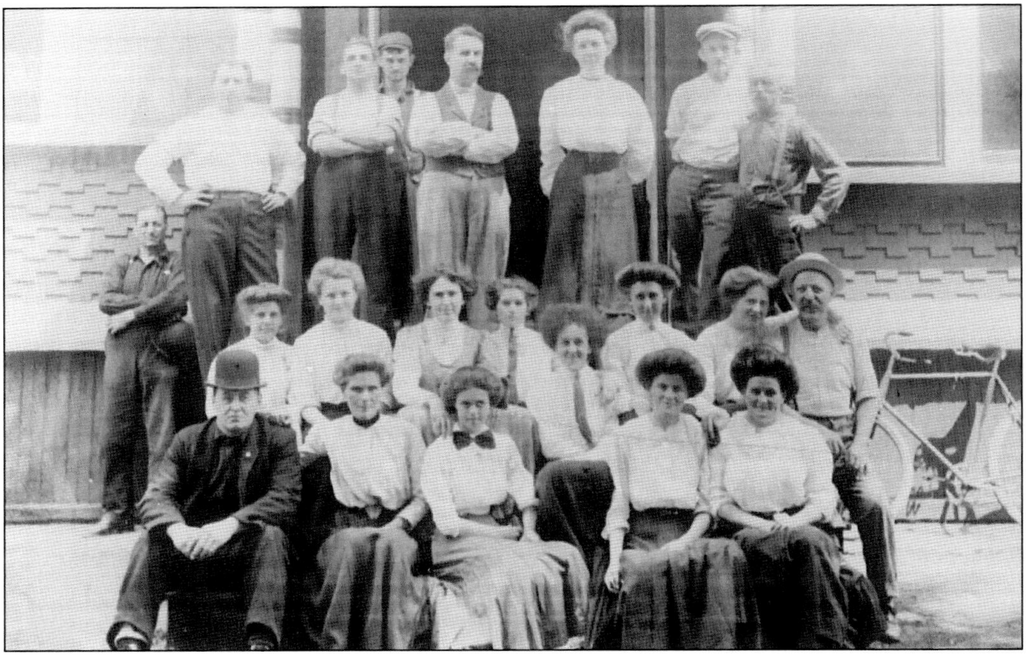

Workers at the Champion Card and Paper Company on Lowell Street pose on the steps for their picture. Note that all the women have their hair either rolled up or pulled back to avoid it getting caught in the machinery. One poor unfortunate woman had previously lost some of her hair when it got caught in one of the machines.

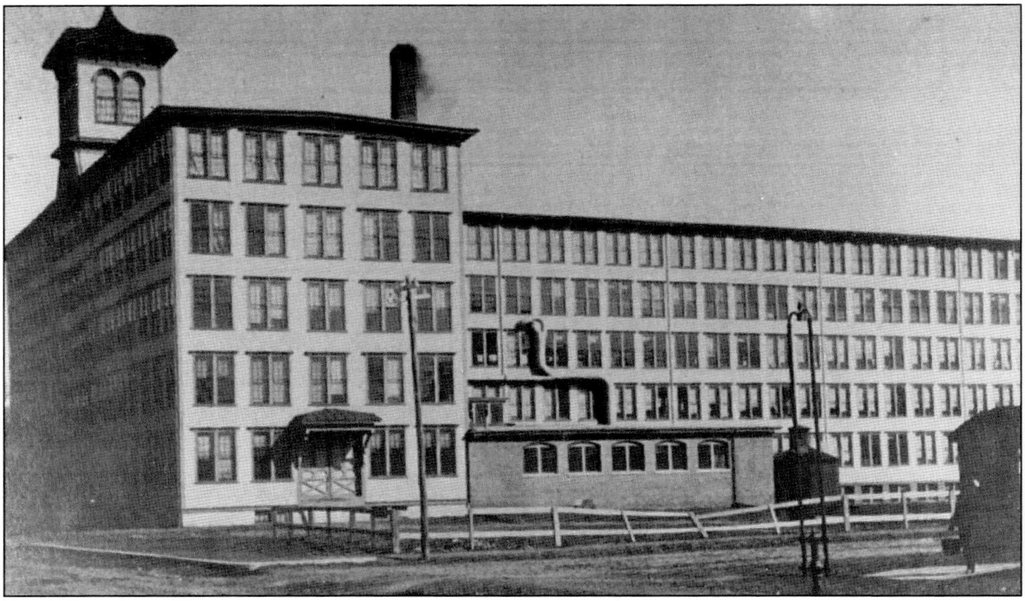

The dedication of the new Leighton Brothers Shoe Factory was held on February 23, 1891, with a grand celebration perhaps unequaled by any other in Pepperell. Decorations adorned the building to welcome the numerous expected guests. After the arrival of the noon trains in Railroad Square, a parade led by the Pepperell Cornet Band brought businessmen and guests via barges to view the new factory. Festivities came to a close with dinner for about three thousand people, followed by dancing late into the evening.

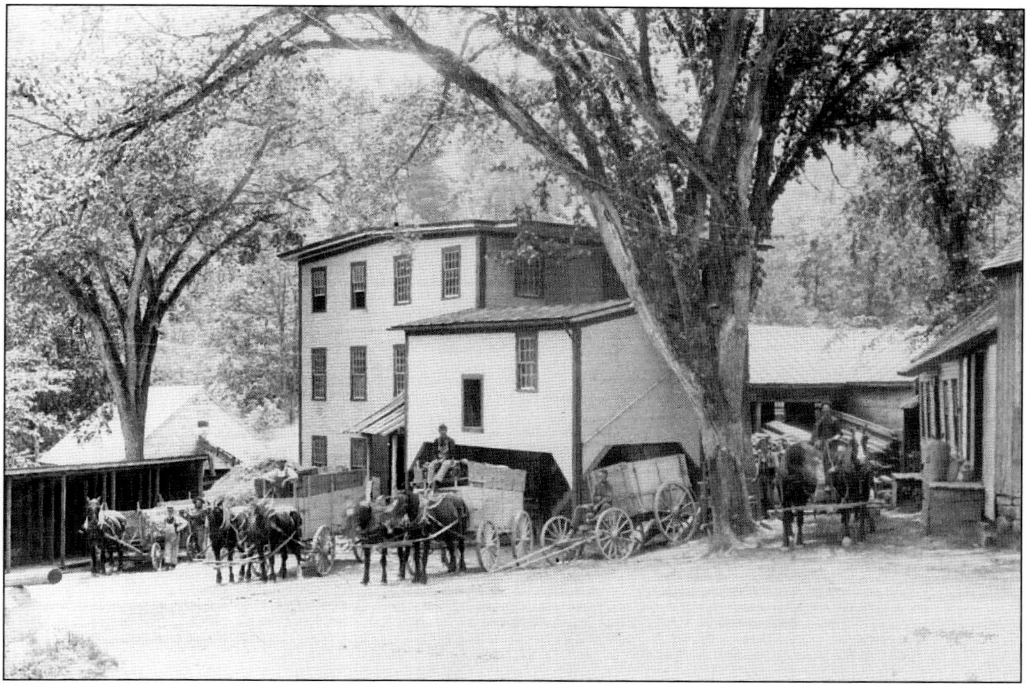

These are two different *c.* 1900 views of the busy Clarence Stickney Mill. There is little other information about this industry, but it was perhaps a sawmill.

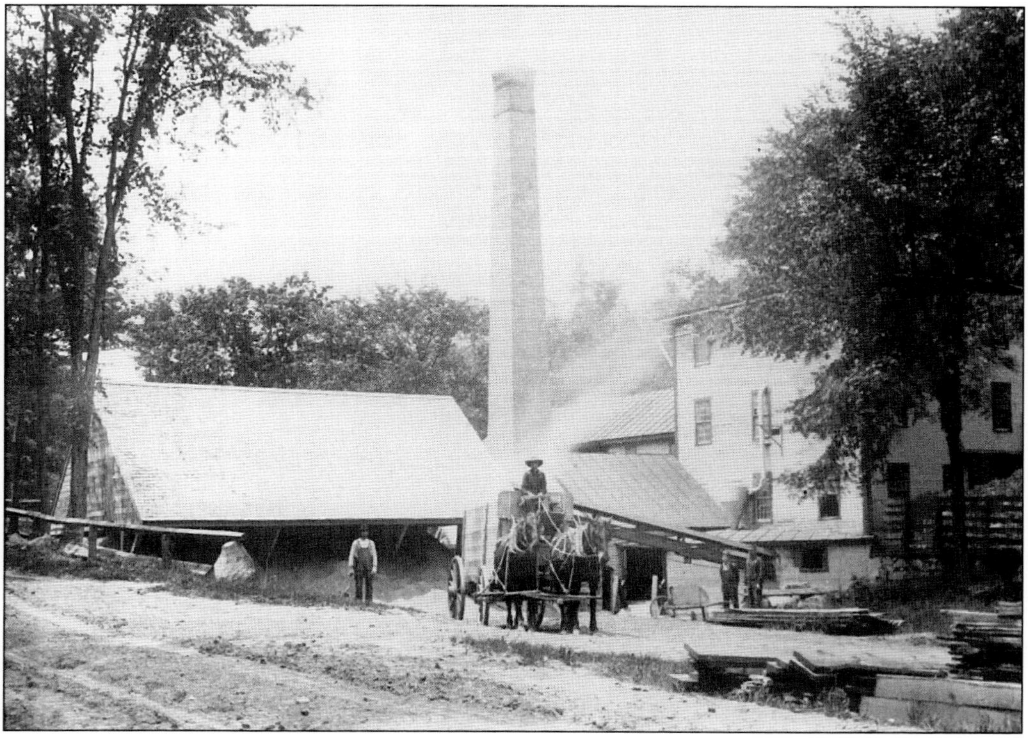

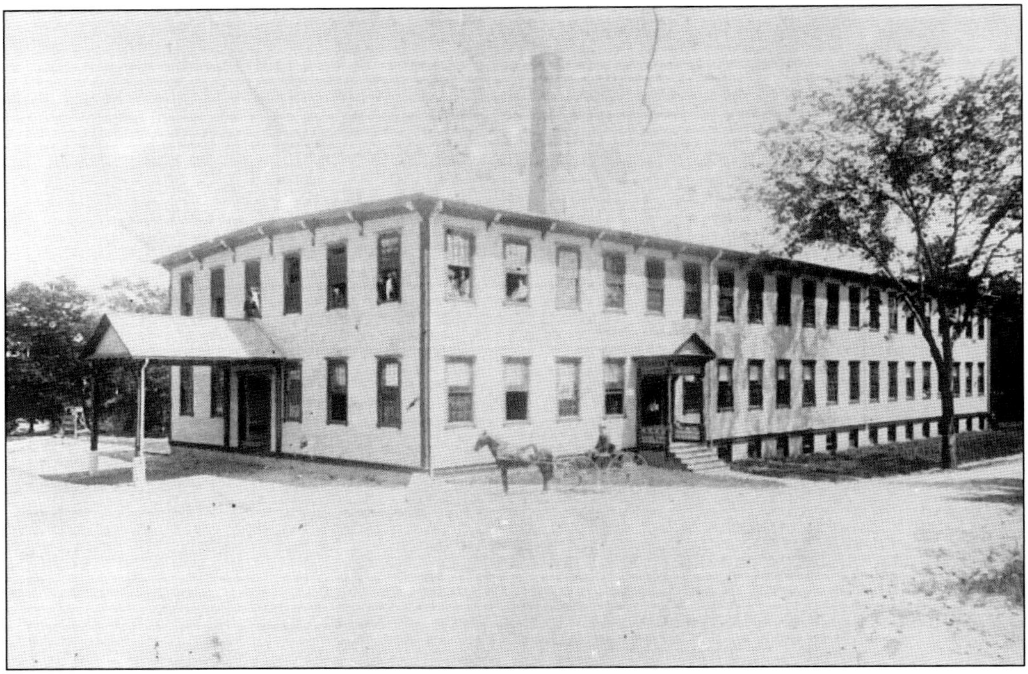

This is a photograph of Pepperell Card & Paper when it was just a two-story building. Production of coated papers was the specialty of this company as well as the Fairchild and Champion Companies, and together the three provided employment for hundreds of people for a number of years.

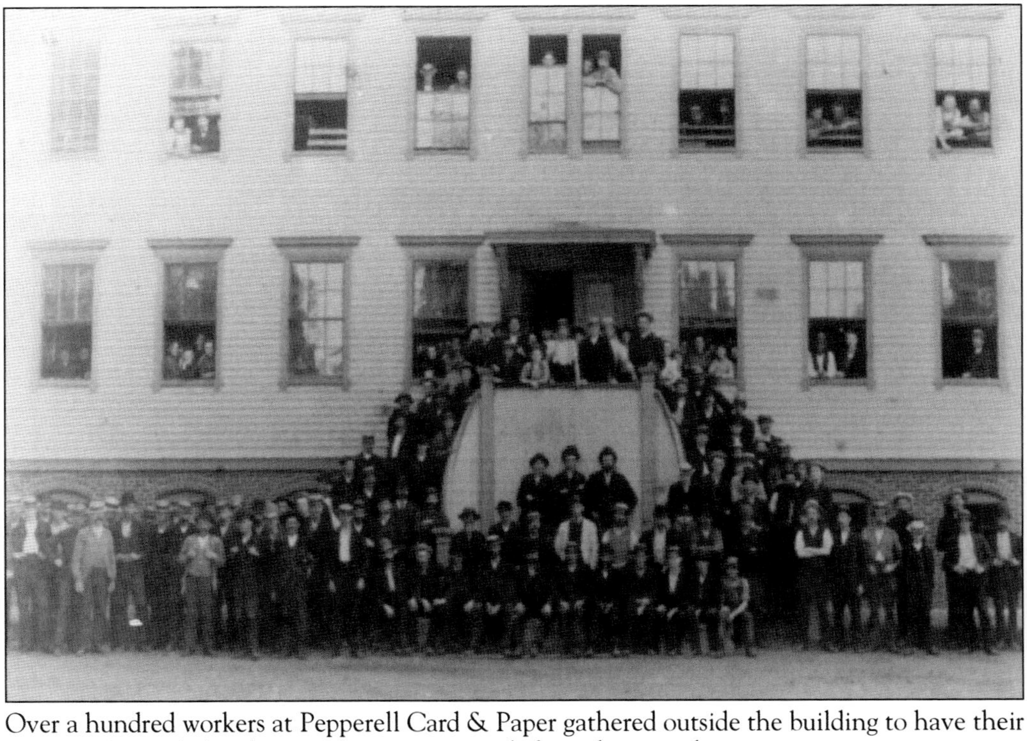

Over a hundred workers at Pepperell Card & Paper gathered outside the building to have their picture taken, while others are content to watch from their windows.

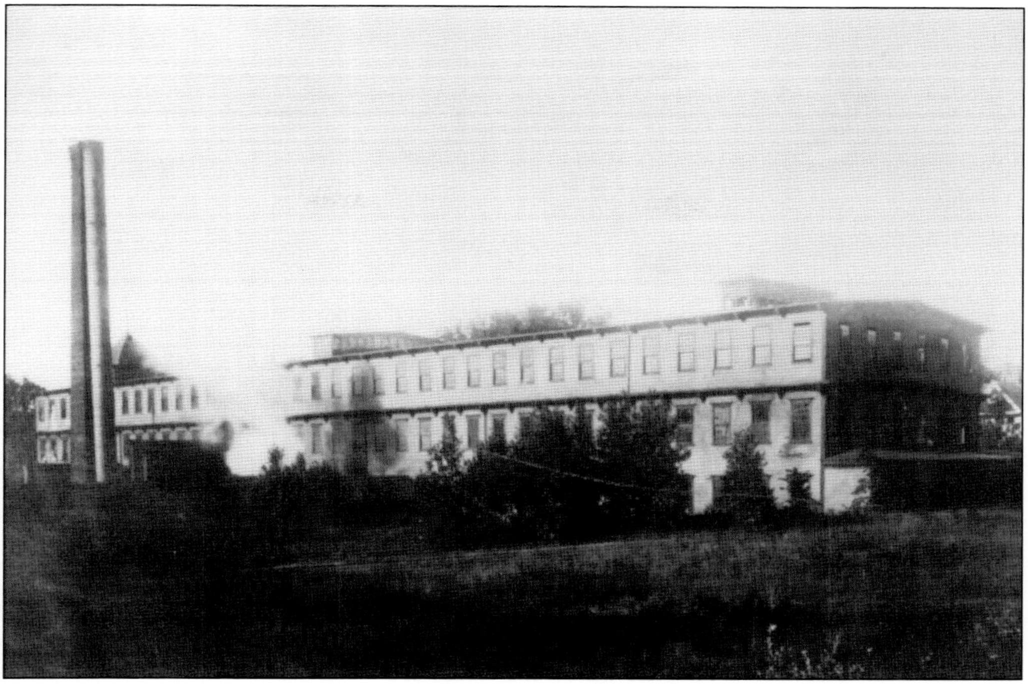

Pepperell Card & Paper is shown here from a distance about 1918.

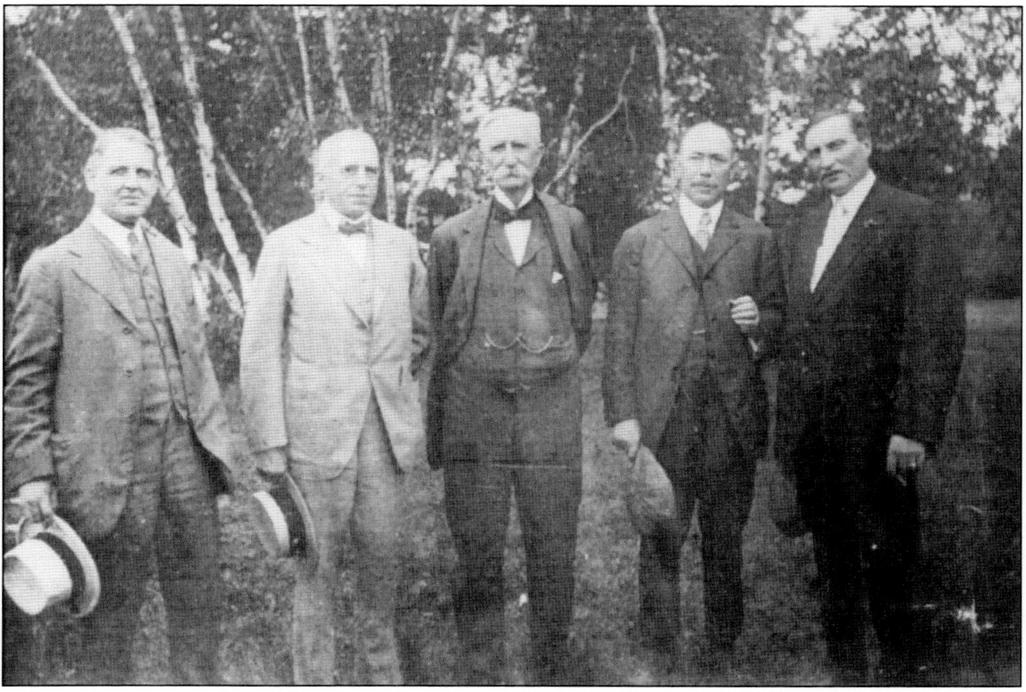

This political group has gotten together to discuss town affairs, in particular the paper industry. From left to right are: Representative Joseph A. Saunders; Honorable George R. Wallace of Fitchburg; Waldo Spaulding, a former president of Pepperell Card & Paper; Max Frank of Boston; and Rainsford Deware, president of Pepperell Card & Paper. This photograph was taken *c.* 1920.

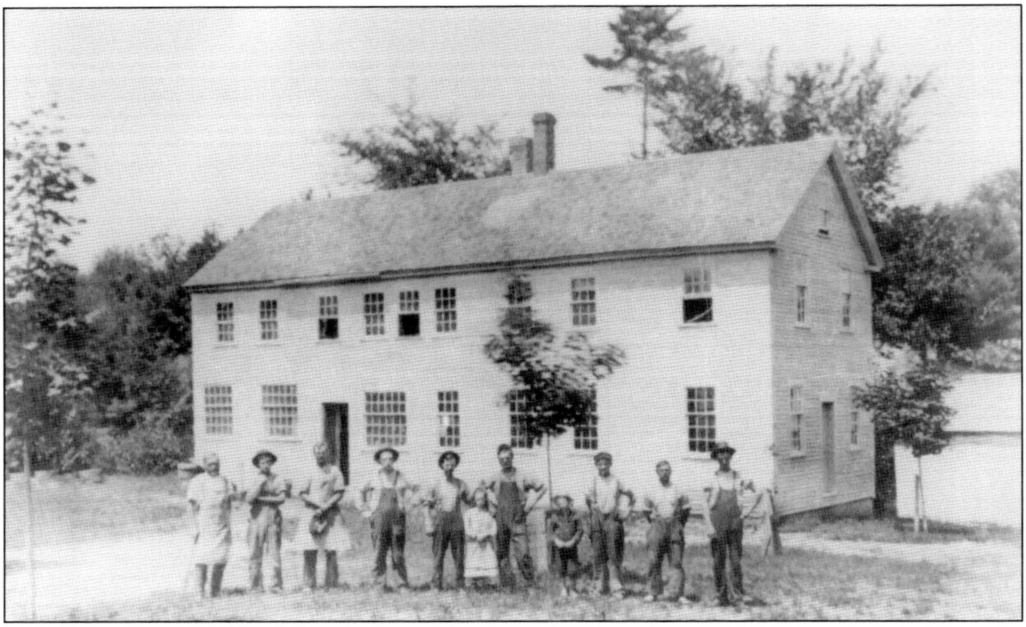

In 1853, Aaron Burkinshaw built a knife factory on Sheffield Street in Pepperell, utilizing water power from a pond that has carried his name ever since. His specialty was making pocket knives, but he later produced kitchen, budding, printing, and even surgical knives of superior quality. Because of the products' renowned craftsmanship, there was an increasing demand for Burkinshaw's knives and the business prospered. This picture of workers standing outside Burkinshaw's factory was taken in the late 1800s.

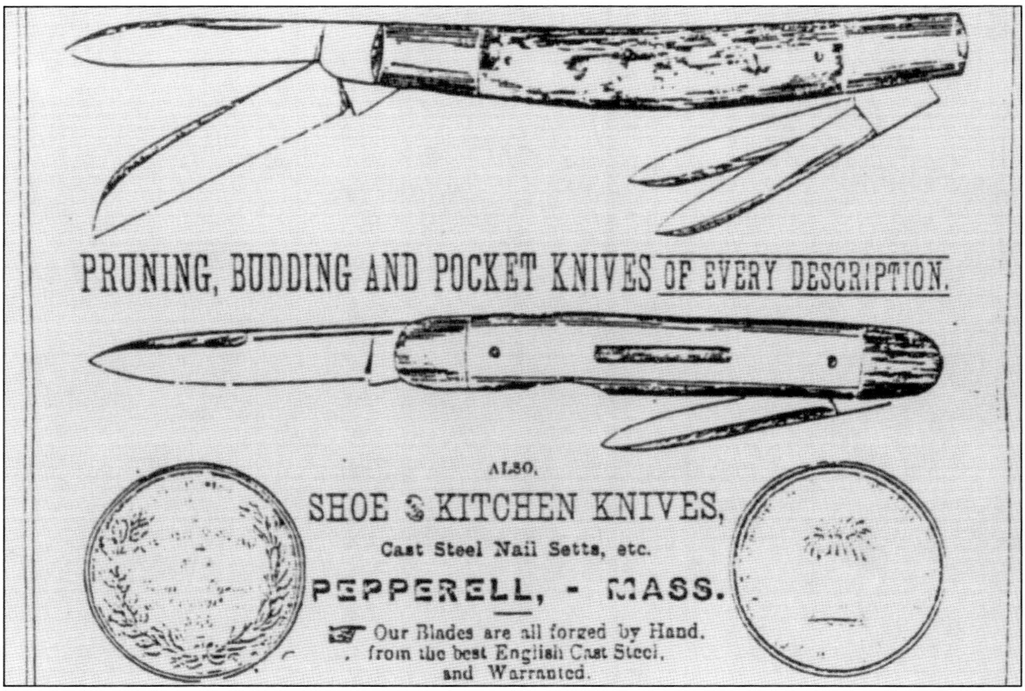

This is an early advertisement for Burkinshaw's knives that calls attention to the fact that the blades were all forged by hand using the best English cast steel.

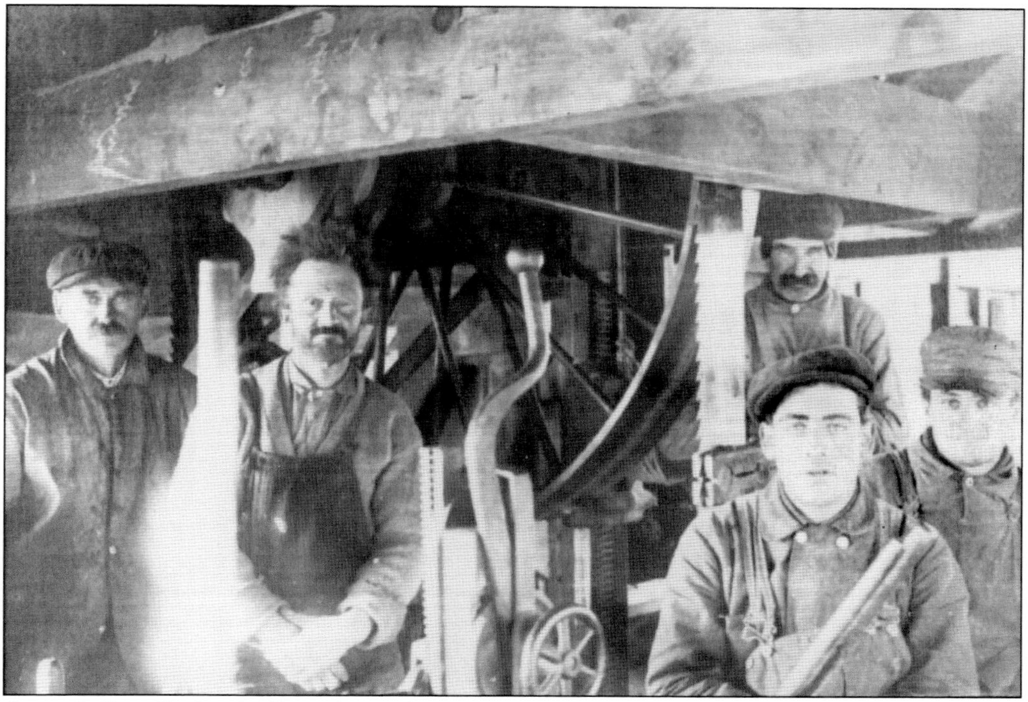

An early Sartelle Saw Mill was located at Trite's Corner in East Pepperell when these employees had their picture taken. From left to right are: Charles Baker, John F. Sartelle, Oscar McDonald, Nelson Archambault, and Dana Bancroft (standing in the back). Sartelle's earliest mill, built in the early 1700s on Sartelle Street, was used as a grist and sawmill, and also produced a variety of wooden products, including the pins for the "Old Covered Bridge."

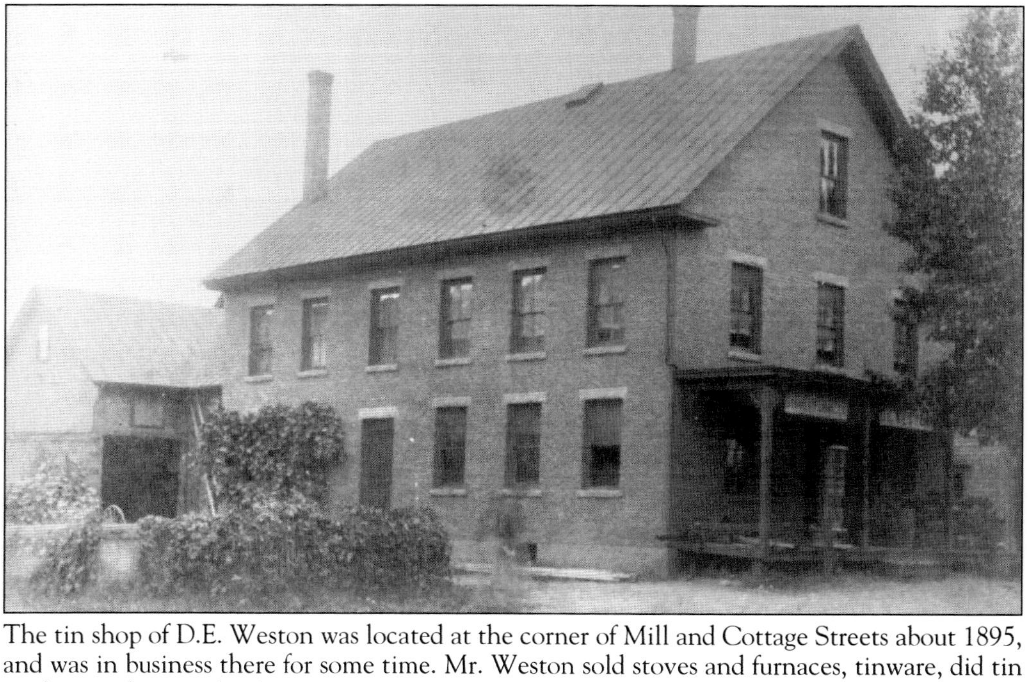

The tin shop of D.E. Weston was located at the corner of Mill and Cottage Streets about 1895, and was in business there for some time. Mr. Weston sold stoves and furnaces, tinware, did tin roofing, and was a plumber.

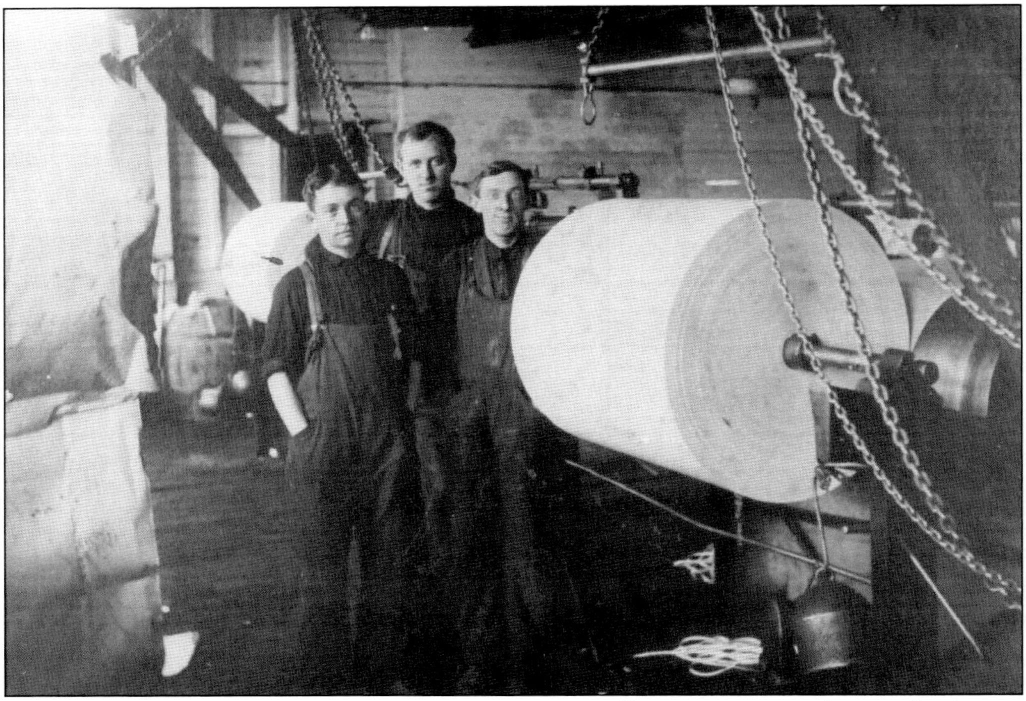

Three young paper workers dressed in their work overalls pose next to a huge roll of paper produced at the mill. This is probably the interior of the Fairchild Paper Company.

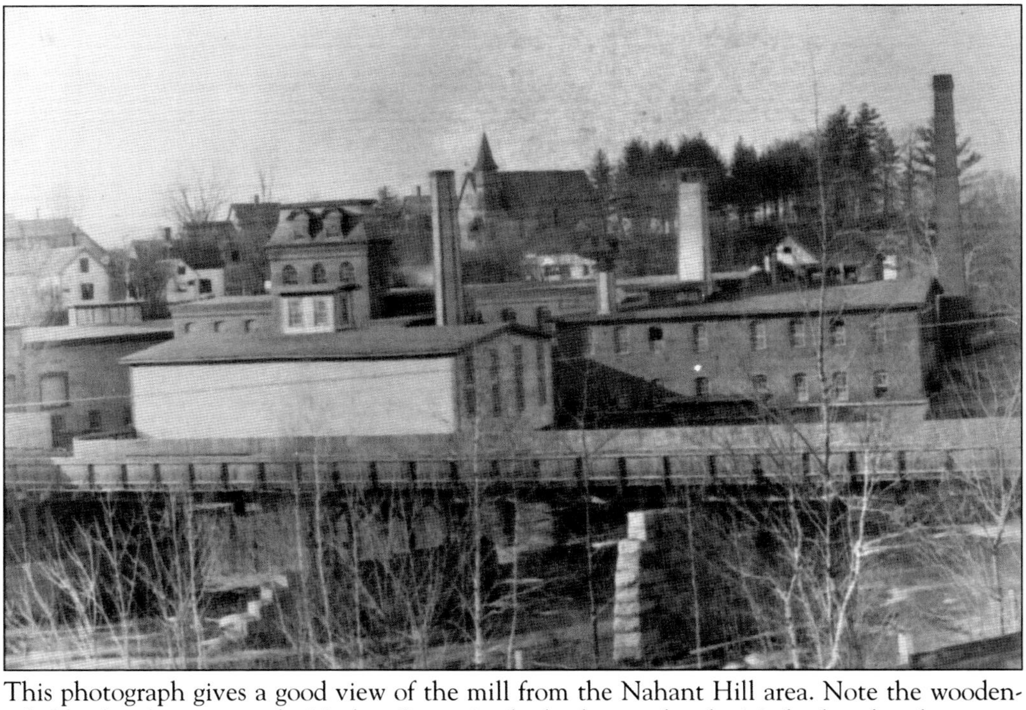

This photograph gives a good view of the mill from the Nahant Hill area. Note the wooden-sided bridge that crosses the Nashua River. In the background is the Methodist church.

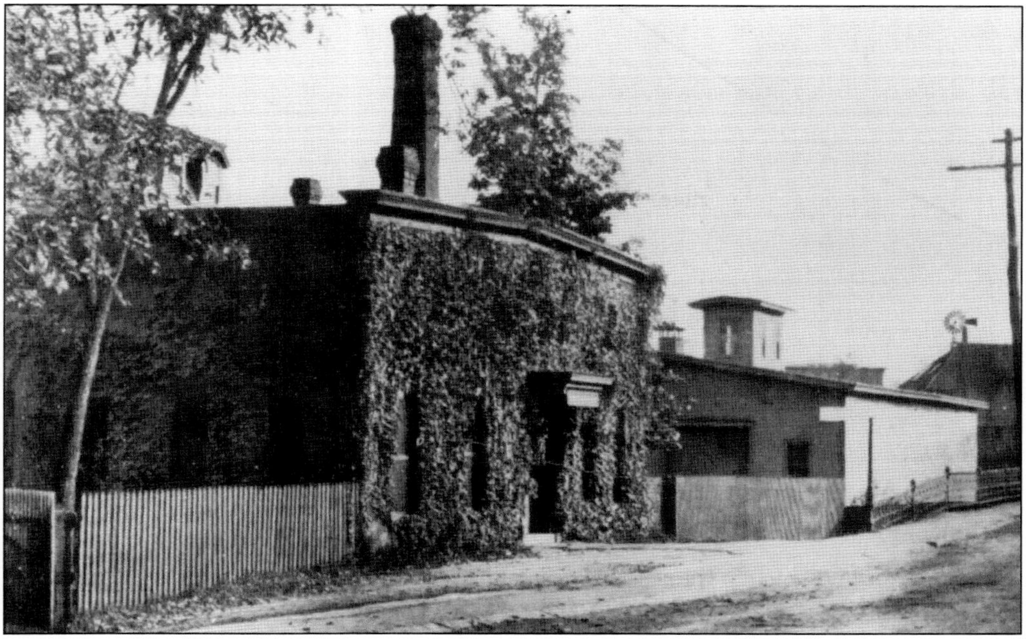

A familiar scene for Pepperellites was the vine-covered office of the Nashua River Paper Corporation of East Pepperell. Note the windmill on the right in this *c.* 1920s photograph.

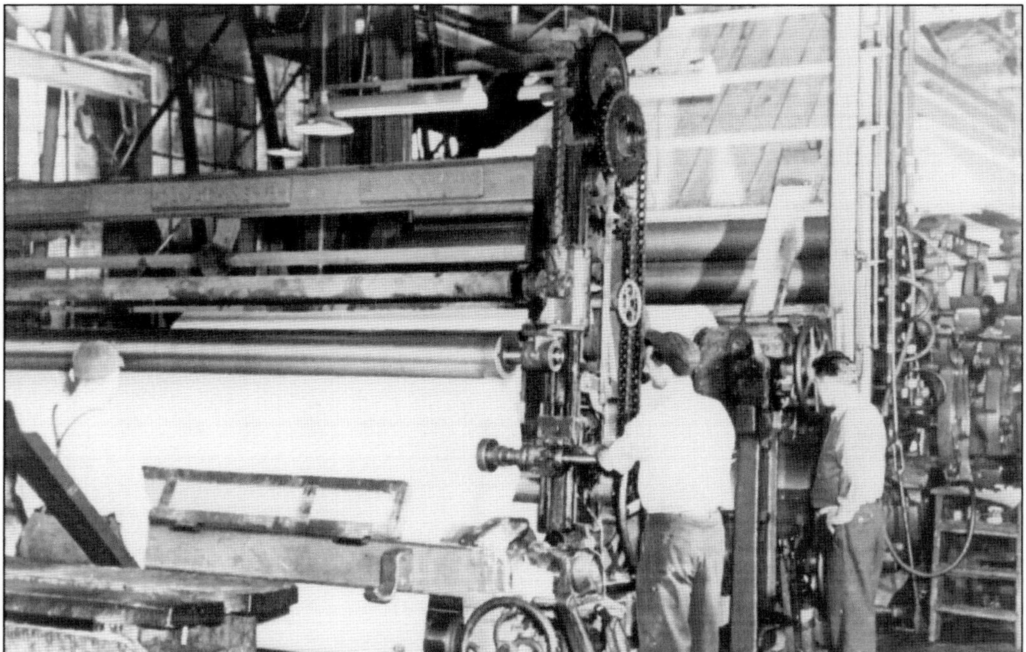

Inside the St. Regis Paper Company these men are tending one of the machines as they watch the huge rolls of paper being wound. In 1946 the St. Regis Paper Company purchased the mill and at that time was the second-largest paper company in the world. There were three fourdrinier machines operating to produce such Kraft specialties as asphalting paper, coating and gumming paper, coin wrap, crepe paper, cable wrap, and gummed sealing tape.

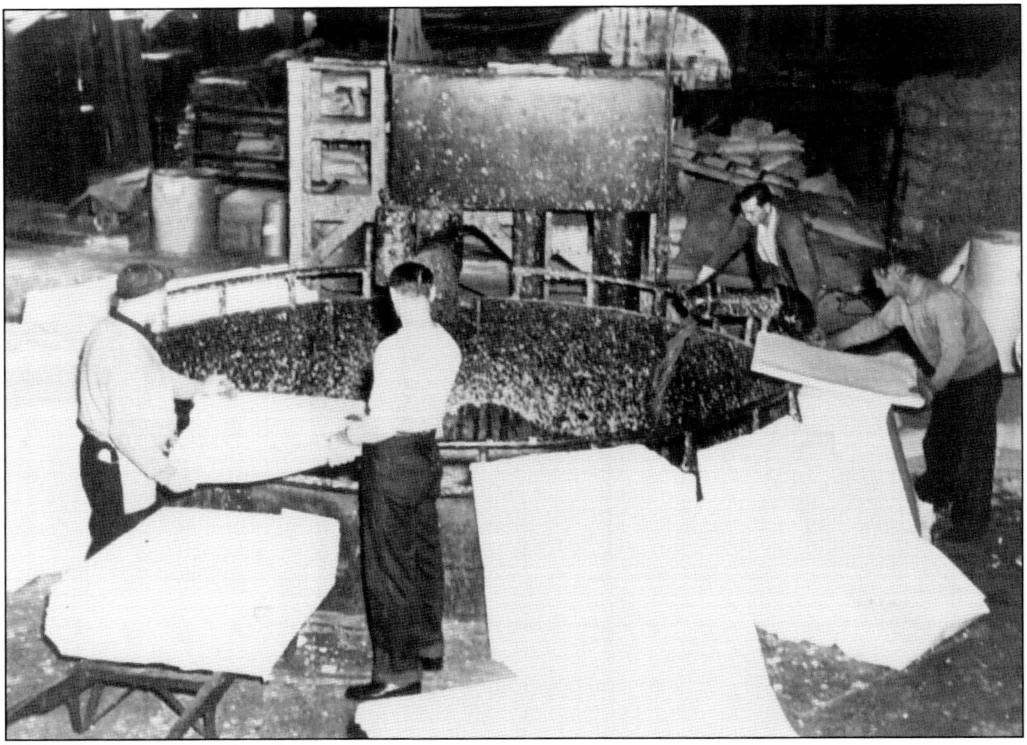

These men are putting paper into the beater-dumper (or hydro-pulper) to prepare it for processing. At this time the mill employed approximately 265 people, and the machines operated twenty-four hours a day with three eight-hour shifts.

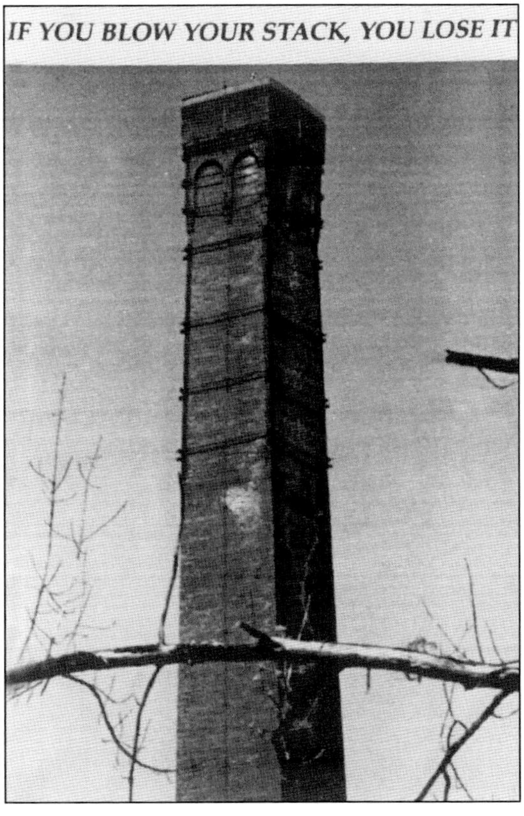

Many people will probably remember the old mill chimney, which in later years became the source of many complaints. To many residents the chimney was part of mill history, perhaps dating back to the earliest Babbitassett Paper Mill, but to others it was only a source of noise and soot. When the old chimney finally became a safety hazard in the 1980s, it was taken down by the Yankee Steeplejack Company.

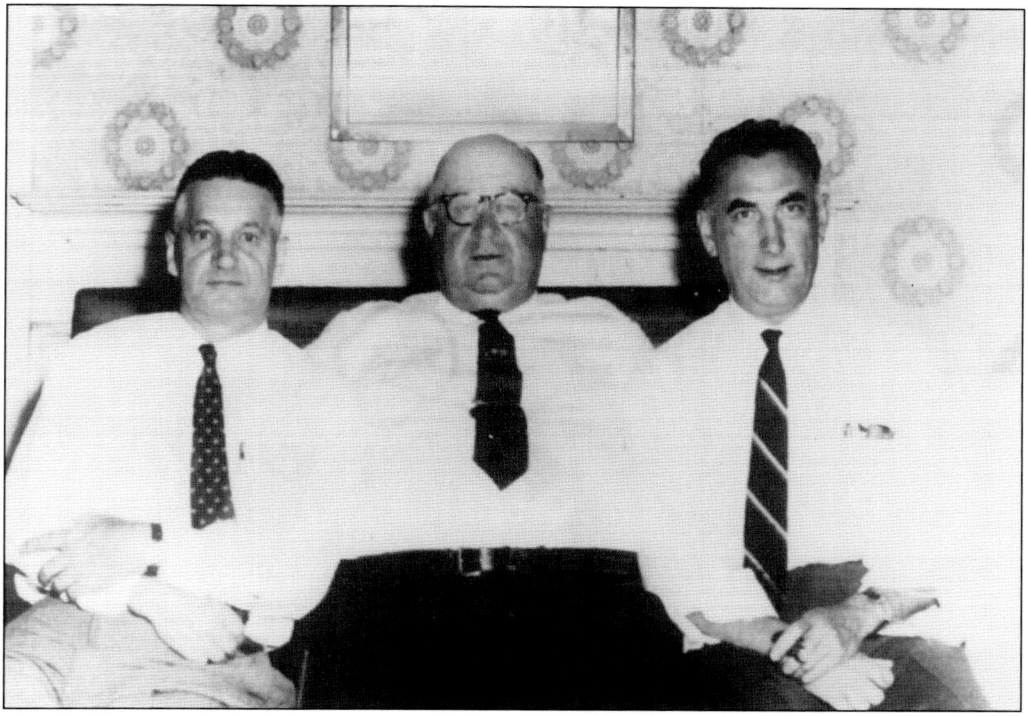

This 1940s photograph was taken of executives at the St. Regis Paper Company. From left to right are: Russell Hamilton (newly appointed general manager), William H. Anders (former president and general manager), and Robert Chase (New England sales manager).

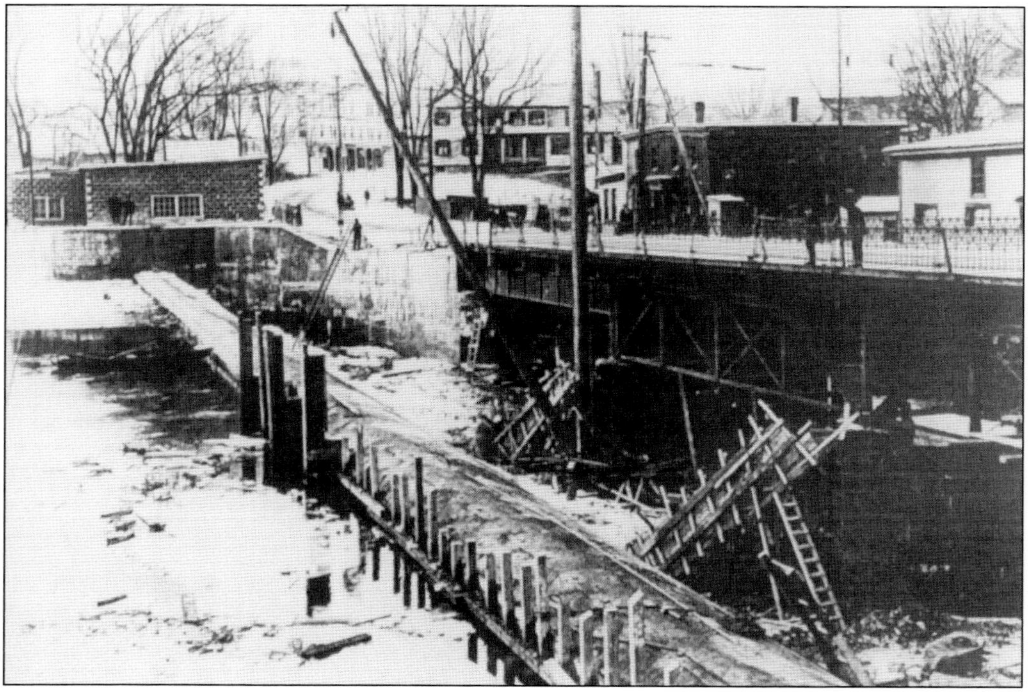

This picture was taken from the east side of the Nashua River looking down on the construction of a new dam.

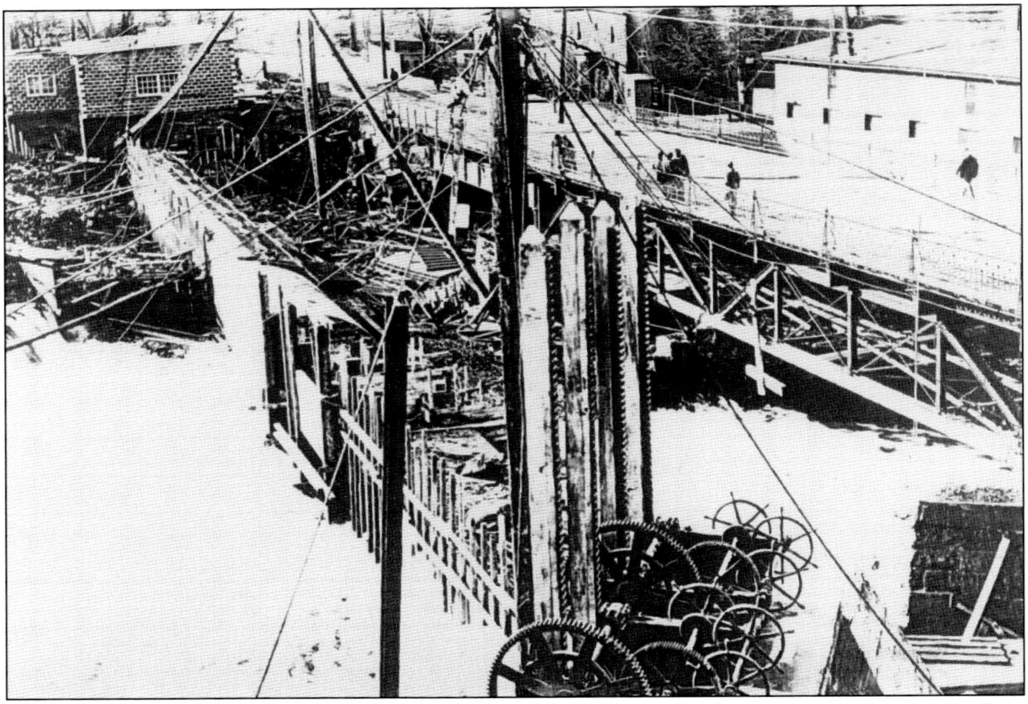

These are the wheels and gears that turned to raise and lower the sluice gates of the Penstock in order to regulate the flow of water going through.

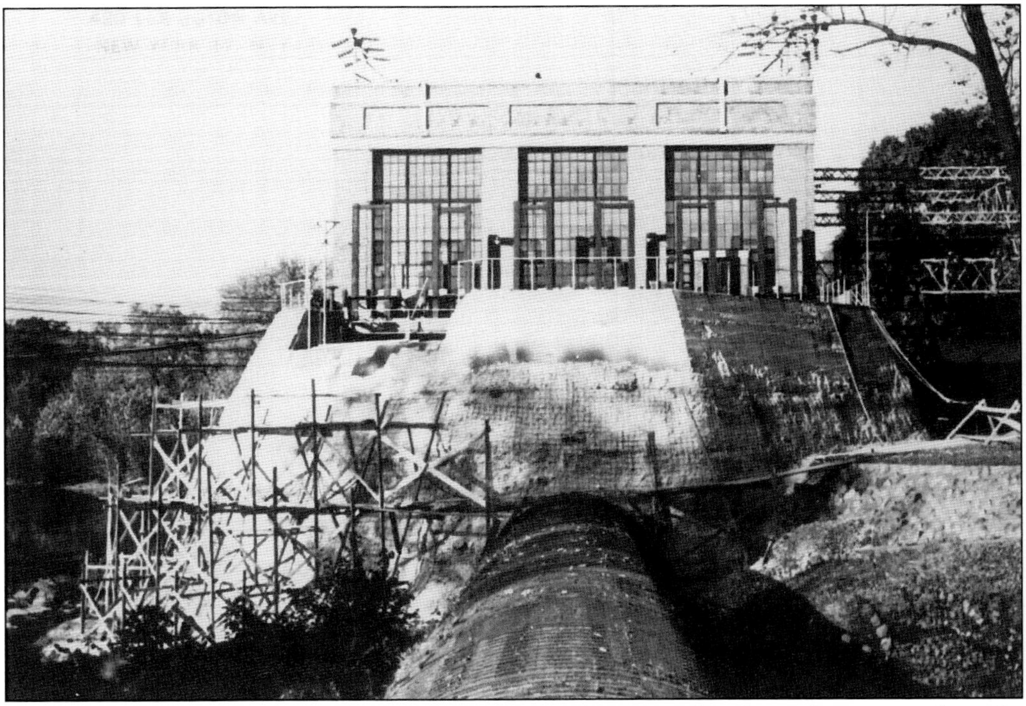

The Penstock, the longest wooden conduit in Massachusetts and perhaps the country, brought water to the electrical generating plant and supplied the mill with power. Work on the generating plant is being done by the Gunite Construction Corporation of New York City.

The Bemis Bag Company was given the Army-Navy "E" Award for excellence above and beyond war contract requirements for production of critical war material. An awards ceremony was held in June of 1944 and programs, such as this one, were passed out to all who attended.

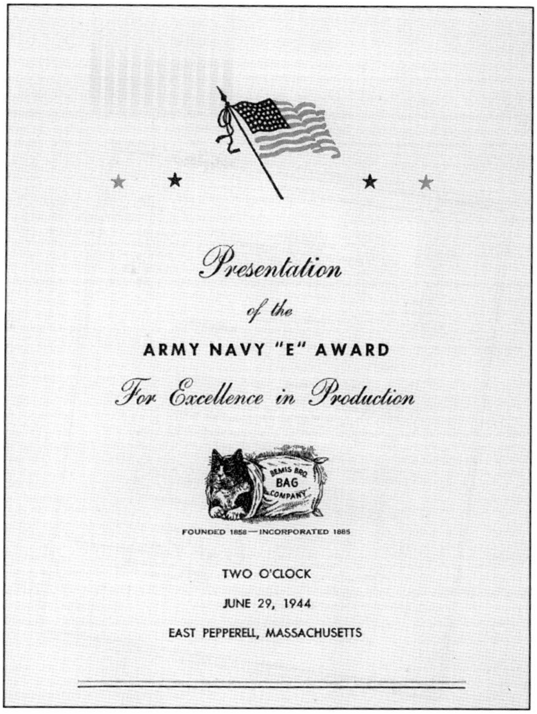

Presentation

of the

ARMY NAVY "E" AWARD

For Excellence in Production

BEMIS BRO BAG COMPANY

FOUNDED 1858—INCORPORATED 1885

TWO O'CLOCK

JUNE 29, 1944

EAST PEPPERELL, MASSACHUSETTS

"V for Victory" and the familiar Bemis "cat in the bag" symbol were displayed above the speaker's platform at the Army-Navy "E" Award ceremony. A military band was also on hand for the festivities. The guest speaker for the occasion was Brigadier General Alden H. Waitt, assistant chief of the chemical warfare service, who came from Washington to present the coveted award.

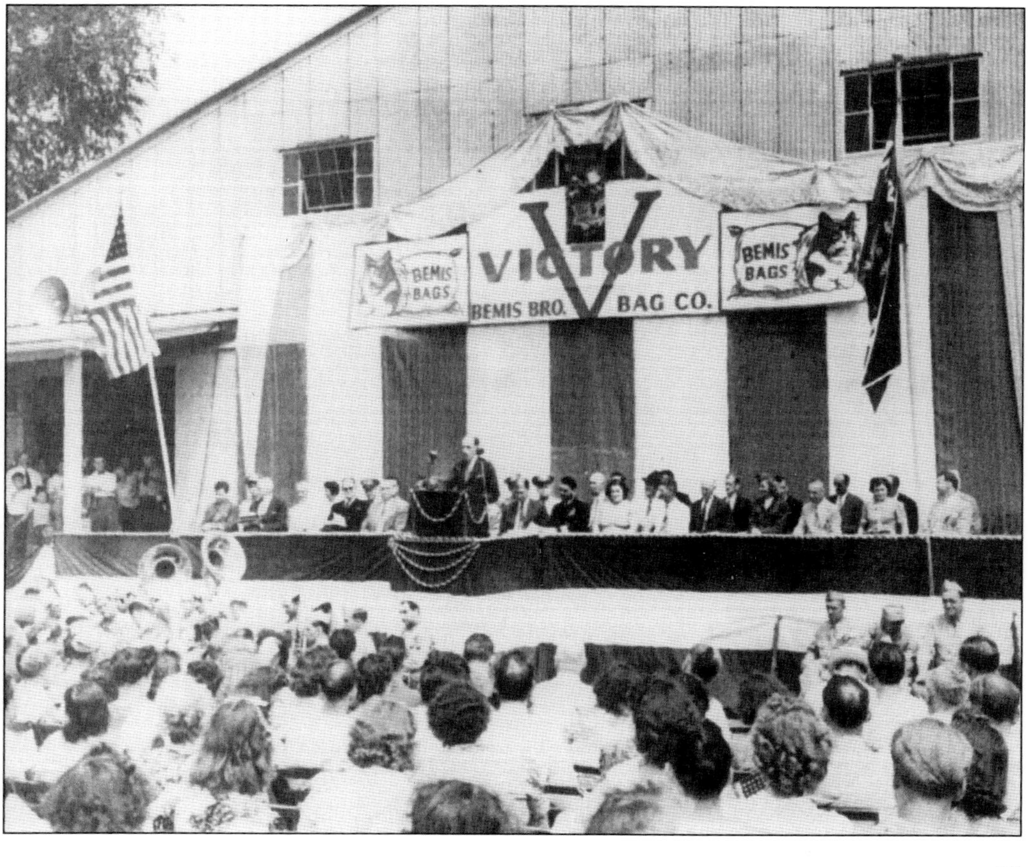

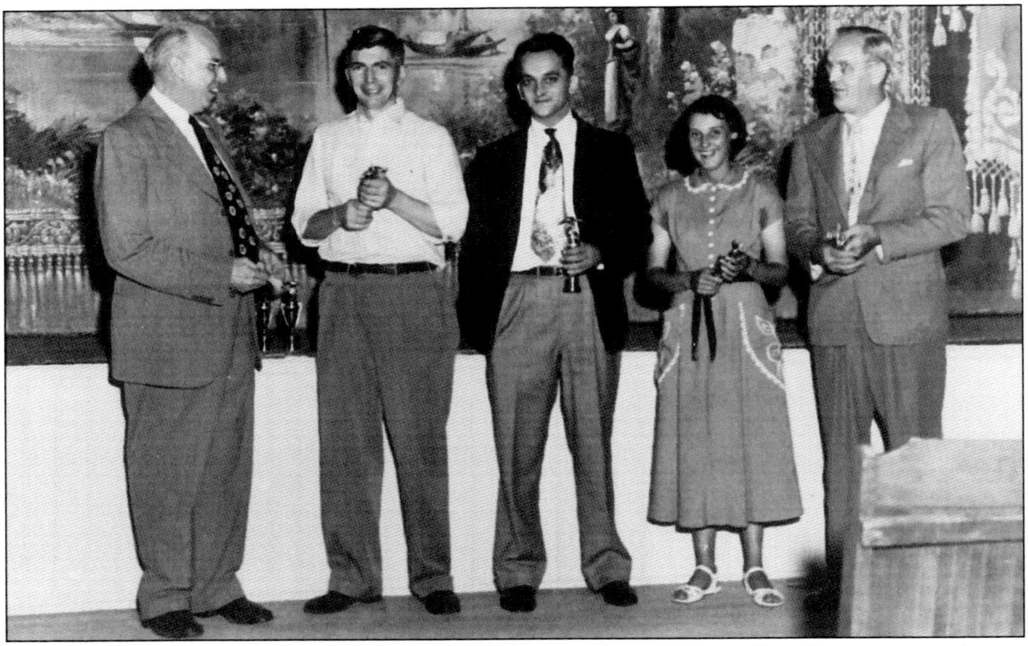

General Manager Arnold Weeks presents bowling trophies to Bemis Bag Company employees Robert Starkey, Roger Hackett, Gertrude Williams Austin, and Frank Scharch. Behind them is the backdrop of the town hall stage.

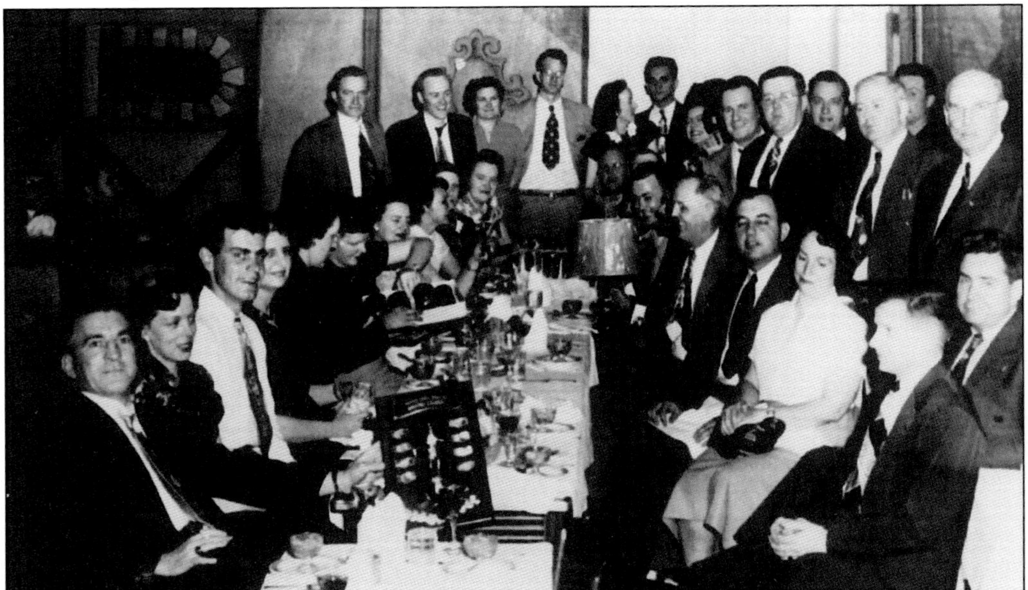

These Bemis employees at a bowling banquet are, from front to back: (left side) Francis Markham, Norma Archambault, Irving Call, Nellie Markham, Ethel Morrill, Mary Tumpney, Lorraine Boutwell, unknown, unknown, and Phyllis Coburn; (right side) Larry Graves, Leige Coakley (to the right), Carolyn F. Reed, Jerry Murphy, Frank Scharch, Bill Lillis, and unknown. In the back row, from left to right, are two unknown men, Eileen Marshall, Bob Carson, Emaline Kiely, Roger Hackett, unknown, Barney Blaney, Charlie Symonds, unknown, Lawrence Sliney, and Arnold Weeks.

Four

Parades and Celebrations

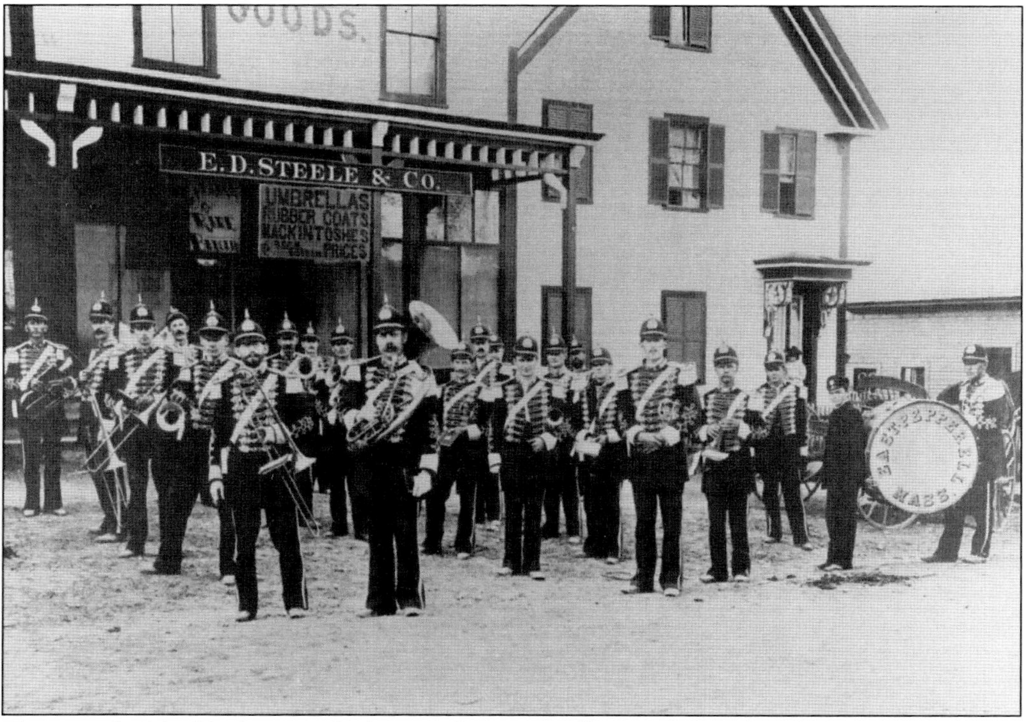

This wonderful old photograph depicts the Pepperell Cornet Band in full regalia, gathered in front of E.D. Steele's men's store in lower Railroad Square. Standing in the middle of the picture with a cornet under his arm is James "Eddie" Dunn, who played with the band for a number of years.

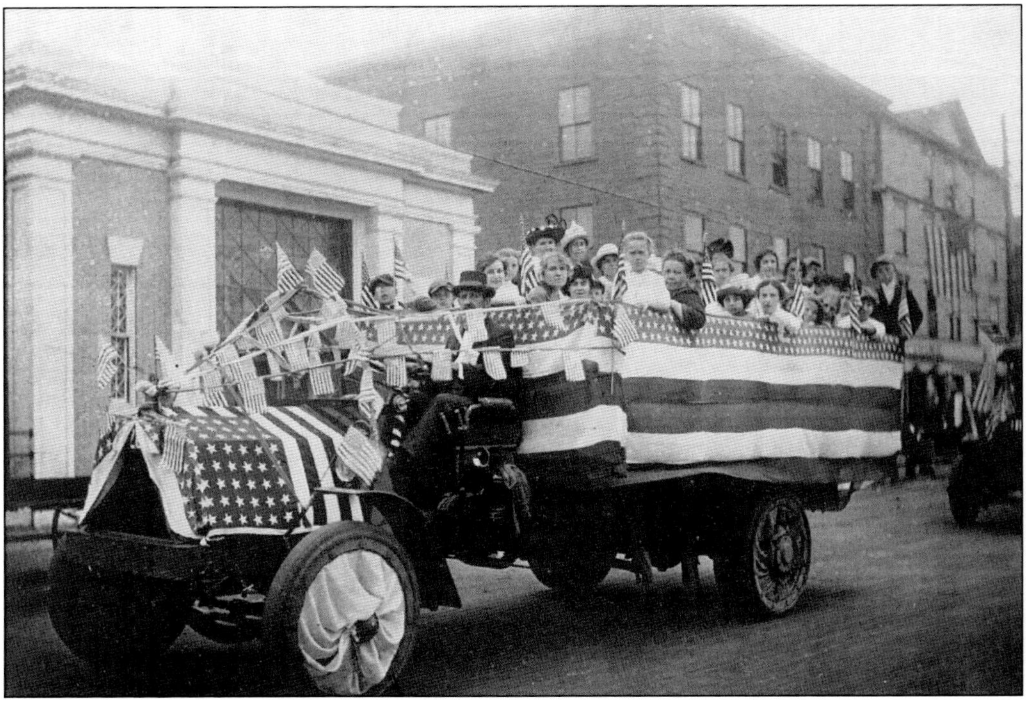

Pepperell's Welcome Home Day of May 26, 1919, was marked by a gala celebration to honor the 152 soldiers and sailors who served in World War I. Industry, stores, and schools were closed, for the day was declared a holiday by the selectmen. Businesses and private homes alike were decorated with red, white, and blue, and everyone turned out for the parade that made its way up Main Street from Railroad Square to the town hall.

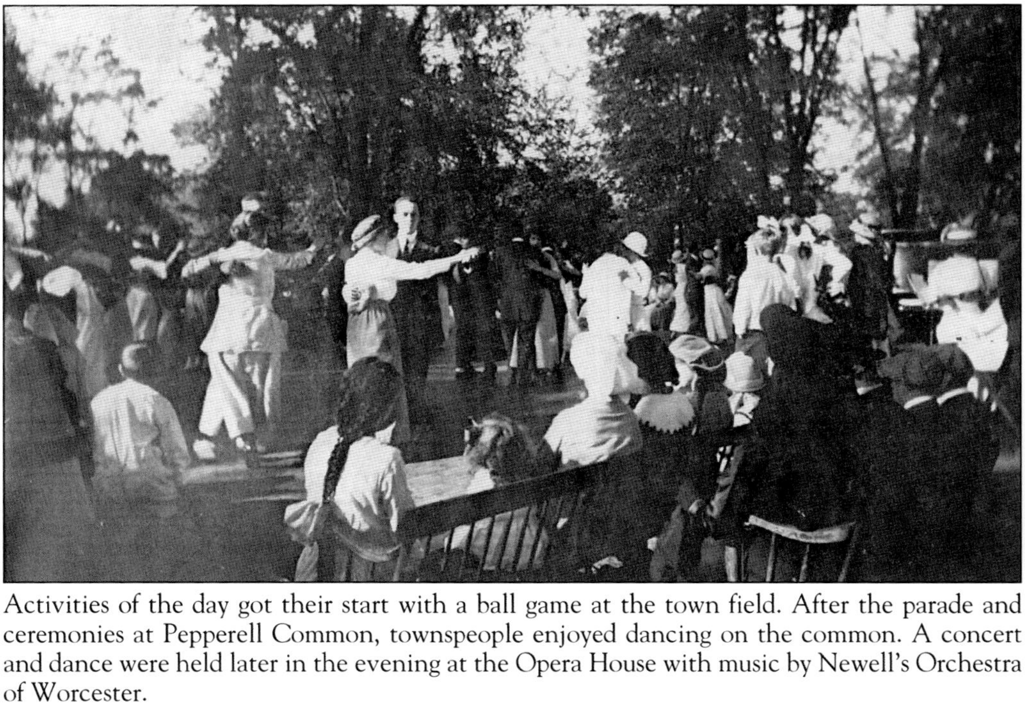

Activities of the day got their start with a ball game at the town field. After the parade and ceremonies at Pepperell Common, townspeople enjoyed dancing on the common. A concert and dance were held later in the evening at the Opera House with music by Newell's Orchestra of Worcester.

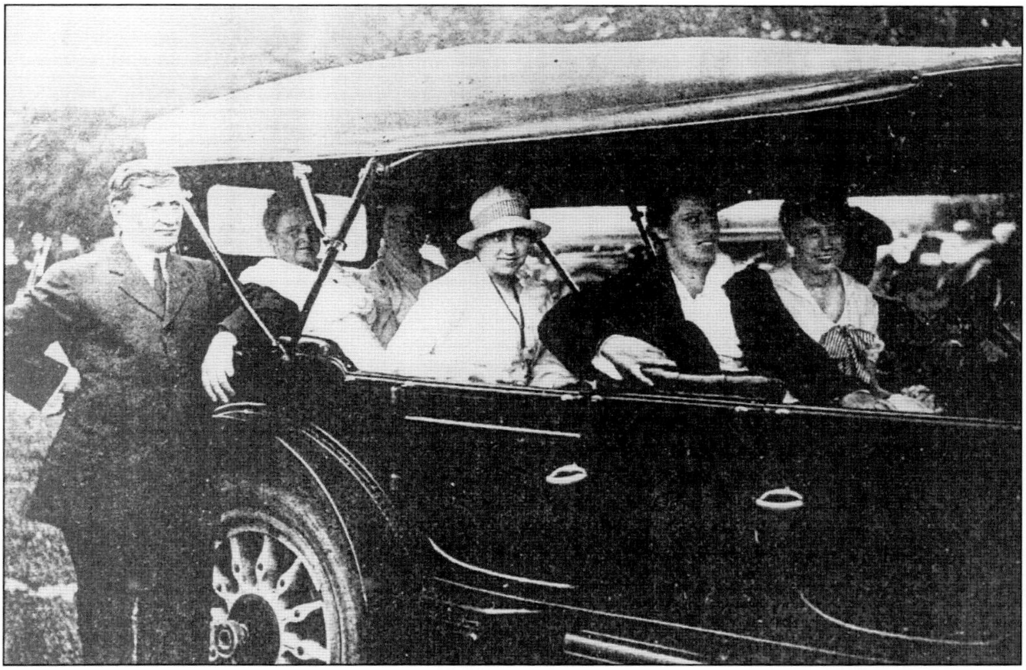

Rainsford Deware, president of the Pepperell Card & Paper Company, was chairman of the Welcome Home Day committee. He is shown here with his family at the celebration.

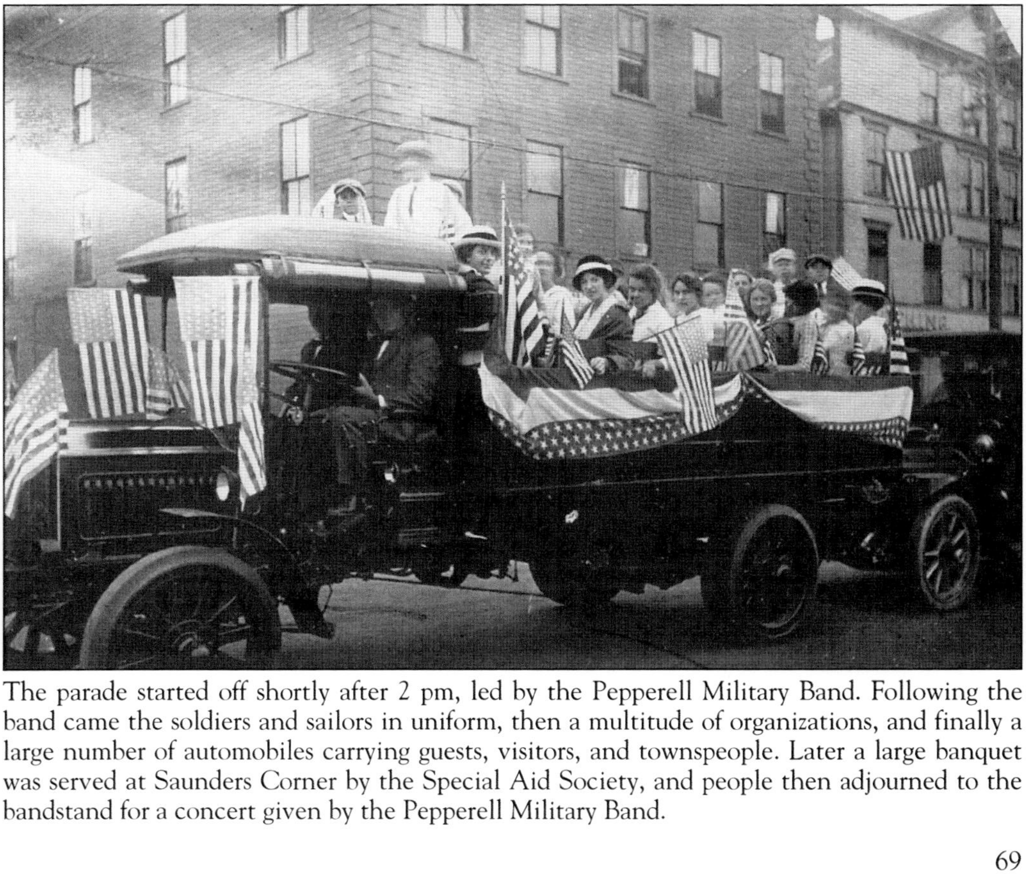

The parade started off shortly after 2 pm, led by the Pepperell Military Band. Following the band came the soldiers and sailors in uniform, then a multitude of organizations, and finally a large number of automobiles carrying guests, visitors, and townspeople. Later a large banquet was served at Saunders Corner by the Special Aid Society, and people then adjourned to the bandstand for a concert given by the Pepperell Military Band.

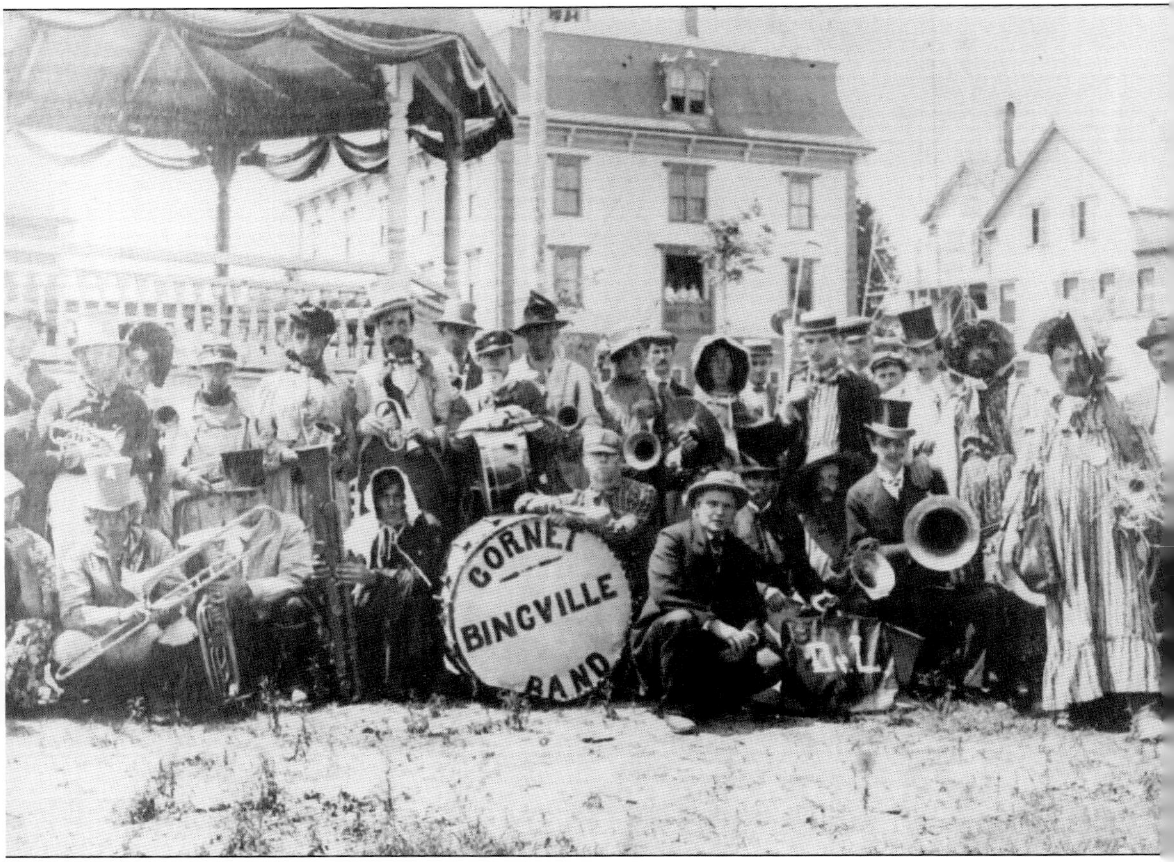

The Bingville Cornet Band must have been quite a sight in their unusual attire as they marched along or played in the bandstand. Kneeling next to the drum and looking too plainly dressed to be part of the group is Dr. Lovejoy. His large barn can be seen in the background. The bandstand pictured here was later moved to the town field, where it was the site of many a band concert.

Many holiday celebrations were held at the Babbatassett Driving Park until the building of the Nashua River Dam flooded the area and put an end to the use of this popular spot. This is the cover from one of the Columbus Day programs.

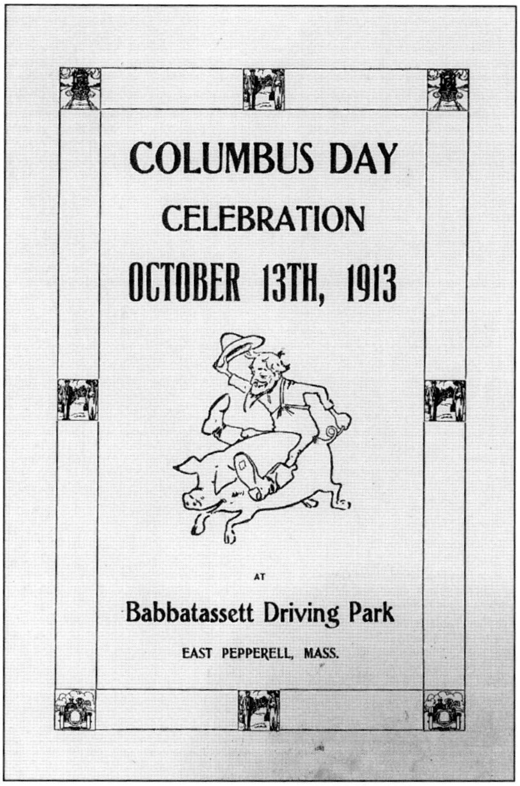

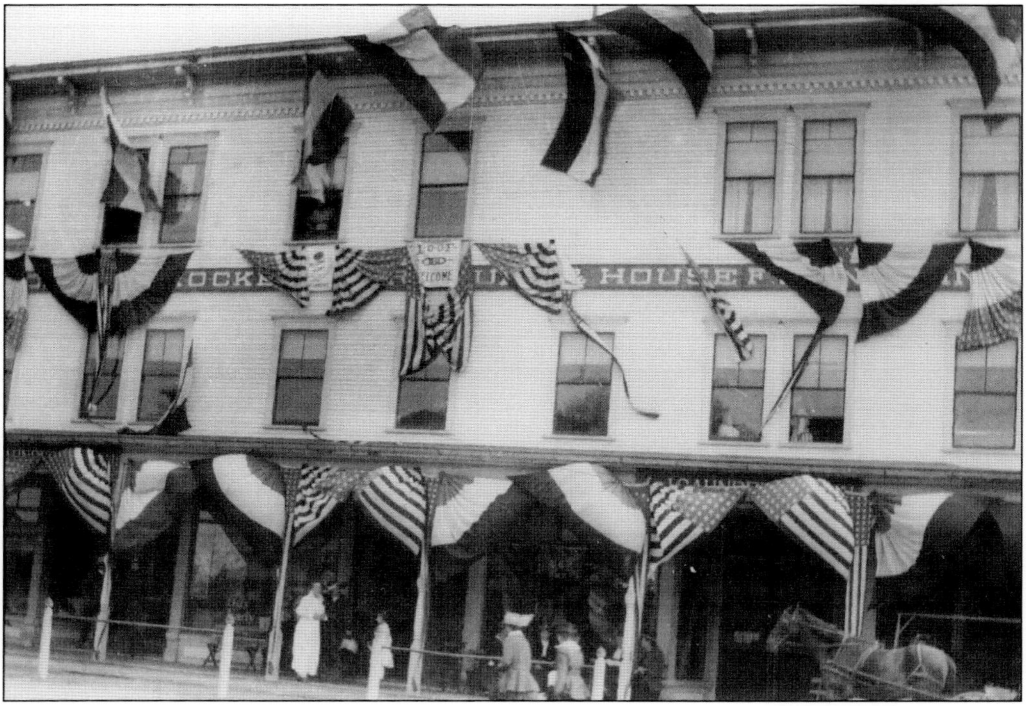

Saunders Corner (now the Odd Fellows Building) is all decked out with flags and banners in readiness for the Welcome Home Day celebration in May 1919.

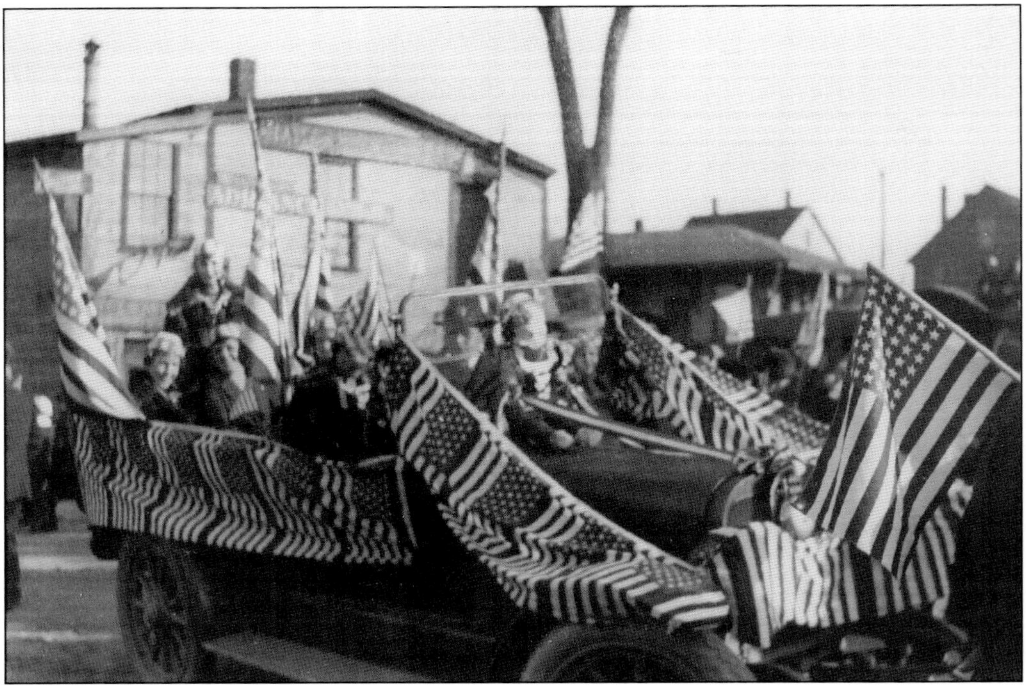

A group of smiling young ladies waits in Railroad Square for the parade to begin. The car is patriotically decorated and appears to have a doll sitting on the hood in front of the windshield. In the background is probably the railroad express office and the Boston and Maine freight house.

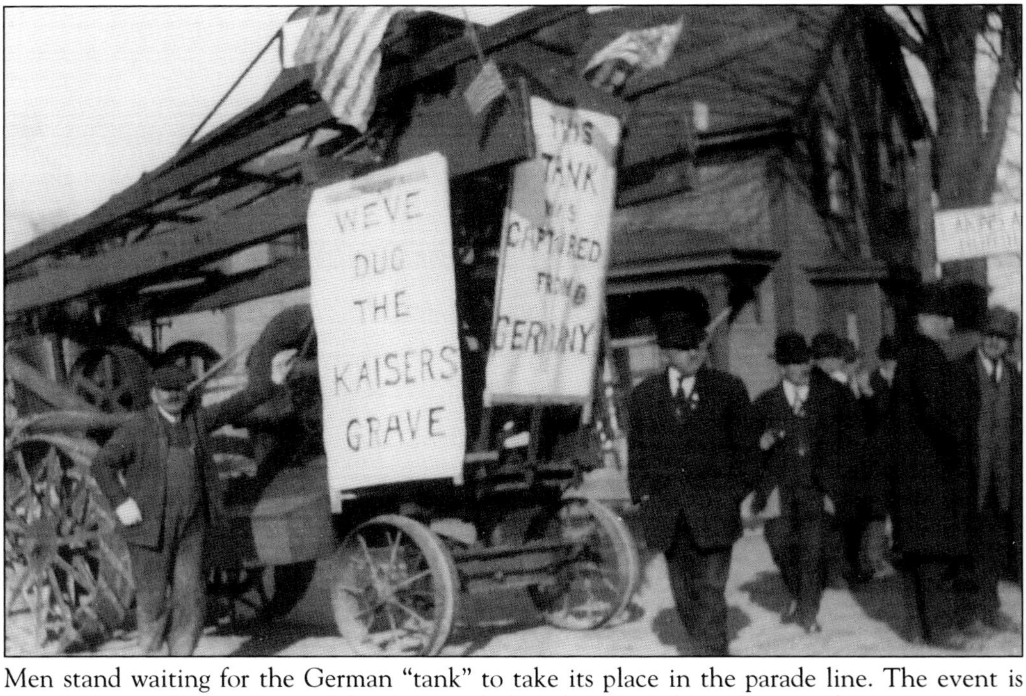

Men stand waiting for the German "tank" to take its place in the parade line. The event is the Welcome Home Day celebration, and the place is Lakins Auto and Horse Barn on Railroad Street.

The highlights of the Labor Day festivities on September 5, 1910, were the races at the Babbatassett Driving Park and dancing later that evening in Lawrence Hall. Horses and horse racing had been a popular pastime for townspeople for some time. Often new horses were exhibited daily on the streets, and a keen rivalry existed between horse owners, occasionally resulting in the challenge of a game of billiards for the ownership of a horse.

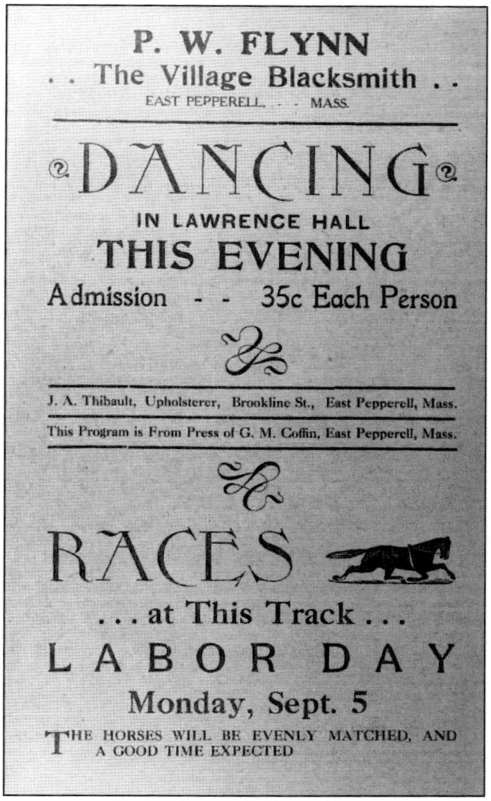
P. W. FLYNN
. . The Village Blacksmith . .
EAST PEPPERELL, . . MASS.

DANCING
IN LAWRENCE HALL
THIS EVENING
Admission - - 35c Each Person

J. A. Thibault, Upholsterer, Brookline St., East Pepperell, Mass.
This Program is From Press of G. M. Coffin, East Pepperell, Mass.

RACES
. . . at This Track . . .
LABOR DAY
Monday, Sept. 5
THE HORSES WILL BE EVENLY MATCHED, AND A GOOD TIME EXPECTED

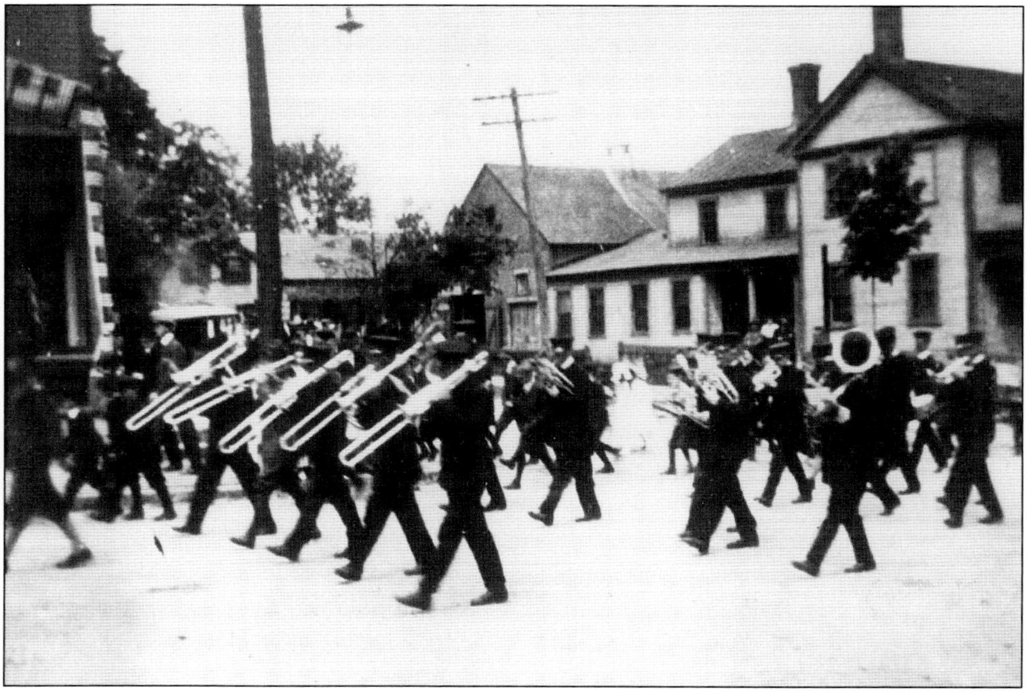

This picture was taken from in front of the Odd Fellows Building around 1900. The band is playing as they march past the corner of Mill and Main Streets.

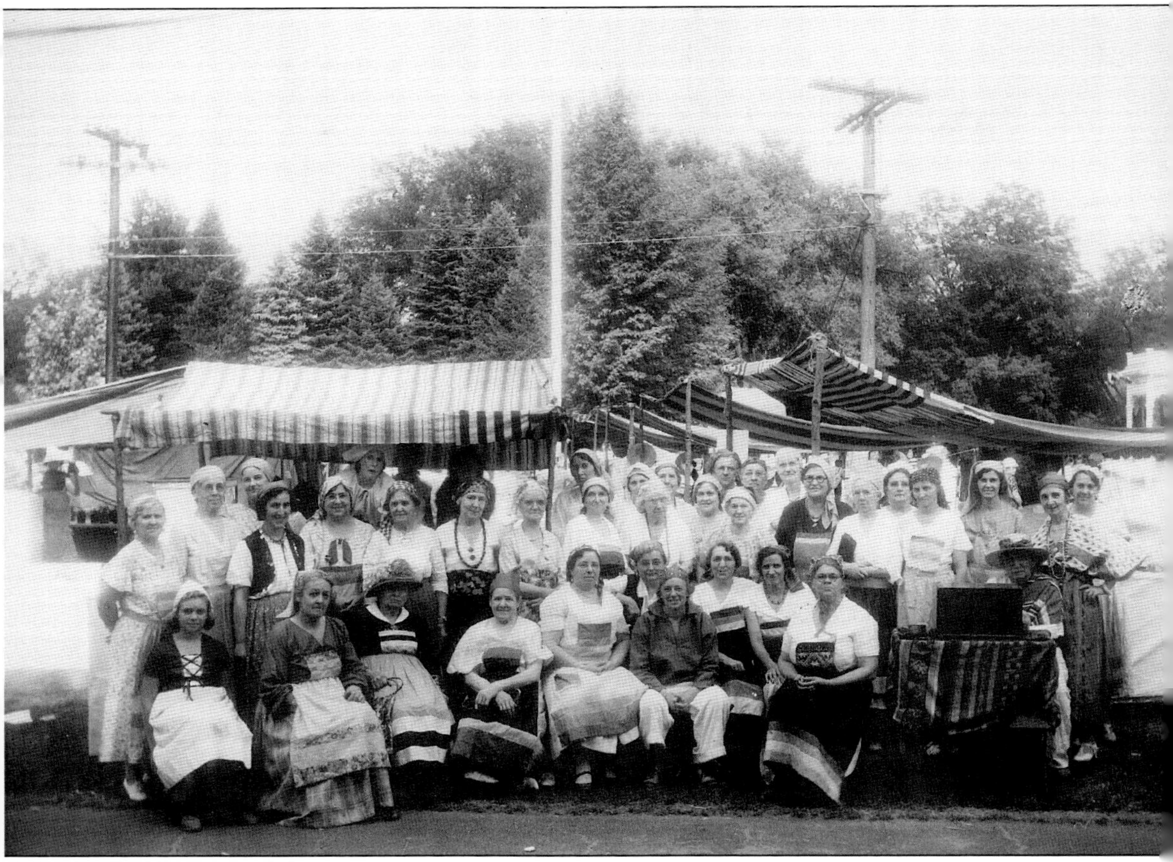

The ladies of the Community Church got dressed up in bandannas and costumes for their street fair in Pepperell. From left to right are: (front row) unknown, Louise Richardson, Fannie Hobart, Idella Annis, Idella Winn, Elizabeth Hutchinson, Katherine Smith, unknown, Irene Attridge, and Mrs. Bessie Olsen; (back row) Marion Mahony, Mrs. P.J. Hayes, Mrs. Butland, Mrs. DeVrees, Mrs. George Parker, Emily Newell, Mary Wood, Mrs. Nellie Harrison, Grace Winch, Mrs. Chester Parker, unknown, Mrs. Charles Miller, unknown, Mrs. Mabel Lane, Mrs. Maude C. Parker, unknown, Mrs. Ida Saunders, Mrs. Maria Loker, Mrs. Julia Dunn, Mrs. Lawrence Morgan, unknown, Alice Greenwood, Mabel Williams, Elizabeth Wright, and May Wiley. Mrs. George A. (Grace) Shattuck is standing under the canopy.

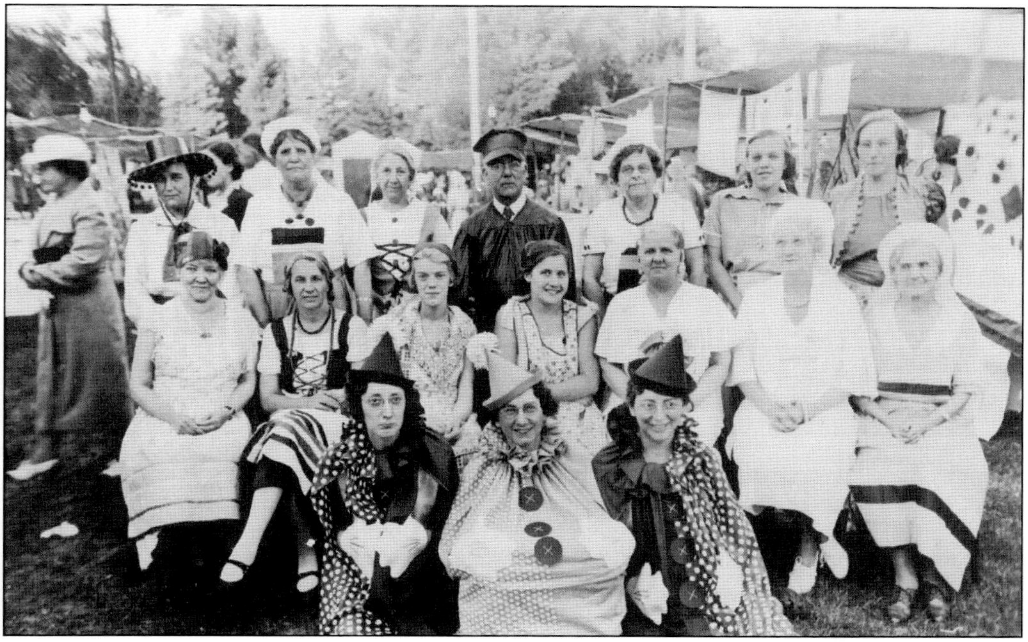

The Pepperell Booth Fair was held on the common and even sported clowns to add to the fun. Unfortunately the names of the clowns are unknown. Identified persons are, from left to right: (second row) Mrs. Ingram, unknown, unknown, unknown, Mrs. Amos Mahony, Mrs. Loker, and Mrs. Durant; (back row) Audrey Burkinshaw, Mrs. James Dunn, Mrs. Mills, Harry Adams Hersey (who tuned pianos in town in the summers of the late 1920s), Mrs. Janes ?, June Kimball, and Lena Kimball.

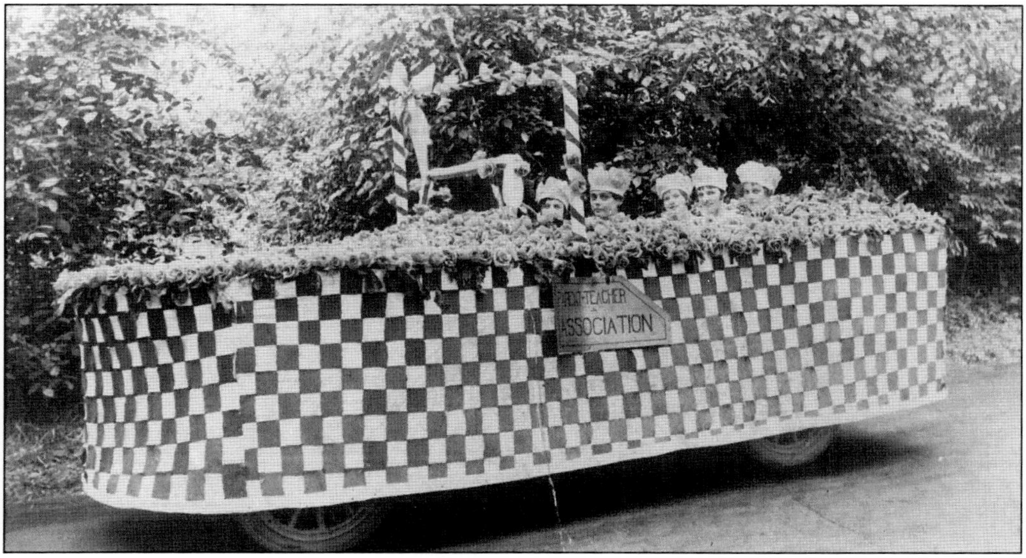

Anna Drumm is driving the Parent Teacher Association float in the Fourth of July "mammoth street parade" in 1928. On her left is her sister, Margie Scullane, and to the right are Charlotte Cotton, Nellie Toomey Markham, and Phyllis Soule. The parade consisted of five divisions: military, organizational, merchant, private car, and "horrible," each division being led by a different band. A total of $500 was given out in prizes for the best-decorated car in each division.

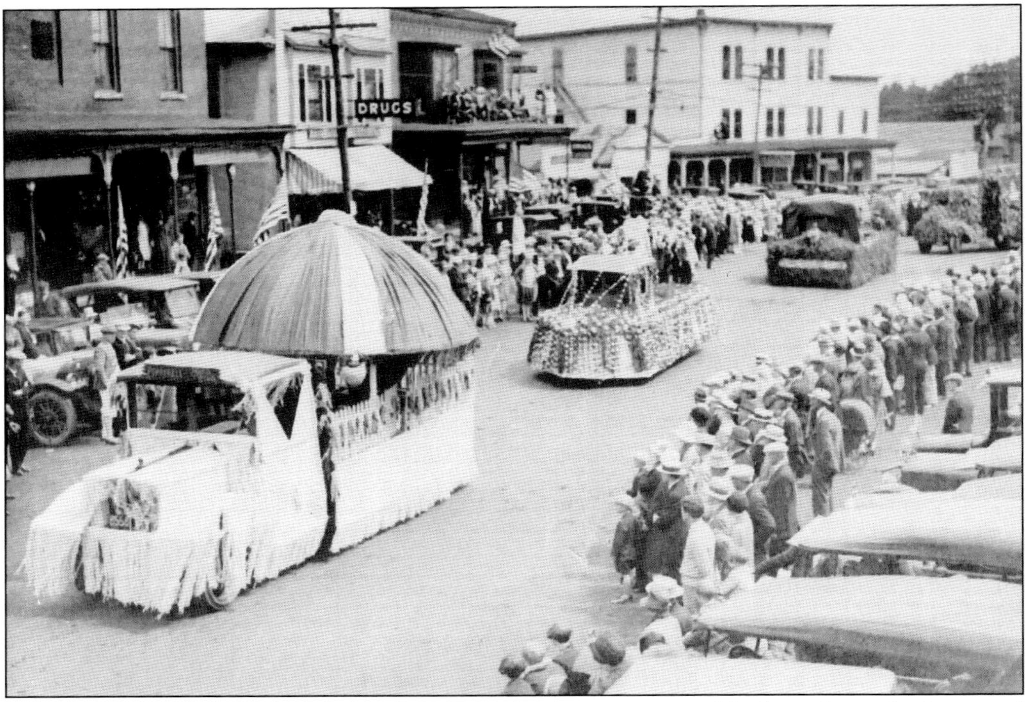

Spectators crowd the street and gather on rooftops to get a good look at the gaily decorated vehicles as the they go through Railroad Square. The Pepperell Town Club's second annual Fourth of July celebration had gotten off to a grand start the evening before with band concerts, magicians, a bonfire, and dancing at Prescott Hall from 12:30 am until sunrise. Still to come was a ball game, vaudeville acts, a firemens' muster, a balloon ascension, and the grand finale: fireworks.

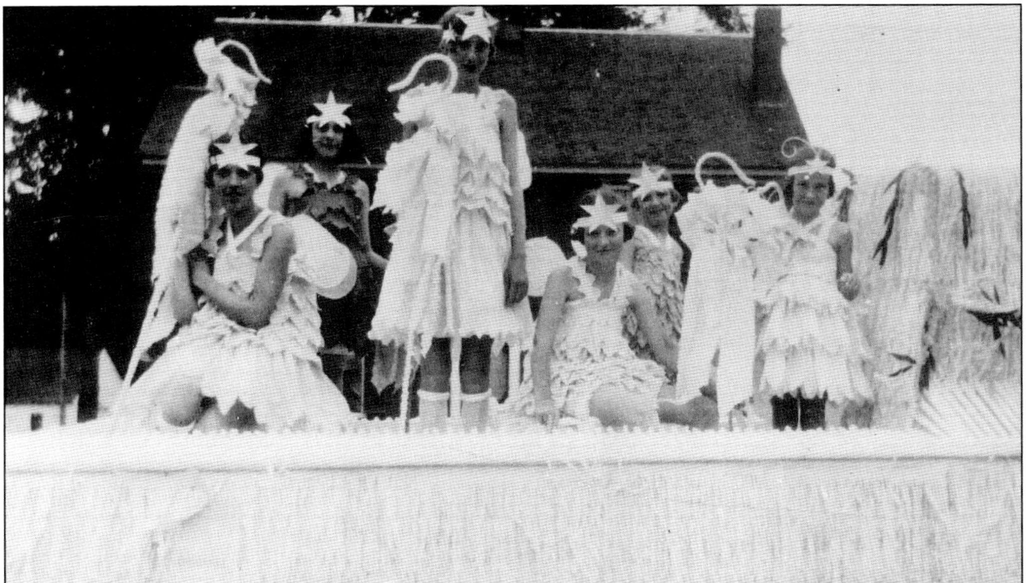

These girls are all prettily dressed to ride in the parade and appear to be sprouting wings as well as stars on their foreheads.

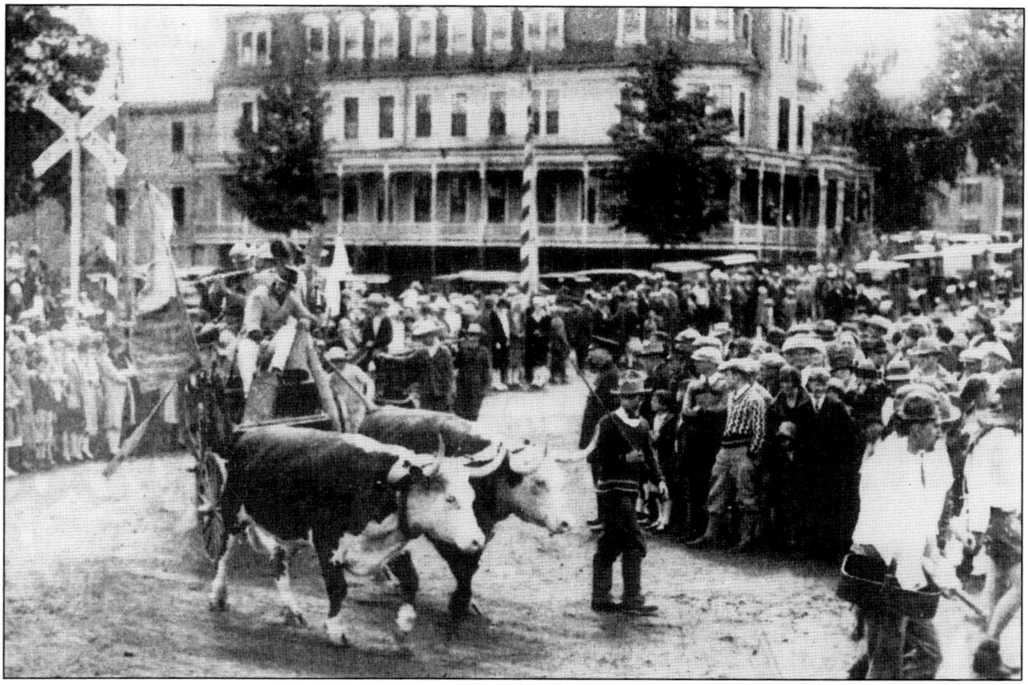

The oxen appear quite unconcerned as they round the corner from Groton to Main Street. However, the driver looks a little precariously perched as the wagon seems to be leaning to one side.

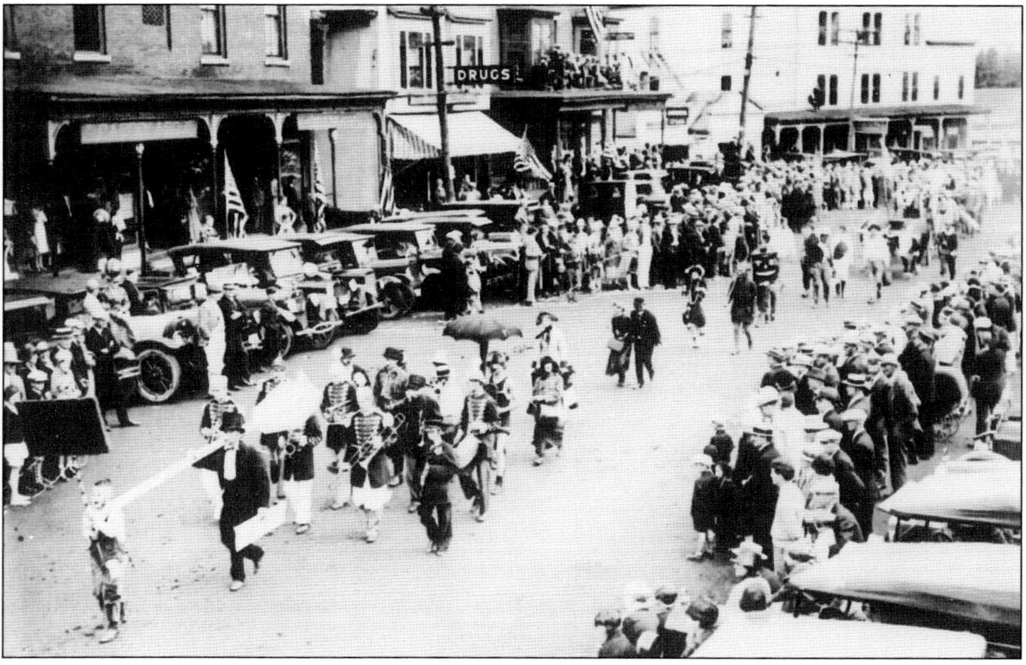

Bringing up the end of the parade was the Laurel Band of Milford, New Hampshire, followed by the "grotesque and horrible horribles." The "horribles" brought much laughter and entertainment along the parade route. Included in this group was the "Hunchback," who won first prize in its class.

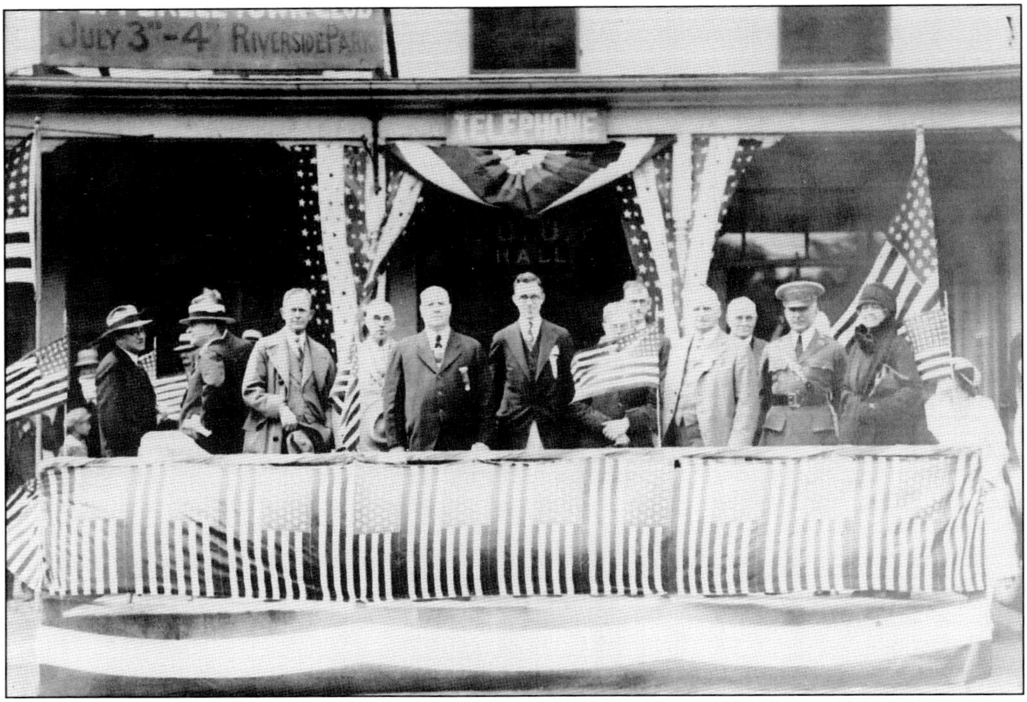

The reviewing stand for the 1927 Fourth of July parade was set up in the front of the Odd Fellows Building. People in the reviewing stand included Congresswoman Edith Nourse Rogers, Major Wahl of Camp Devens, Charles Miller, George Parker, W.C. Fuller, Mr. Cornell of Chicago, Mr. Crandell of New York, Mr. Dowd of Nashua, and Frank Torrey of Groton. The guests in the reviewing stand were later entertained at lunch at the Villa Lorraine.

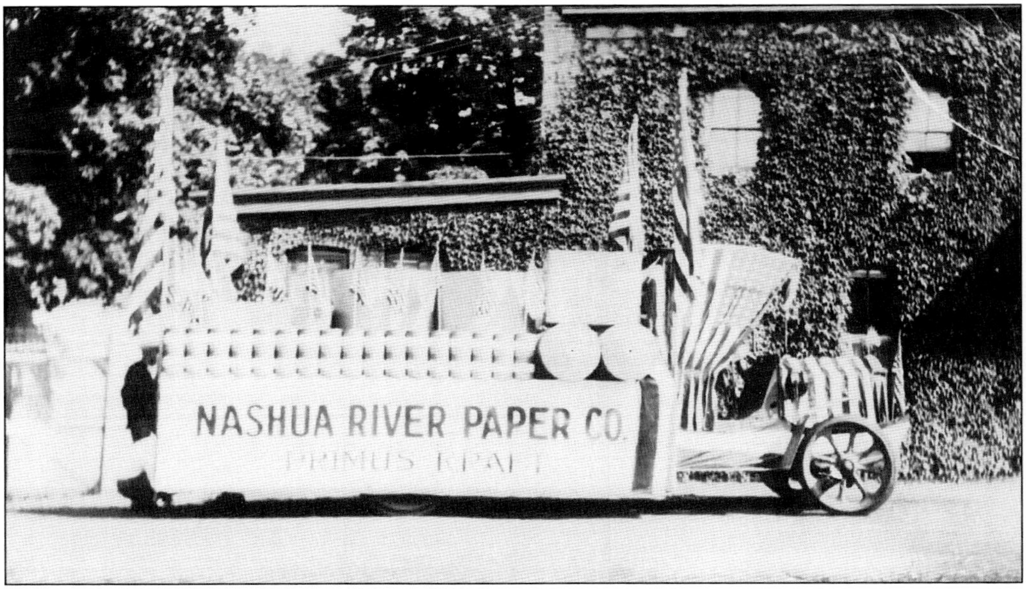

Parked outside the mill office is the Nashua River Paper Company's contribution to the 1927 Fourth of July parade.

Five

Fires and the Fire Department

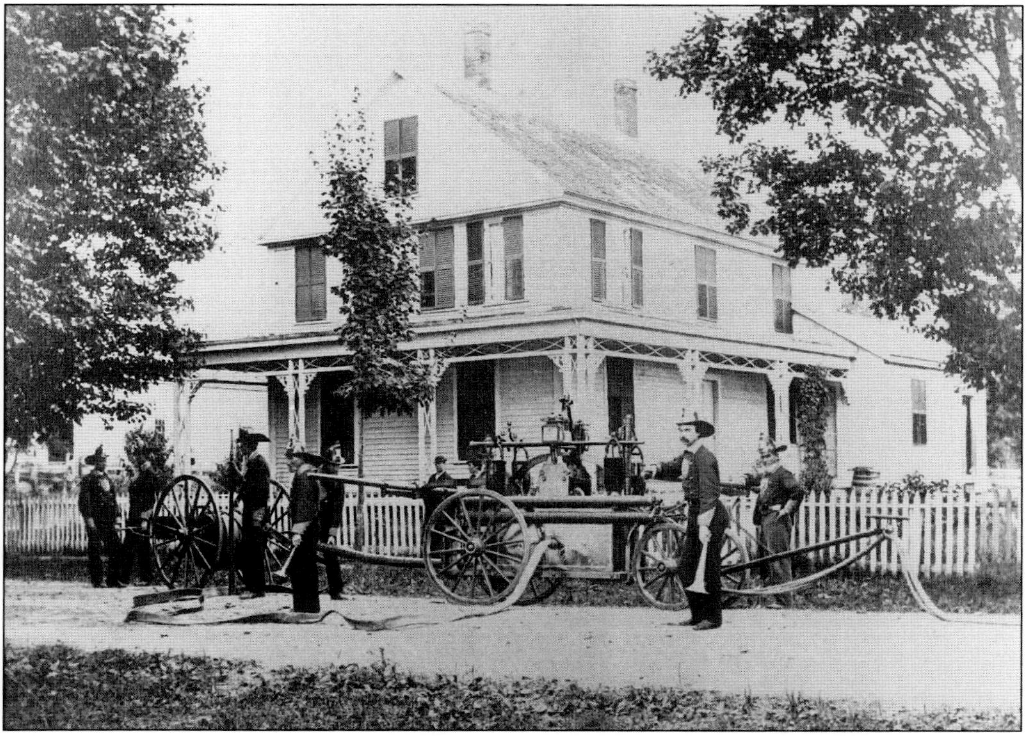

The fire department was temporarily located on Cottage Street in 1891 when Pepperell firemen, out in the street for a drill, stopped briefly to have their picture taken.

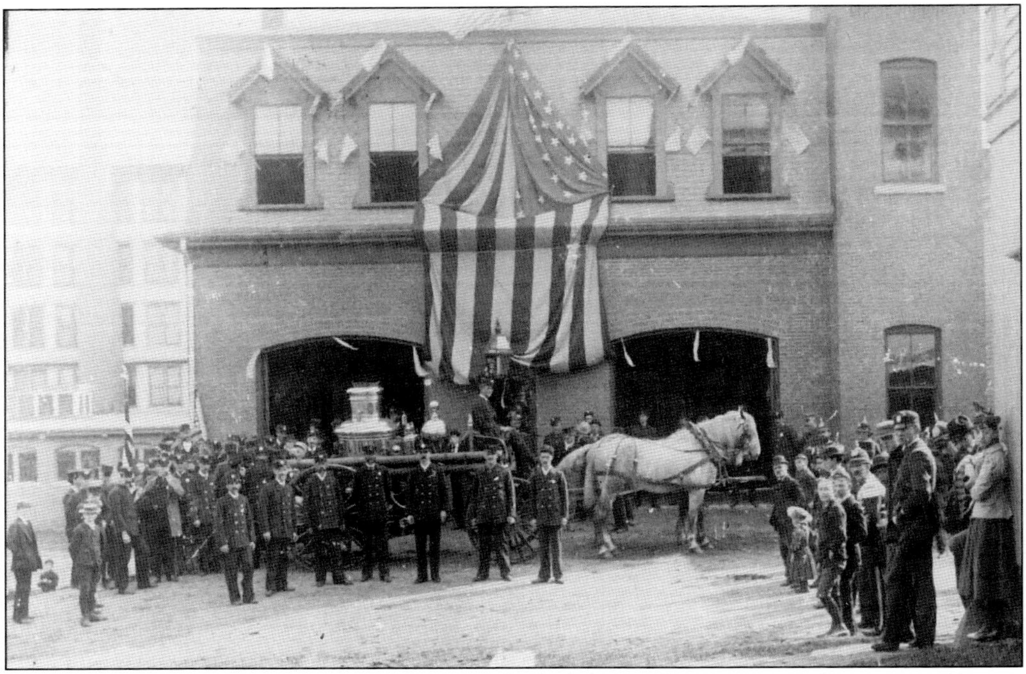

The Foster Street firehouse is decked out for the holiday as the steamer and its team of horses stand quietly by while the firemen pose for a picture. The Leighton Shoe Factory can be seen on the left in the photograph, which was taken prior to the fire of 1903.

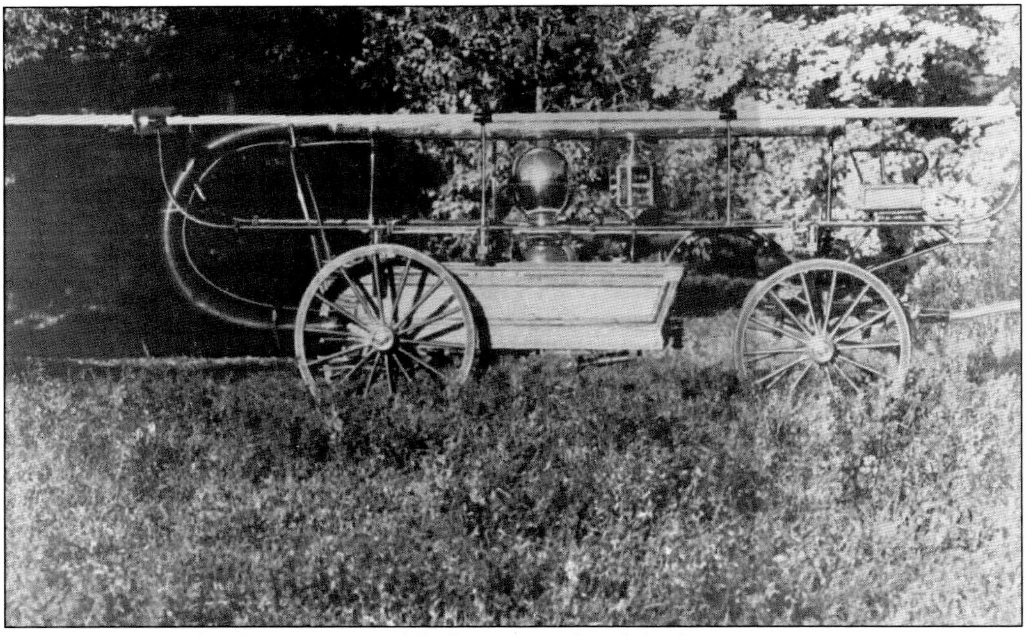

The Warren Hand Tub was renowned for having produced the longest stream at many a muster, her record at one meet reaching over 238 feet. This record, set at the turn of the century, was still unchallenged over twenty years later. The engine made the best average record in New England in 1898.

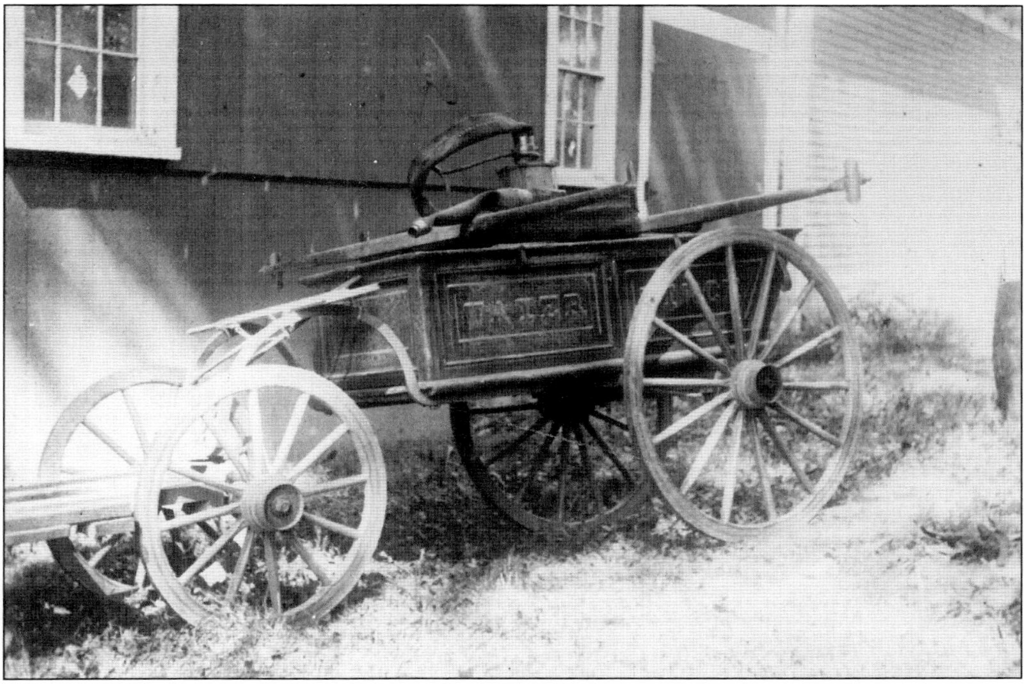

Pepperell's first purchase of fire apparatus was made in 1831 when two small hand engines were bought. The "Water Witch" was built for Pepperell in Belchertown, Massachusetts. When remodeled years later it was based at East Village. The other engine was destroyed at the Cutter fire in 1853.

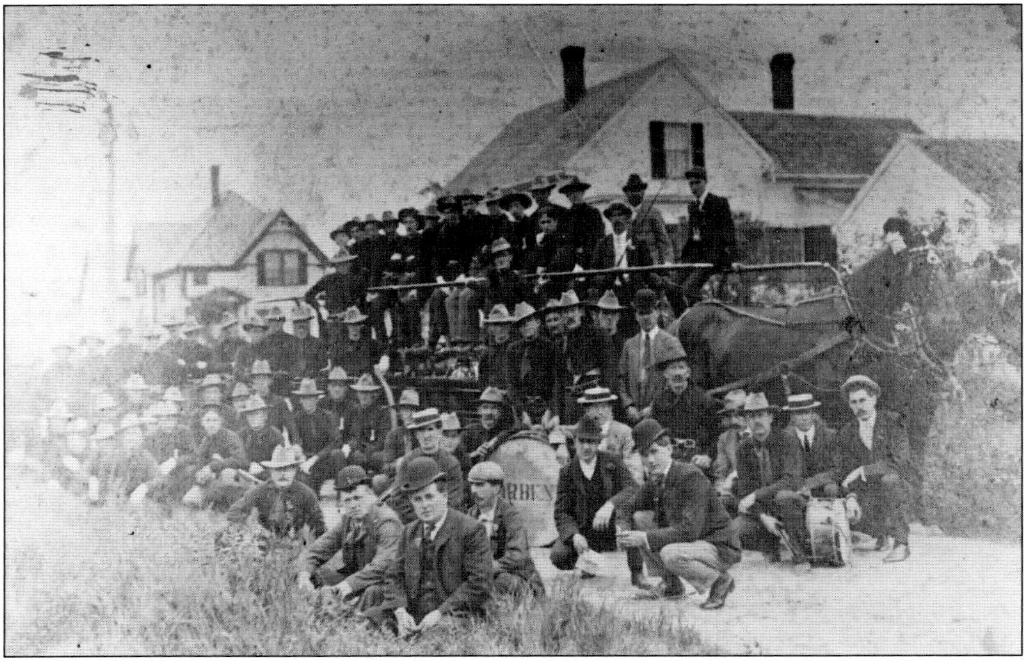

This photograph was taken of the Warren and her men at a muster in Winchendon, Massachusetts, on June 23, 1900. The Warren won the muster and $300 prize money. The winning stream was 222 feet and 11 inches.

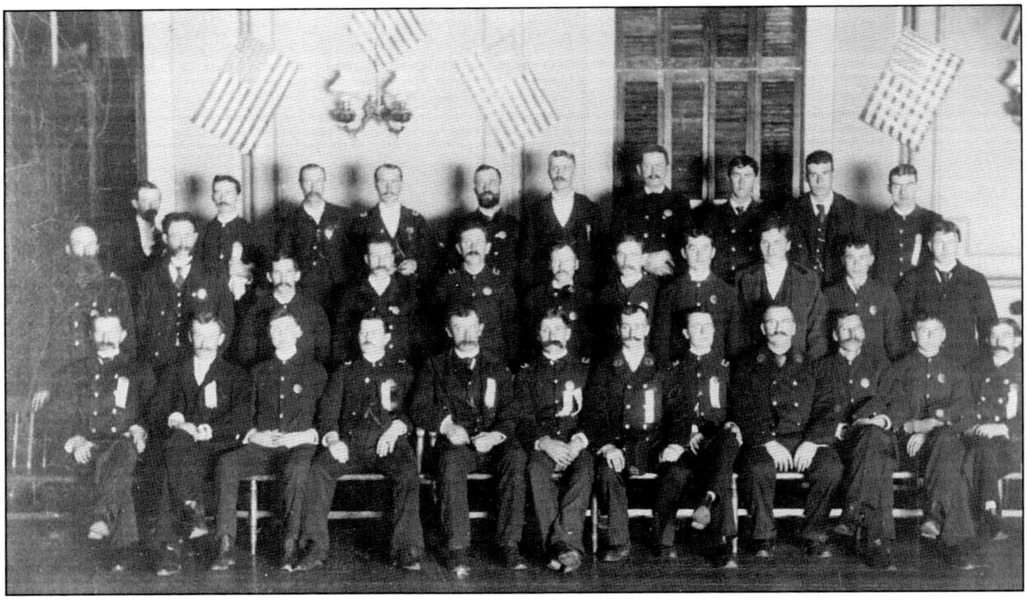

The Third Annual Concert and Ball of the Pepperell Fire Department was held at Prescott Hall on Friday, January 4, 1895. Brigham's Orchestra provided the music and pictures were taken by Kimball & Caswell of Fitchburg. From left to right are: (front row) John Bartz, unknown, unknown, Jack Boon, L. Gilman Robbins, Warren M. Blood, Albert Deware, John Farrell, Frank Morrill, Lincoln Johnson, George Willett, unknown, and unknown; (middle row) James Mock, Jonas E. Andrews, Mr. Whalen, Ed Lamsin, unknown, Frank D. Bolles, W.C. "Putt" Shattuck, unknown, Rainsford Deware, unknown, and Phil Leahy; (back row) E.S. Durant, William G. Rouse, unknown, L.P. Shattuck, Fred J. Dunlap, E.L. Tarbell, Fred Stevens, Frank S., Bert Ripley, and unknown.

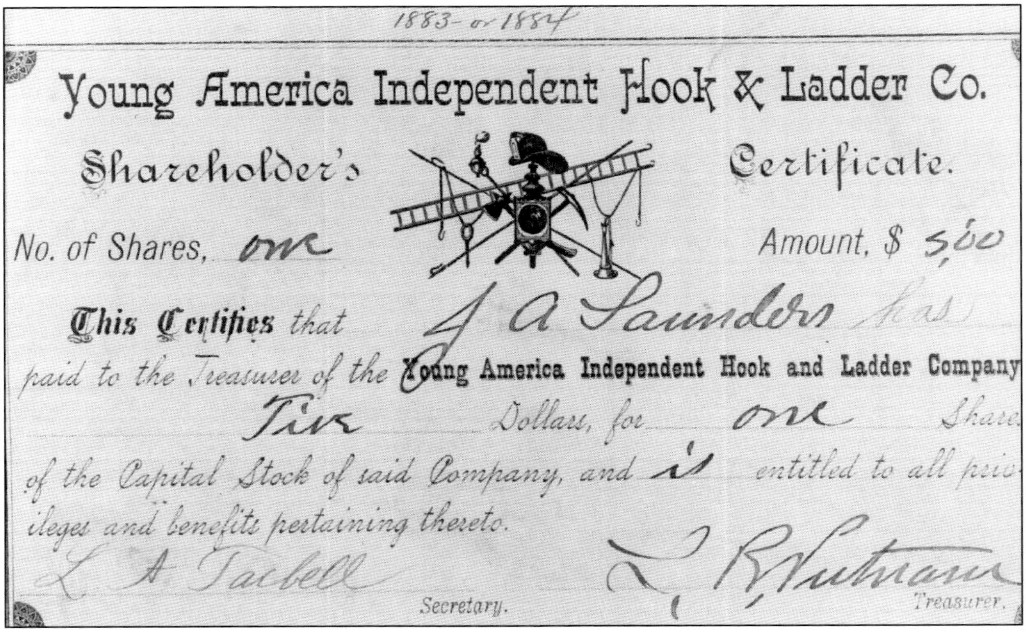

1883 or 1884

Young America Independent Hook & Ladder Co.

Shareholder's Certificate.

No. of Shares, one   Amount, $ 5.00

This Certifies that J A Saunders has paid to the Treasurer of the Young America Independent Hook and Ladder Company Five Dollars, for one Share of the Capital Stock of said Company, and is entitled to all privileges and benefits pertaining thereto.

L A Tarbell, Secretary.   L R Putnam, Treasurer.

In the early 1880s the Young America Independent Hook & Ladder Company sold shares of their stock for $5 apiece.

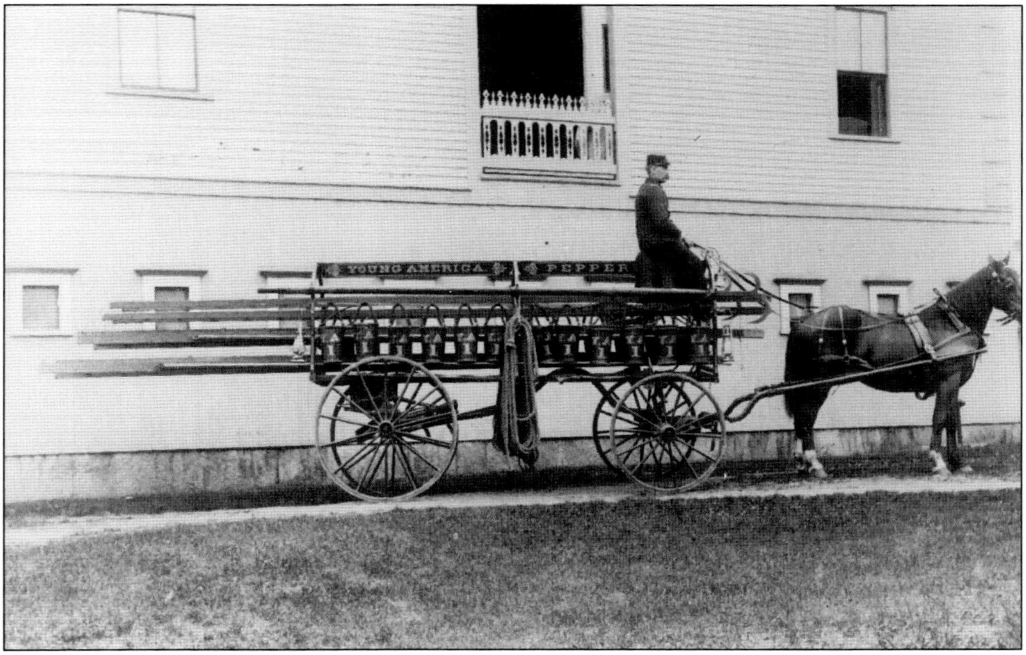

Sitting in front of Lovejoy's barn is the Young America Hook & Ladder truck. With its fire buckets hanging in a row along the side, a large coil of rope, ladders, and long-handled hooks neatly stacked, the truck offers a good look at what early fire-fighting equipment was all about.

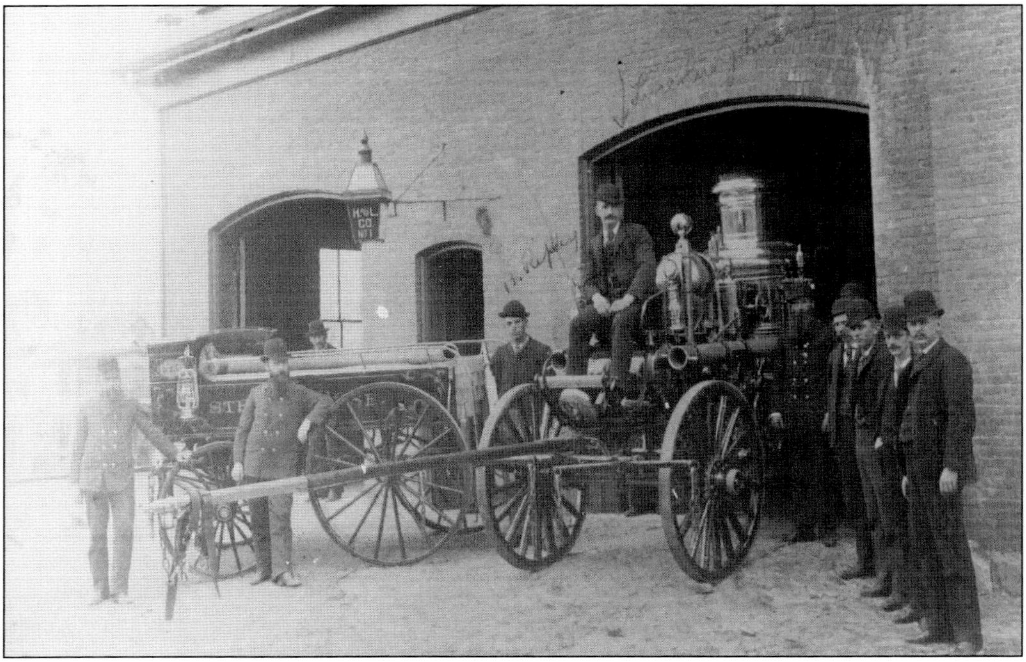

The steamer and hose wagon were purchased in 1891. In April 1891 the fire department was reorganized and Union Engine Co. #2 was disbanded, the steamer then taking its place. When the new Foster Street fire station was completed in 1892, the steamer shared the space with the Hook and Ladder Co. #1. Sitting on the steamer is Lincoln Johnson and standing next to him is B. Ripley.

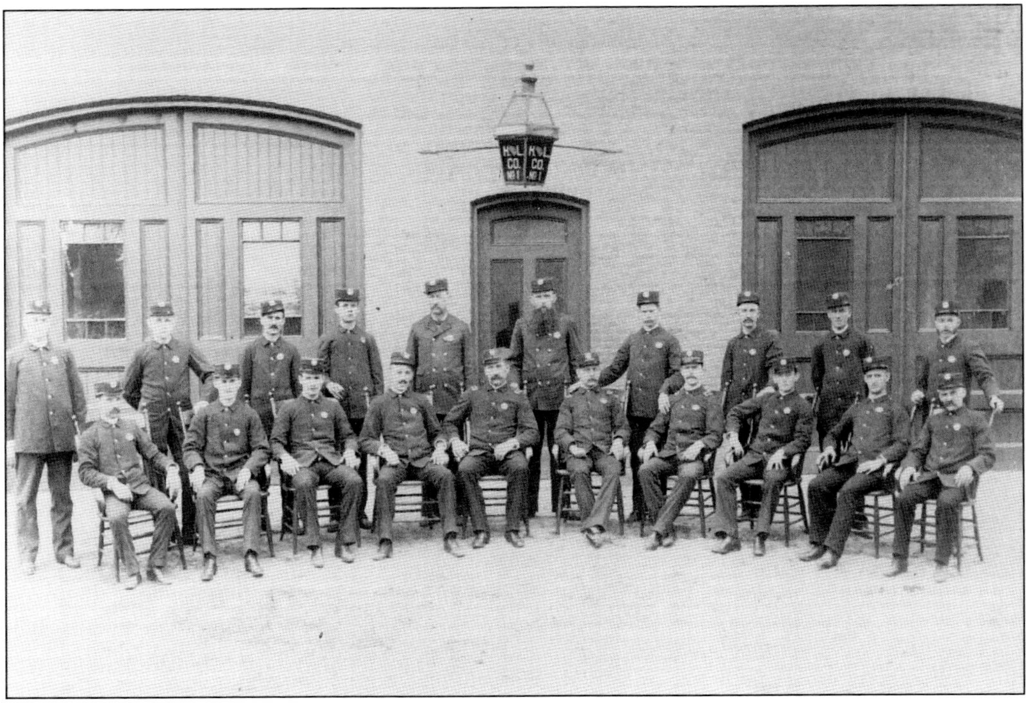

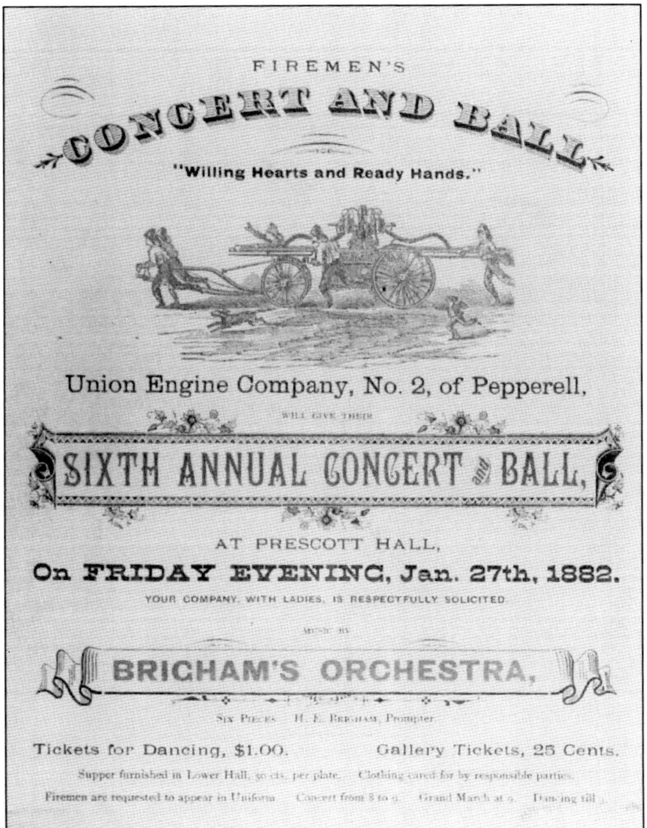

This early photograph shows the men of Hook and Ladder Co. #1 sitting outside the fire station.

Prescott Hall was the scene of many festivities in its early years. On January 27, 1882, the Union Engine Company #2 held their Sixth Annual Concert and Ball at the hall. Here is an interesting program from that ball. One could come and eat supper in the lower hall, or for 25¢, just sit in the gallery and watch. A one-hour concert preceded the Grand March and—imagine!—dancing continued until three am.

In 1902, while on the way to a fire, the steamer and its team of horses went into the canal. Mr. Gebhart was the driver (who also went into the canal, but came out safely). Unfortunately, one horse drowned and the other had to be shot. This scene, though somewhat faded, appears to depict spectators watching as the steamer is pulled from the canal.

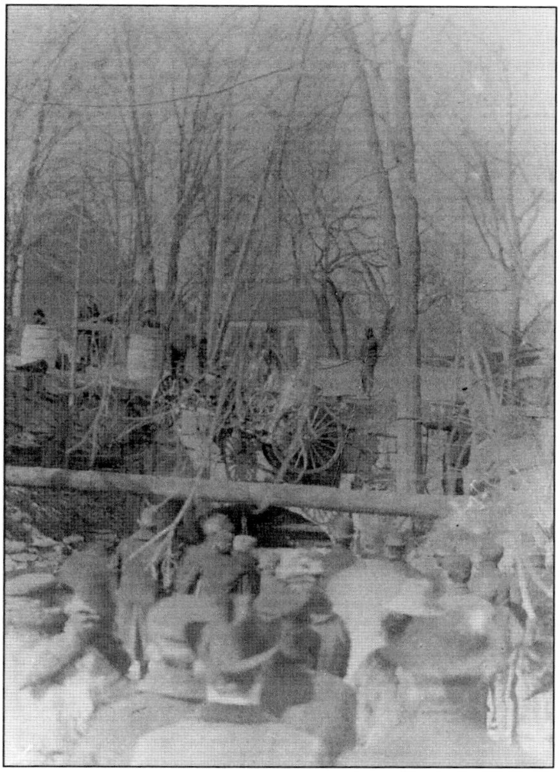

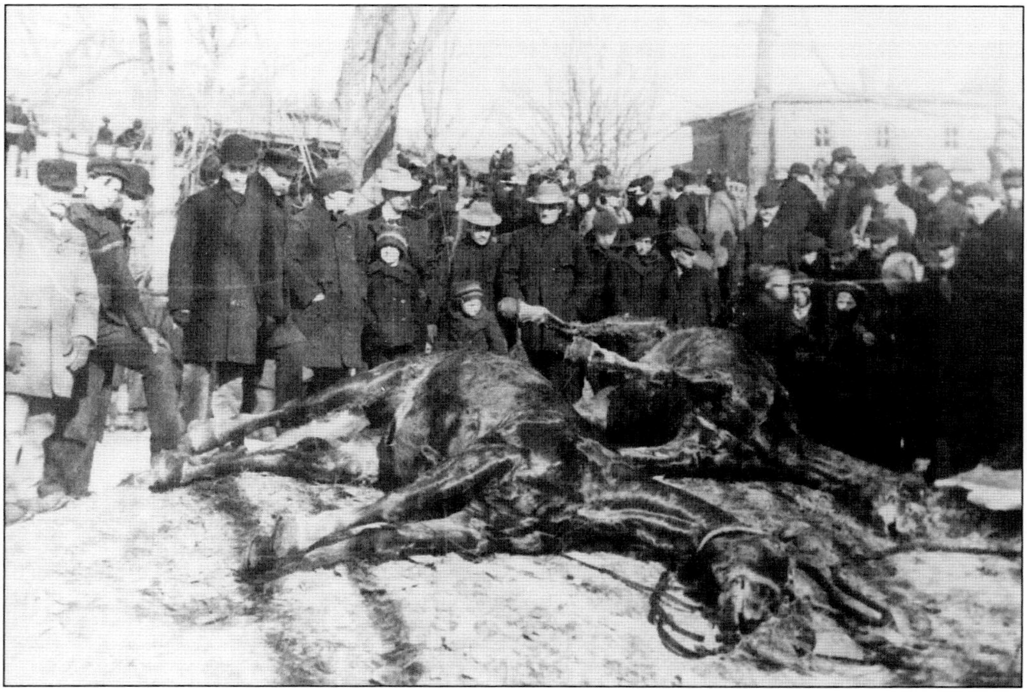

Townspeople sadly view the dead horses as they lie on the bank next to the canal. The cause of the accident was apparently due to icy roads and the driver being new and unfamiliar with the team of horses.

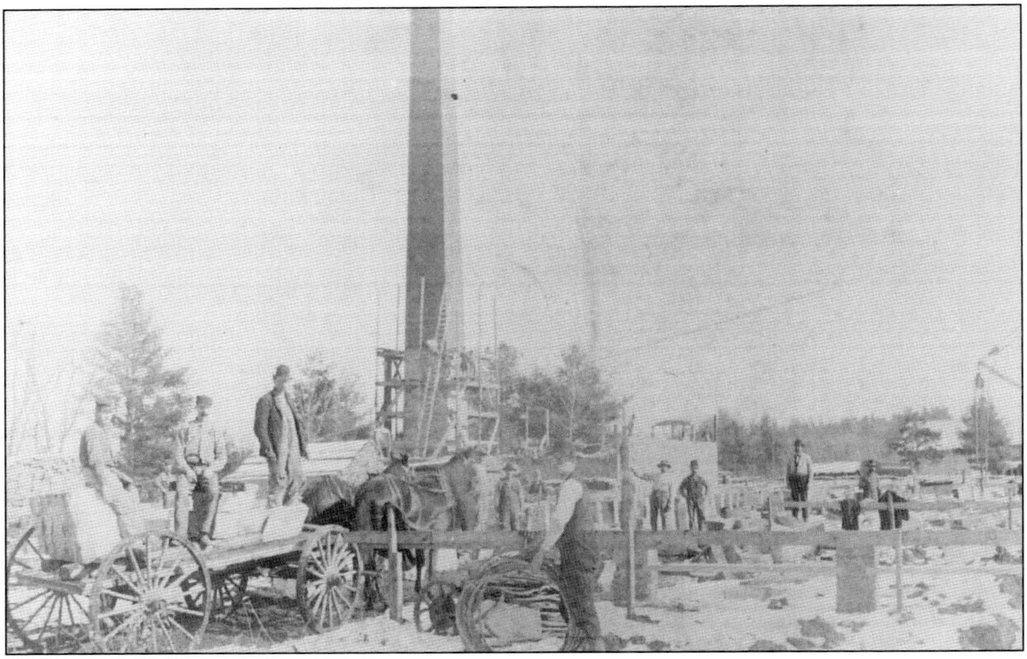

This is what remained of the first shoe shop after the fire of 1879. The first Leighton Shoe Factory was built at the corner of Main and Foster Streets where the Robbins Block now stands.

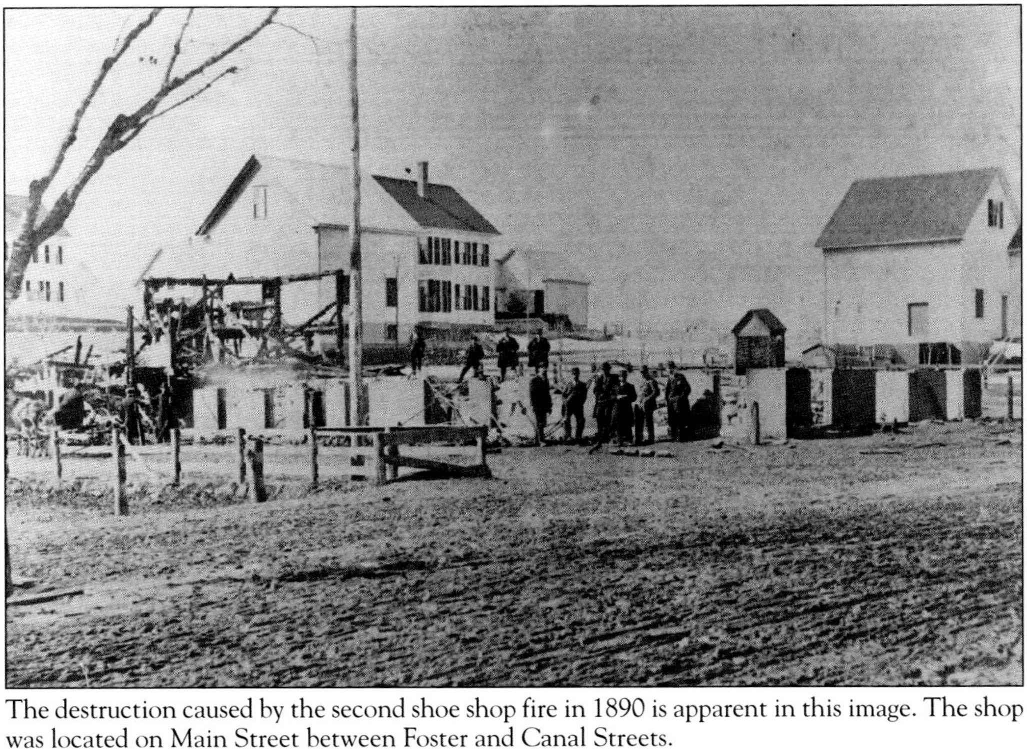

The destruction caused by the second shoe shop fire in 1890 is apparent in this image. The shop was located on Main Street between Foster and Canal Streets.

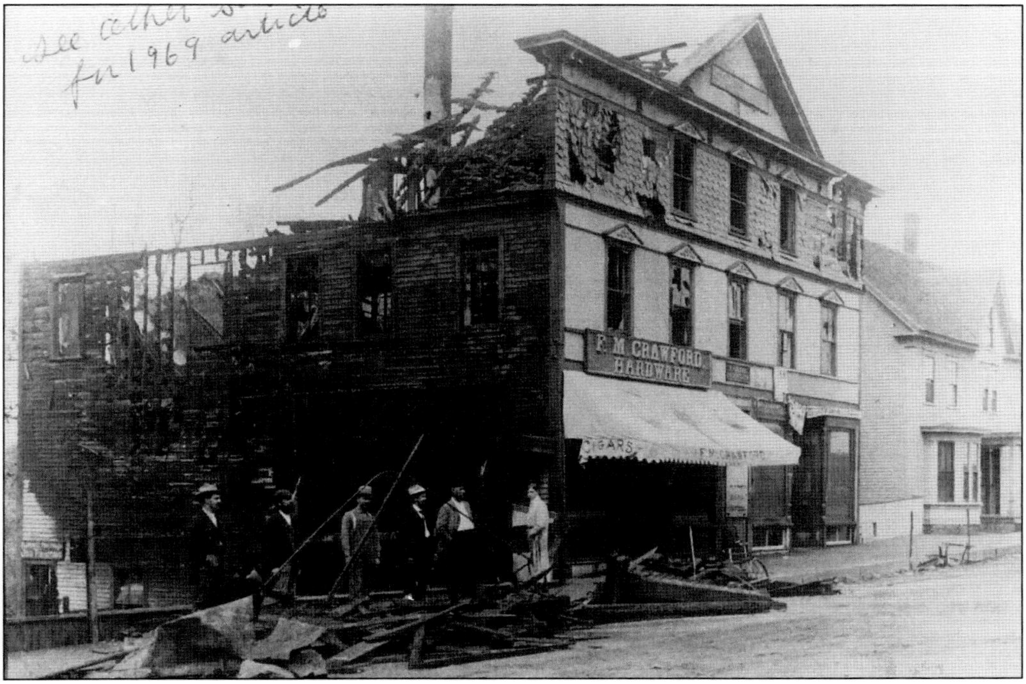

Crawford Hardware was located in the Aldine Block at the time of a fire there. The building housed many different businesses over time: Mansfield's Pharmacy, a restaurant and lunchroom, a men's clothing store, and Arthur Bartlett's Hardware Store. The telephone exchange and suites of offices were located on the second floor.

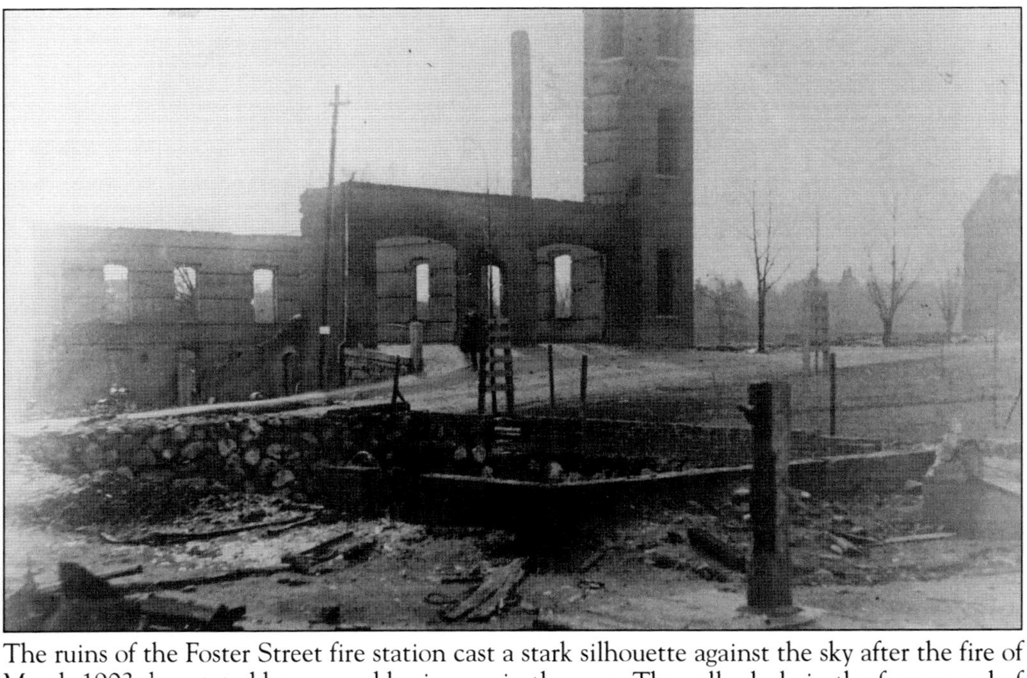

The ruins of the Foster Street fire station cast a stark silhouette against the sky after the fire of March 1903 devastated homes and businesses in the area. The cellar hole in the foreground of the picture is probably that of Kemp's Restaurant, which sat directly behind Kemp's Store in the Robbins Block.

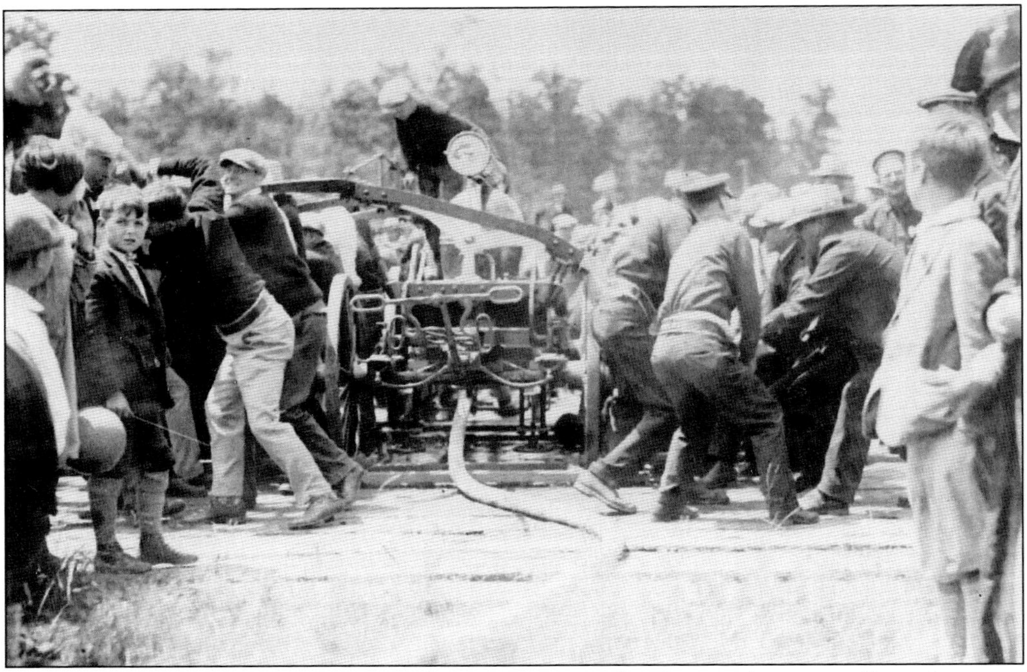

One of the most popular activities of yesteryear was the firemens' muster. Over the years its popularity has continued, and the competition with teams in the surrounding area has remained keen. In this photograph, taken in the late 1920s, onlookers lend a helping hand during the muster.

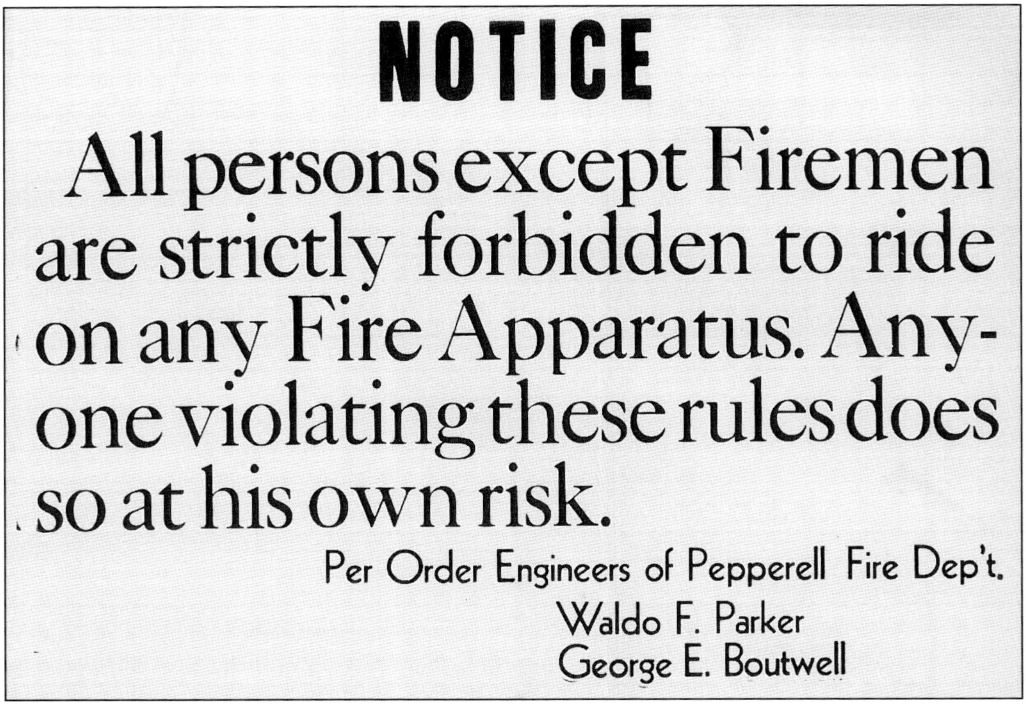

NOTICE

All persons except Firemen are strictly forbidden to ride on any Fire Apparatus. Anyone violating these rules does so at his own risk.

Per Order Engineers of Pepperell Fire Dep't.

Waldo F. Parker

George E. Boutwell

Large cards were printed by the fire department to warn people that anyone riding on any fire apparatus would do so at their own risk.

Six

SCHOOLS

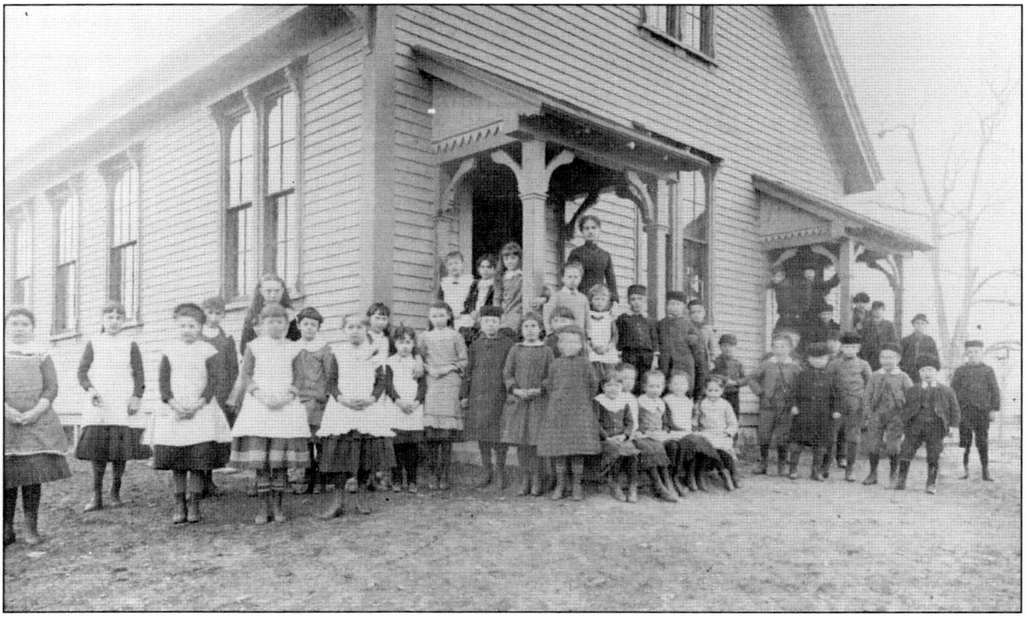

Teacher Anna Boynton poses with students in front of the Babbitassett School. The school stood about where the Clara M. Shattuck School/Pepperell Police Department now stands. It was reportedly faded green in color and had two porches on the front, one for the girls and one for the boys. Inside stood a pail of water drawn from a nearby pump with a long-handled dipper hanging close by. The seats accommodated two pupils; boys sat on one side of the room, girls on the other.

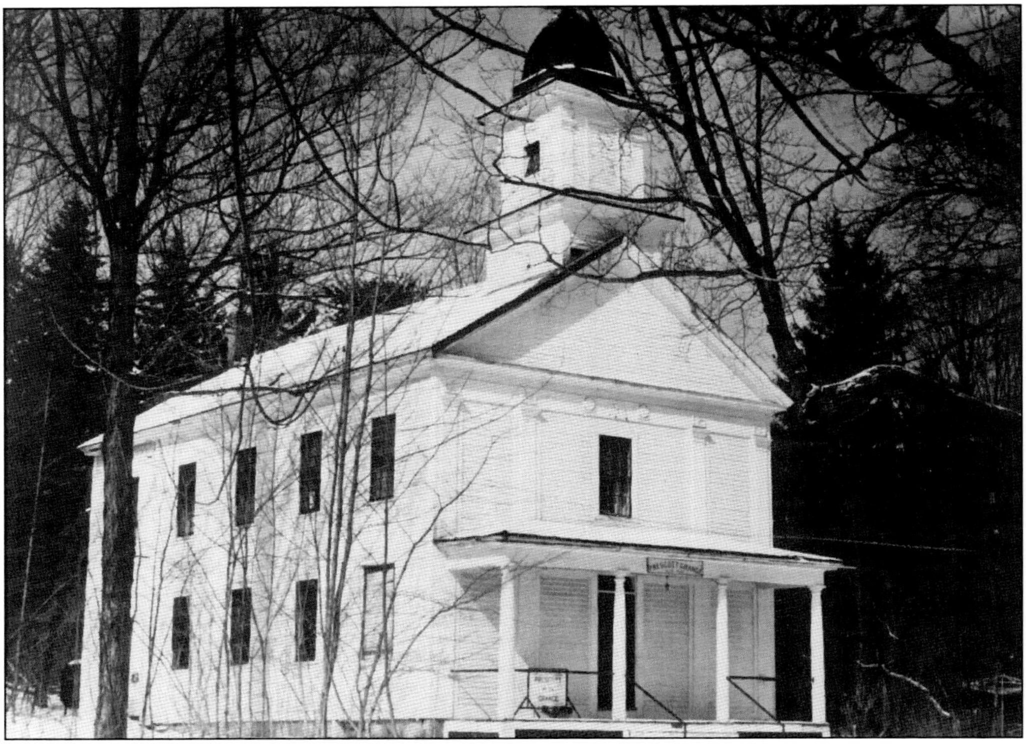

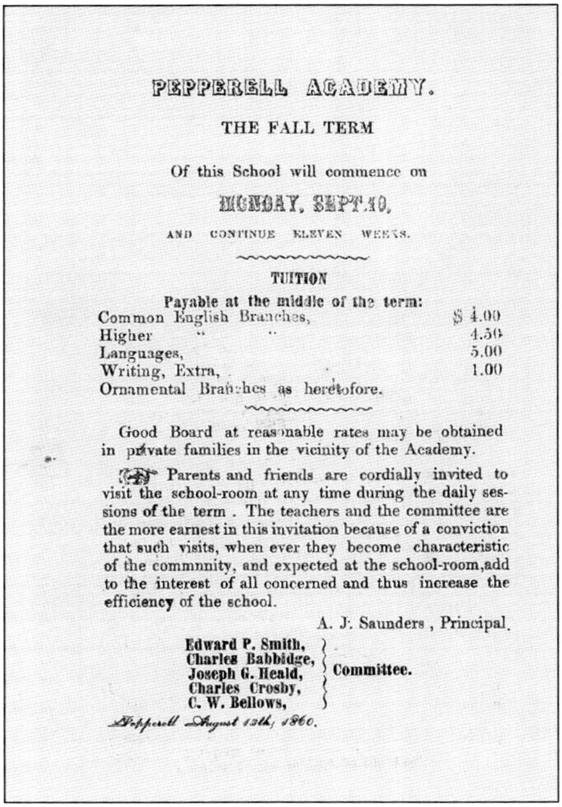

PEPPERELL ACADEMY.

THE FALL TERM

Of this School will commence on

MONDAY, SEPT. 10,

AND CONTINUE ELEVEN WEEKS.

TUITION

Payable at the middle of the term:

Common English Branches,	$ 4.00
Higher " "	4.50
Languages,	5.00
Writing, Extra,	1.00
Ornamental Branches as heretofore.	

Good Board at reasonable rates may be obtained in private families in the vicinity of the Academy.

Parents and friends are cordially invited to visit the school-room at any time during the daily sessions of the term . The teachers and the committee are the more earnest in this invitation because of a conviction that such visits, when ever they become characteristic of the commnnity, and expected at the school-room,add to the interest of all concerned and thus increase the efficiency of the school.

A. J. Saunders , Principal.

Edward P. Smith,
Charles Babbidge,
Joseph G. Heald, **Committee.**
Charles Crosby,
C. W. Bellows,

Pepperell August 13th, 1860.

Pepperell Academy was built in 1834 and opened that spring with fifty-two pupils and Mr. Eldridge as the teacher. Shares were sold to defray the building costs of $900 and to pay for the land. The academy became well known, attracting pupils from as far as 30 miles away. In 1836 it was necessary to build a 12-foot addition to the building as enrollment had increased to 172 students.

This is the announcement of the fall term of 1860 at the Pepperell Academy which ran for a period of eleven weeks. Visits to the school, closer contact with the teachers and school committee, and good and reasonable board with private families were incentives intended to increase interest in the academy, which had been waning in the last five or six years.

Amos J. Saunders came to Pepperell as the principal of Pepperell Academy in 1860, a position he kept until becoming principal of the high school several years later. He was called an "unusual" teacher: one who exacted high standards while at the same time holding the attention and good will of his students. In 1867 he left teaching to open a general store at Babbitassett Village and continued in this endeavor until his death in 1900.

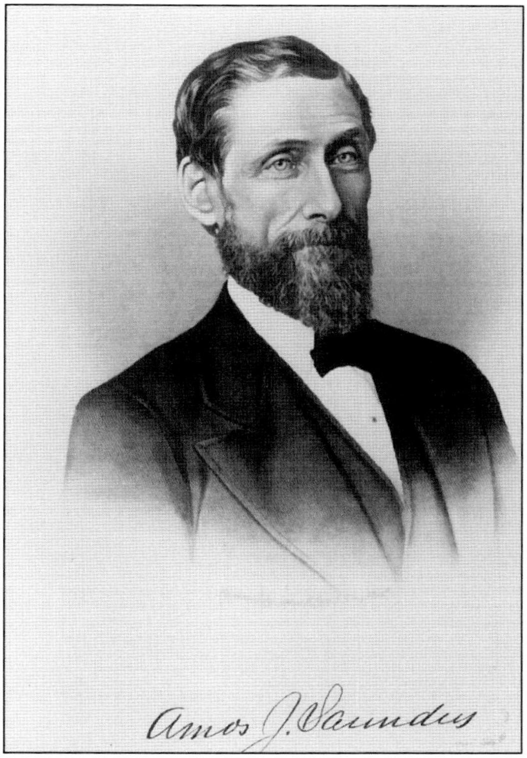

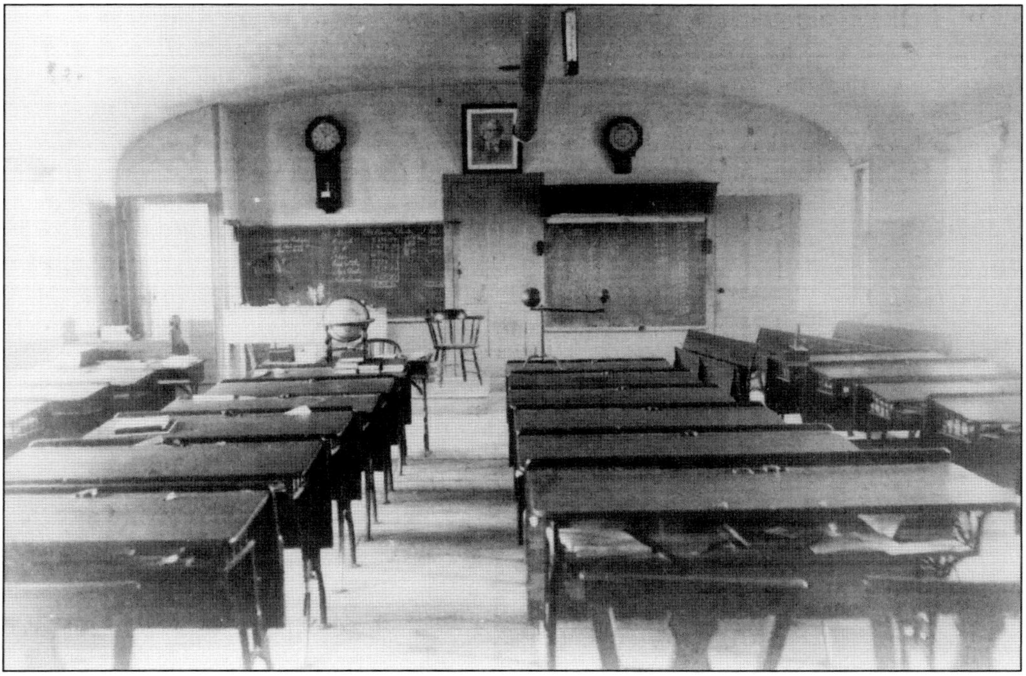

This interior view of the Pepperell Academy was taken about 1888 while the school was still in use. The next year the grammar and high school students were moved from the academy to the newly built schoolhouse at Chase Hill. The building is now owned and used by the Prescott Grange.

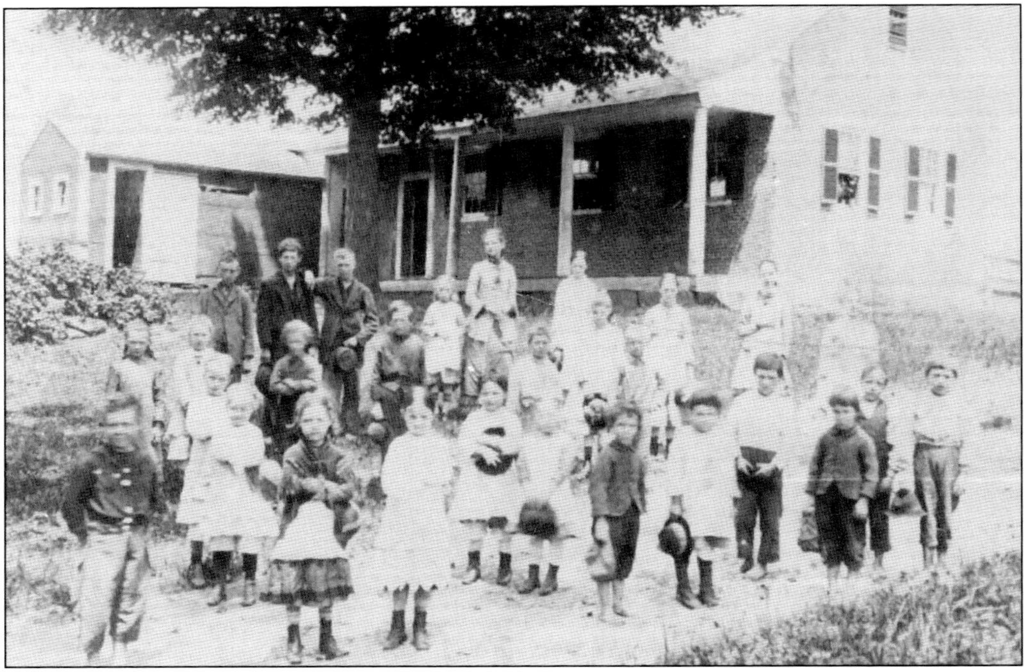

This stereoscopic view depicts the District # 4 North Village School at the corner of North and Prescott Streets. Built before 1772, it was often called "Fog End School House" and was the only school that had a bell. When the school closed, the bell was taken down and moved to the DAR building. Although the schoolhouse remained unoccupied for many years, it was eventually renovated by William Graves and made into a residence.

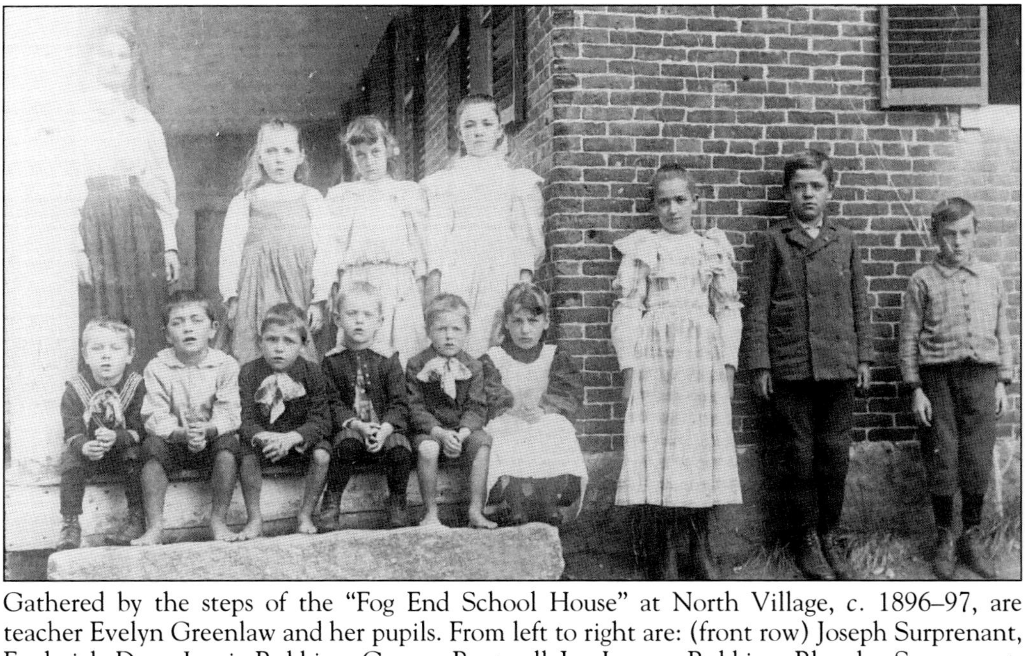

Gathered by the steps of the "Fog End School House" at North Village, c. 1896–97, are teacher Evelyn Greenlaw and her pupils. From left to right are: (front row) Joseph Surprenant, Frederick Dow, Lewis Robbins, George Boutwell Jr., Lyman Robbins, Blanche Surprenant, Annie Dow, Eben Stevens, and Edmund Surprenant; (back row) Effie Welch, Grace Stevens, and Ella Dow.

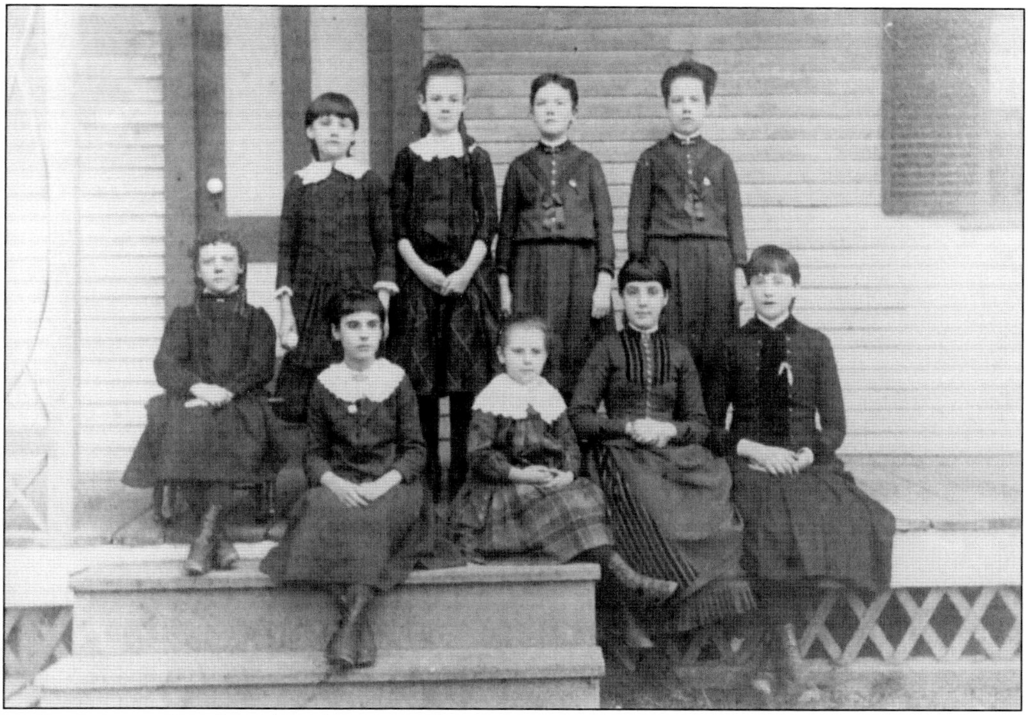

Looking somewhat less than happy as they pose around 1878 on the steps of what is perhaps a private school, these girls are dressed as proper young ladies of the day. The two girls on the right in the back row are Stella F. and Mary H. Saunders, sisters of Joseph A. Saunders.

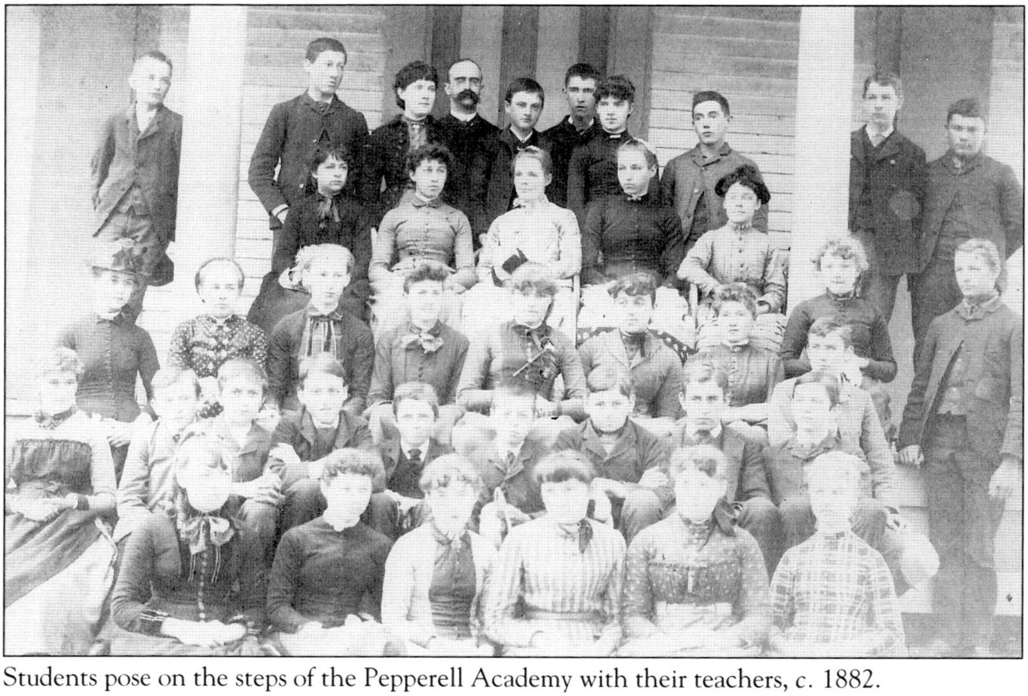

Students pose on the steps of the Pepperell Academy with their teachers, c. 1882.

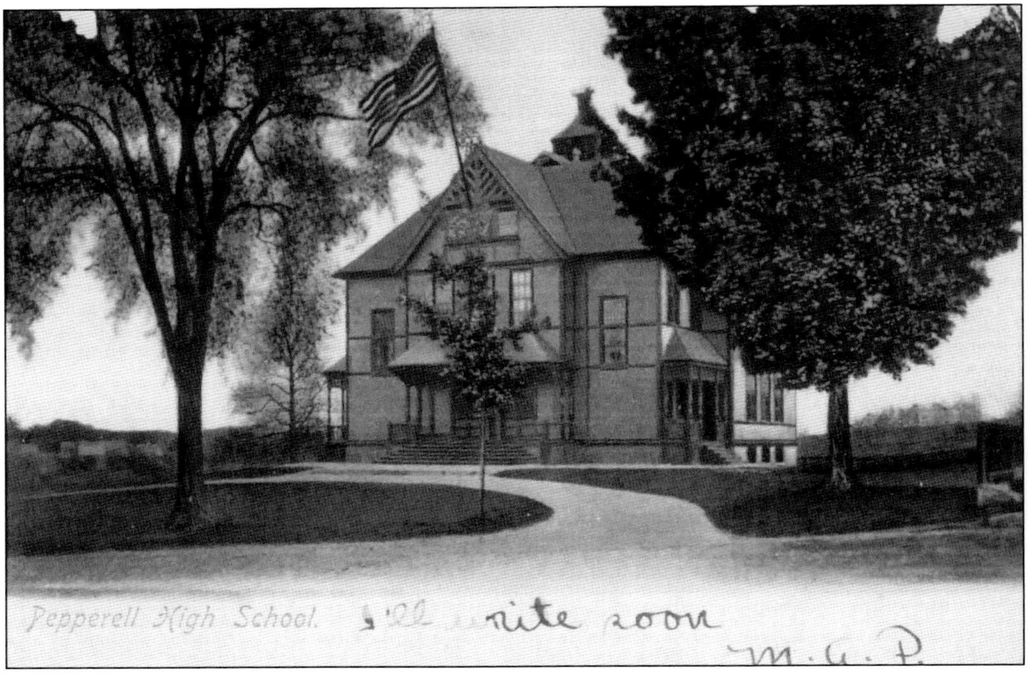

Building was started on the high school in 1888 and it was ready for occupancy by the spring of 1889. Although the school's construction was of questionable quality—with poor heat, freezing water pipes, and rattling windows—it remained in use for the next fifty years. It was painted gray and sported a cupola on the top. Climbing the cupola and writing one's name on its roof became a symbol of daring.

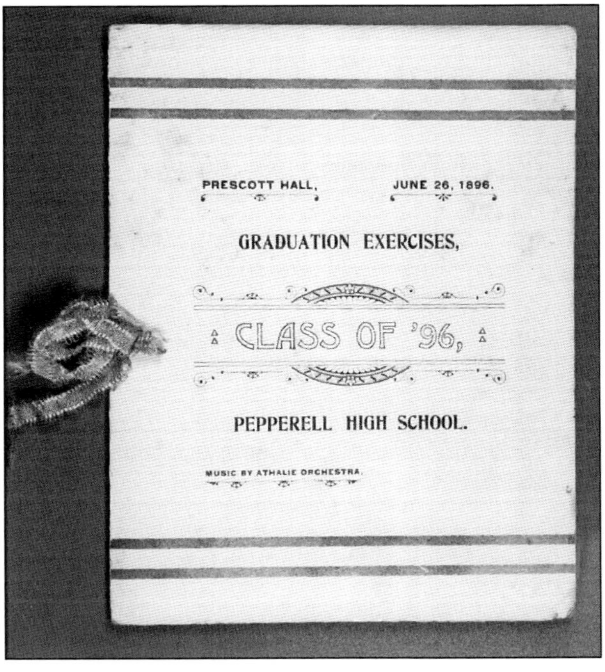

Programs for the graduation exercises of the "Class of '96" were rather fancy little keepsakes announcing the contents of the program, the class ode, and the class motto, which was, "Not Finished, Only Begun." There were but four graduates that year: Edith Margaret Baker, Florence Louise Merrill, and Arthur John Stevens in the English course, and Ethel Medora Wells in the Latin-English course.

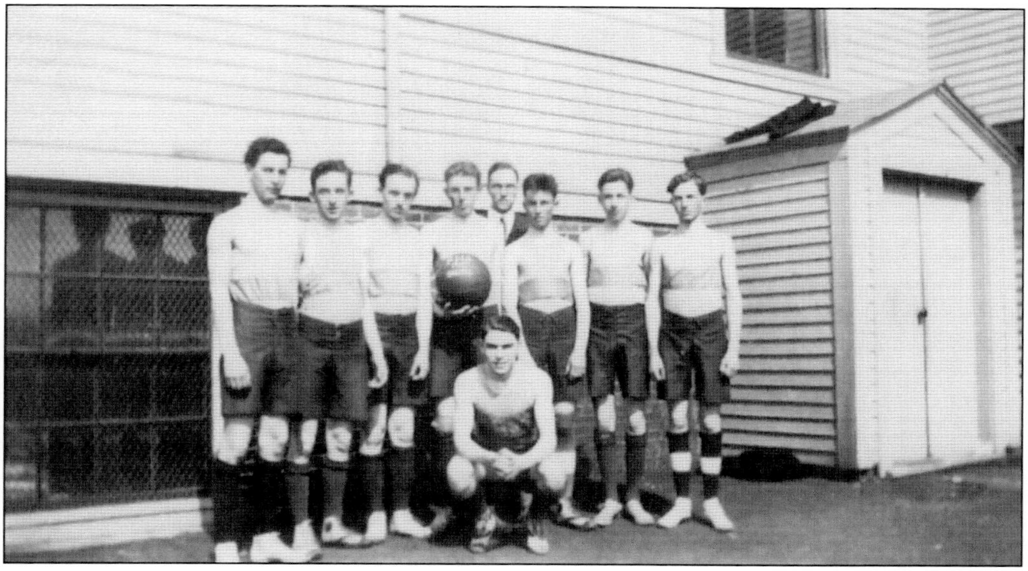

The Pepperell High School basketball team posed with their coach outside the school around 1916.

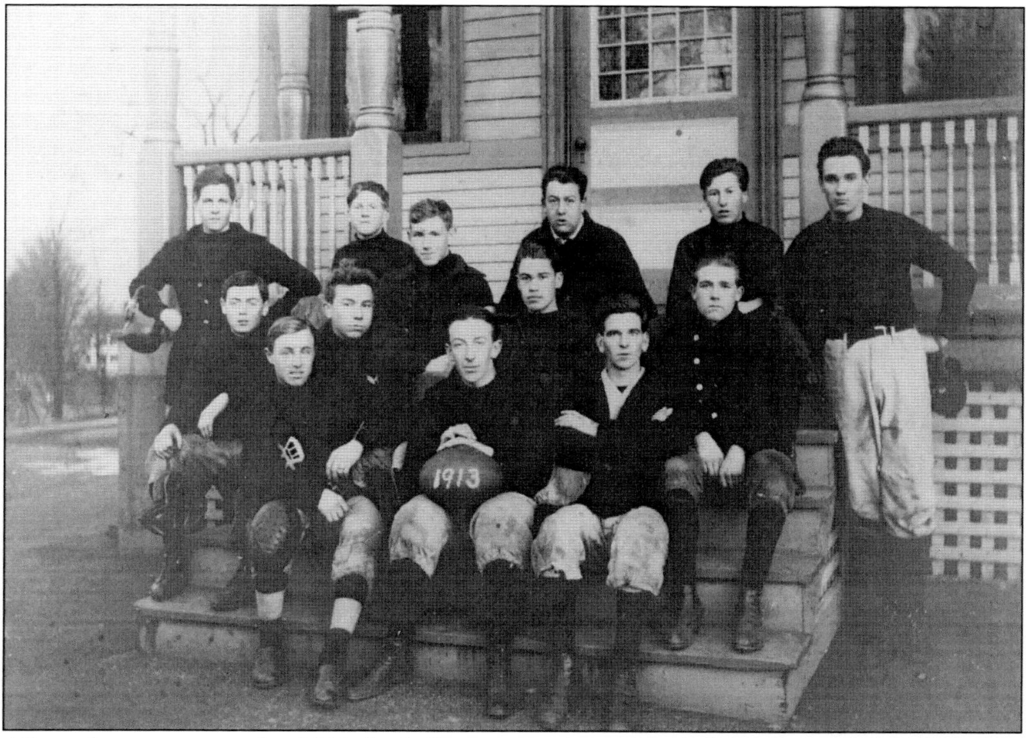

All set for practice is the 1913 football team on the steps of the high school. From left to right are: (front row) Melvin Alden, Thomas Sullivan, and James Breen; (middle row) Harry O'Toole, Albert Pillsbury, Roscoe Hayes, and Raymond Chinn; (back row) Gay Rouse, Origen Kimball, I. Tower, Fred Tarbell, Fred Hall, and Gerry Nutting.

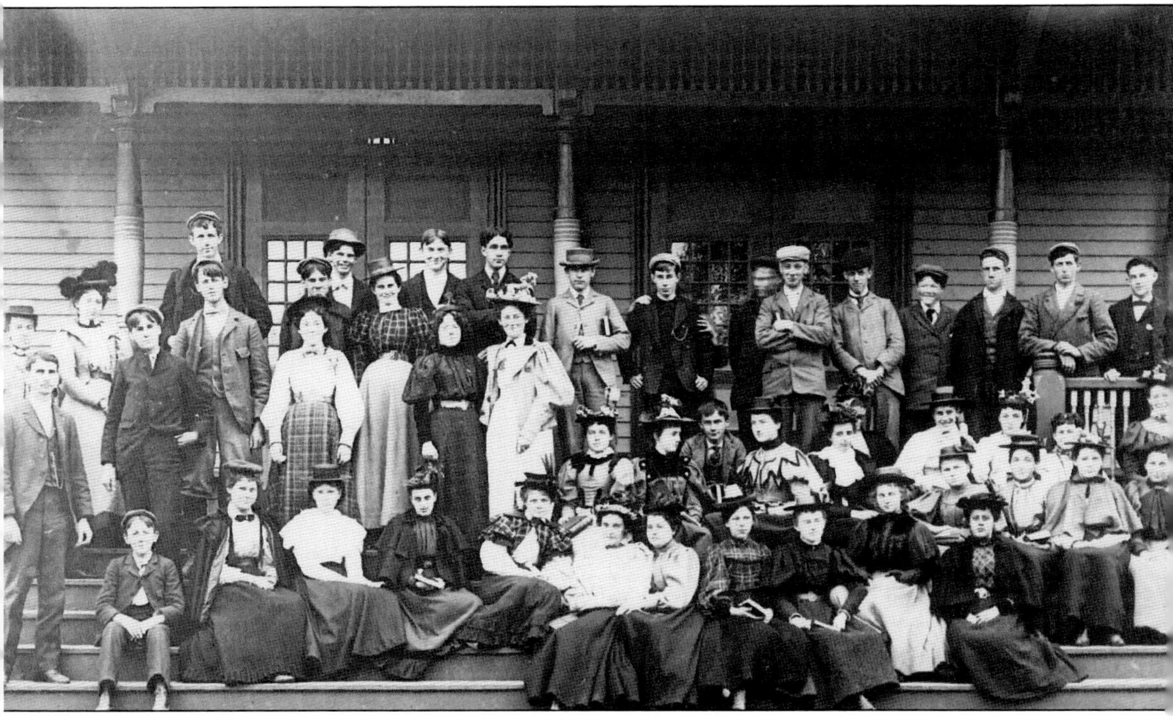

This photograph of happy students gathered on the steps of the high school with their teachers (on the left) was taken in 1898. At that time the school had been in use at this location for nearly a decade.

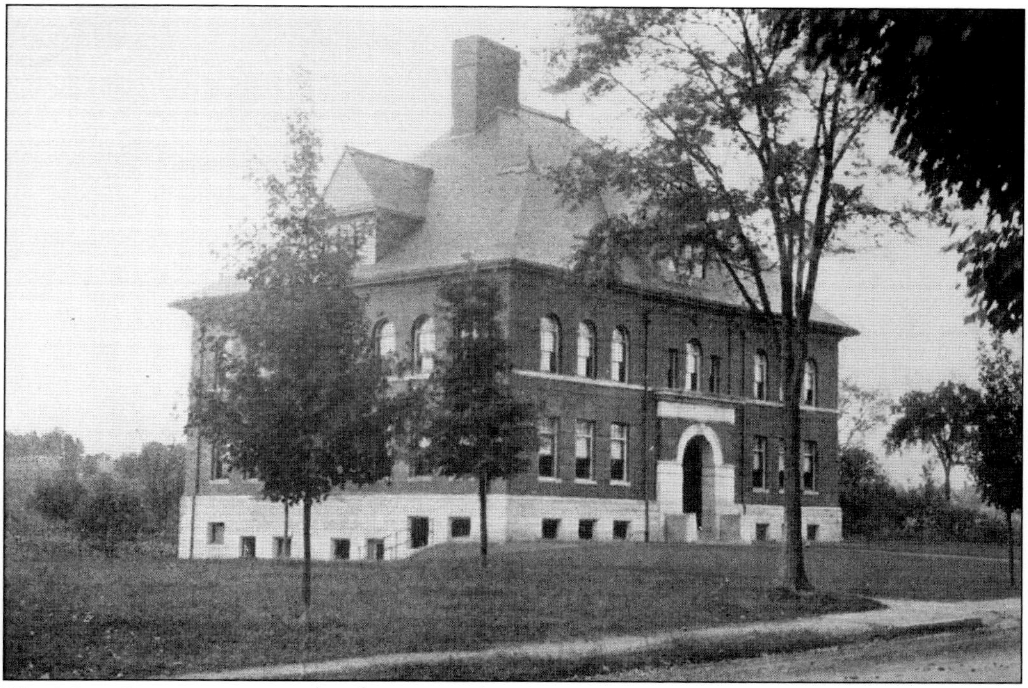

The Main Street grammar school was completed in 1898 but did not receive the name of the Clara M. Shattuck School until 1920. Miss Clara M. Shattuck was appointed principal of the new school in 1889, and stayed there until her retirement in 1922 after fifty years of service as a teacher.

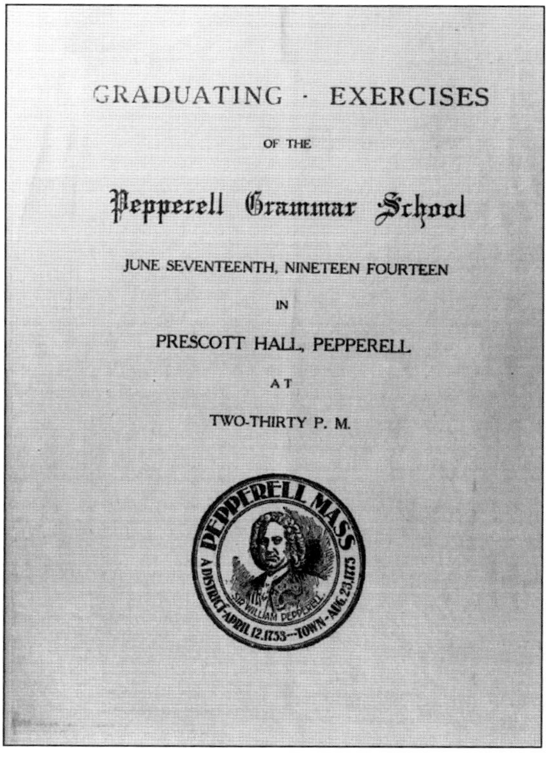

GRADUATING · EXERCISES

OF THE

Pepperell Grammar School

JUNE SEVENTEENTH, NINETEEN FOURTEEN

IN

PRESCOTT HALL, PEPPERELL

AT

TWO-THIRTY P. M.

Graduation exercises were held at 2:30 pm for the twenty-seven students finishing grammar school in June of 1914. Programs were handed out announcing the songs and poems to follow, with diplomas to be handed out at the end of the exercises.

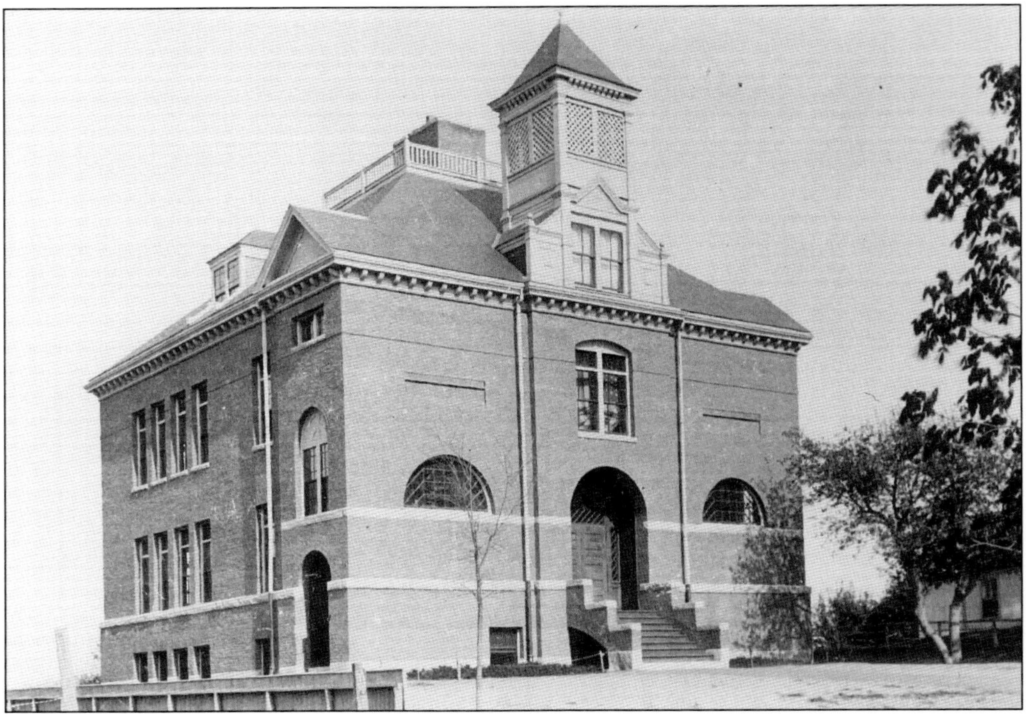

The Groton Street School was built at Depot Village in 1893 for a cost of $14,000. Although the school had seating for 250 students, it was not filled to capacity, owing to the fact that the old Tarbell Street School (the American Legion Hall) was still in use at the time. Five years later the enrollment had dropped from 200 to 166 pupils.

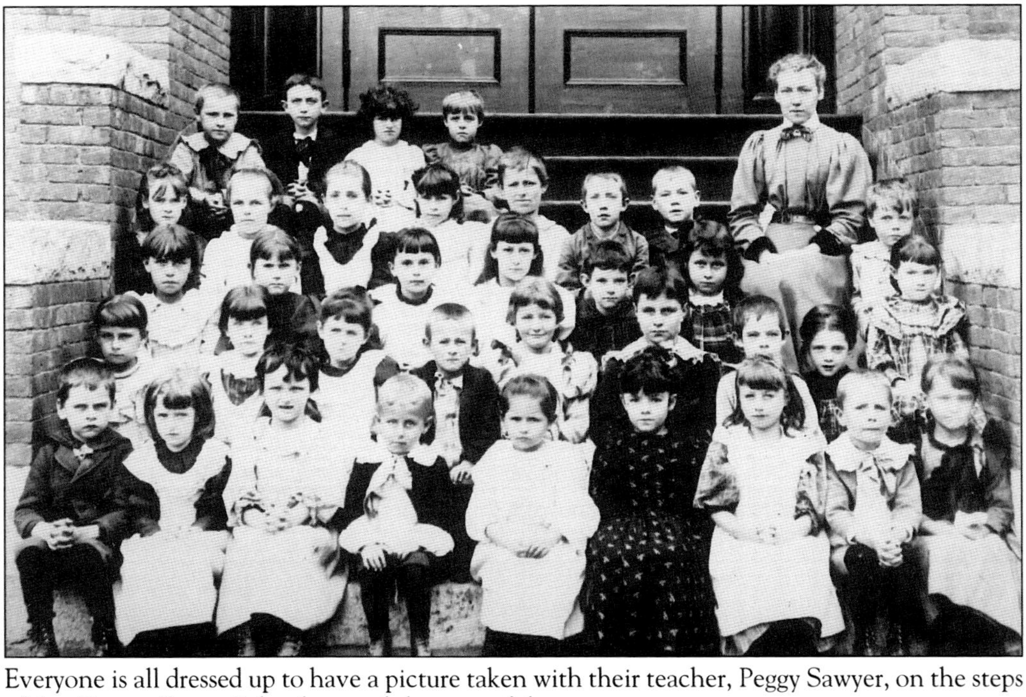

Everyone is all dressed up to have a picture taken with their teacher, Peggy Sawyer, on the steps of the Groton Street School around the turn of the century.

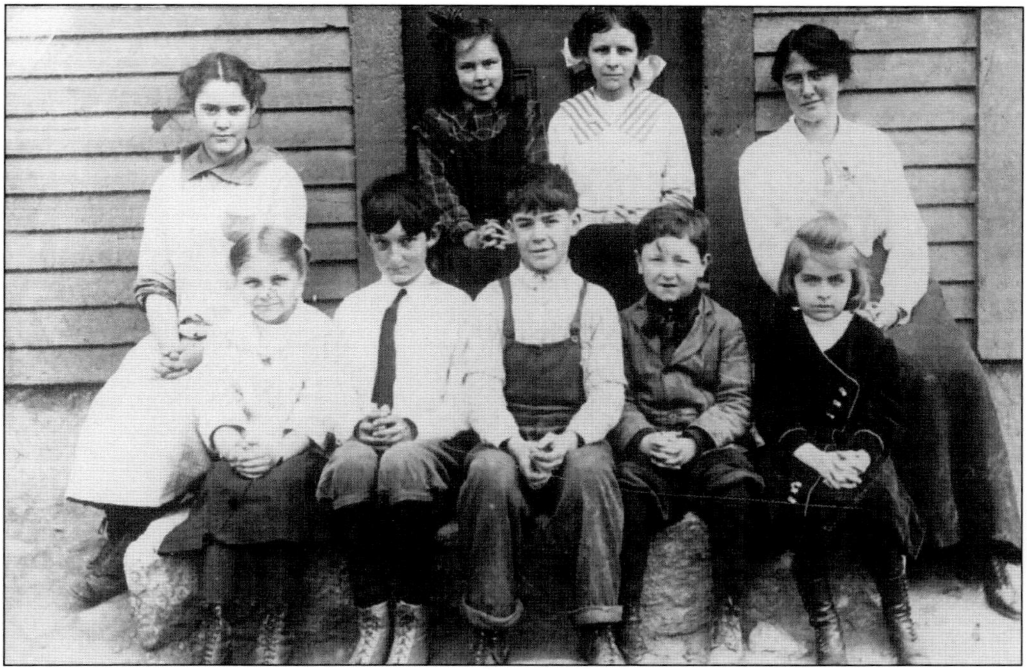

This photograph was taken on the steps of the Oak Hill schoolhouse, located at the corner of Oak Hill and Lawrence Streets. This was the District No. 2 School and was built in the late 1700s, remaining in existence as a school until 1916. From left to right are: (front row) Edith Stuart (who died young), Roger Ryan, Albert Parker, Charlie Allen, and Anita Marston; (back row) Berenice Parker, Sybil Stuart, Maude Stuart, and Jesse Flynn (teacher).

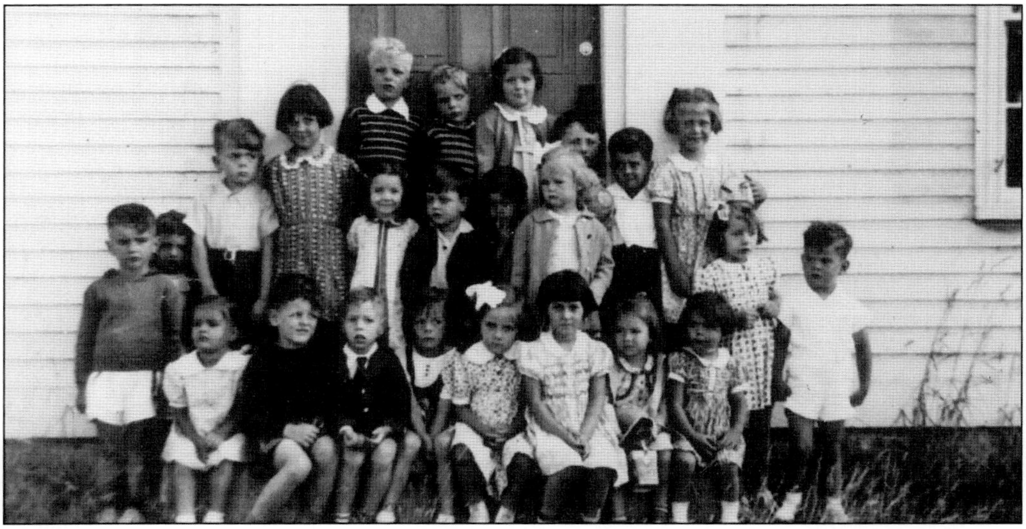

In 1939 Hannah Aldrich ran a kindergarten and nursery school in the old Varnum house on Hollis Street across from the town field. From left to right are: (front row) Kenneth Wright and Lenora Melindy (both standing), unknown, Richard Stevenson, unknown, Jackie Rondeau, Joan Morrill, Jean Duprey, Glenice Stavely, unknown, and Betsy Curtis and William Sherwood (standing); (middle row) Richard Parker, M. Haggarty, Helen Knight, unknown, George Rice, Meredith Frazer, Leroy Schofield, and Mildred Slocum; (back row) Emery Barkhouse, Ernest Barkhouse, Joanne Saunders, and Hank Milroy.

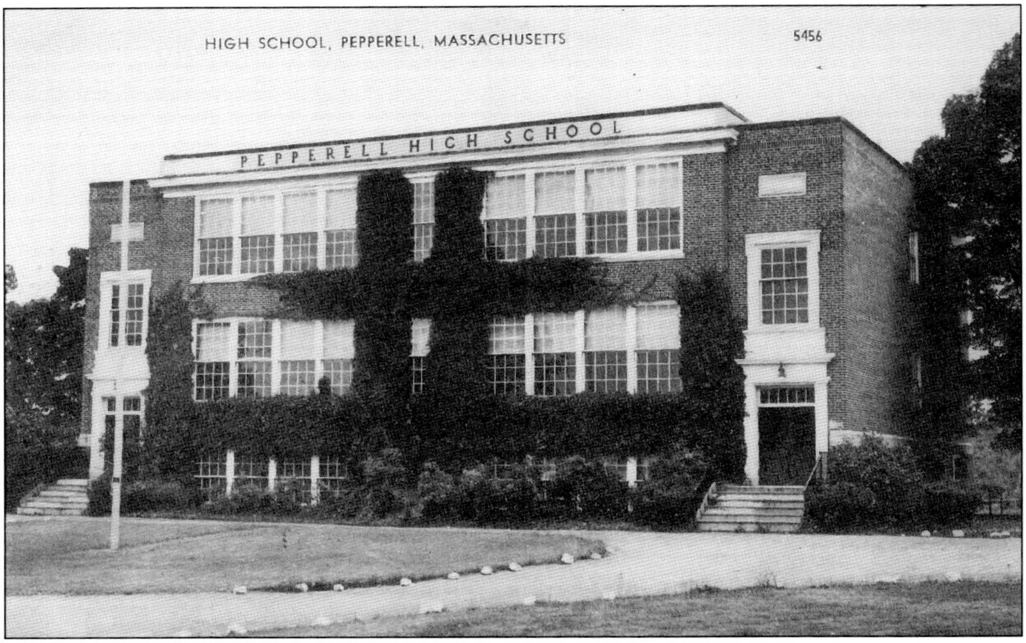

The "new" Pepperell High School was built in 1938–39 directly behind the existing one. Junior high students (grades seven and eight) from both the Groton Street and Shattuck Schools also attended classes here. The school was later named for Peter Fitzpatrick, the well-respected school custodian, who is also remembered for organizing the Green Waves, Pepperell's championship basketball team.

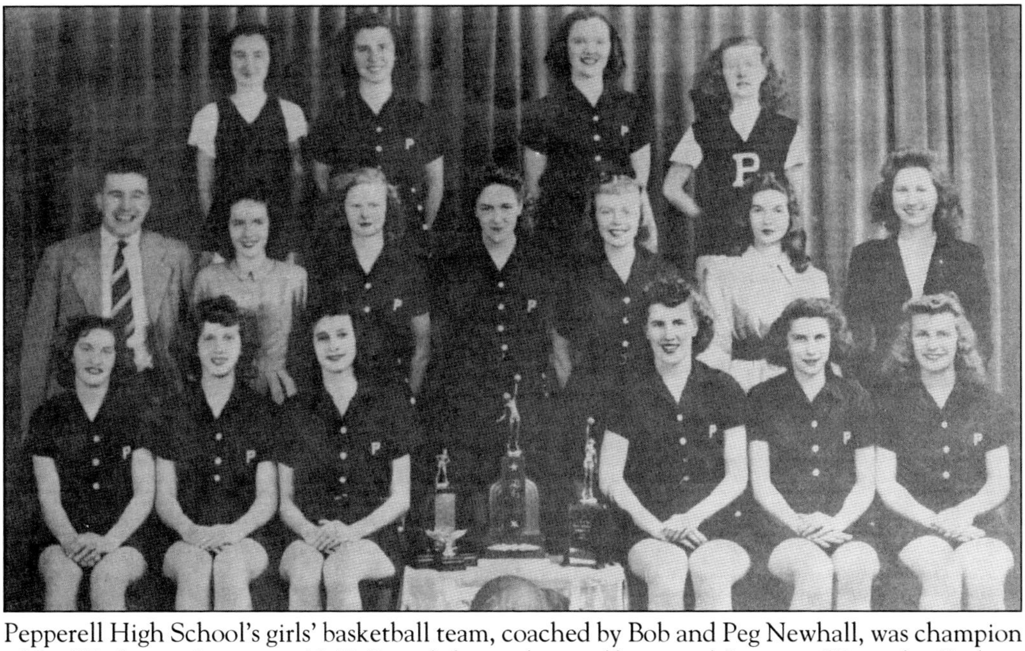

Pepperell High School's girls' basketball team, coached by Bob and Peg Newhall, was champion of the Wachusett League in 1947. From left to right are: (front row) Lorraine Wisnosky, Barbara Toomey, Evelyn Baraby, Kay Lorden, Anna Duda, and Mary O'Brien; (middle row) Coach Bob Newhall, Jackie Dee, Donna Conley, Betty Dow, Nancy Bowen, Natalie Blood, and Coach Peg Newhall; (back row) Jackie Brew, Dolly O'Brien, Anne Abele, and Sis McGrath.

Seven

CHURCHES

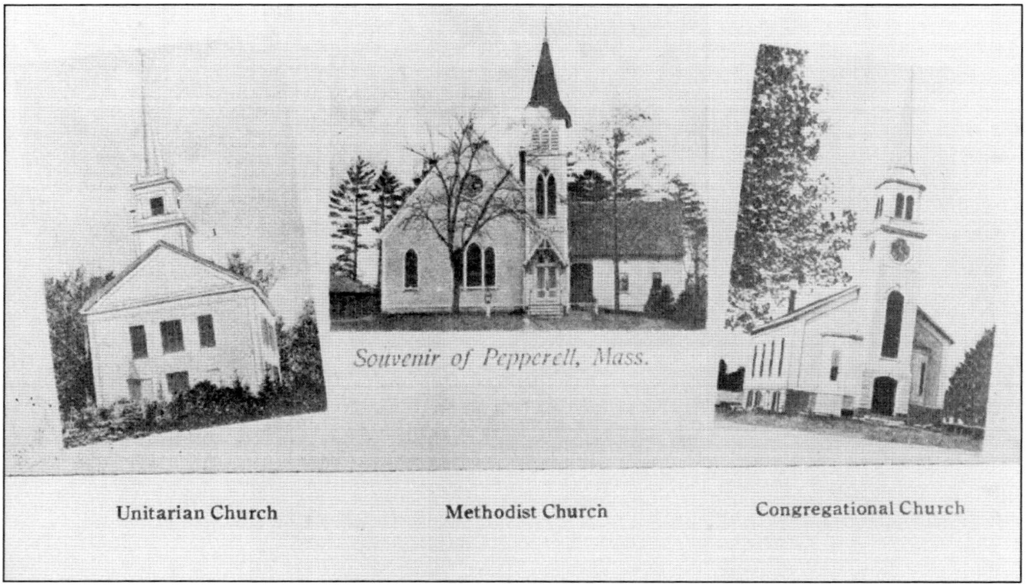

This *c.* 1900 postcard view shows three of Pepperell's early churches.

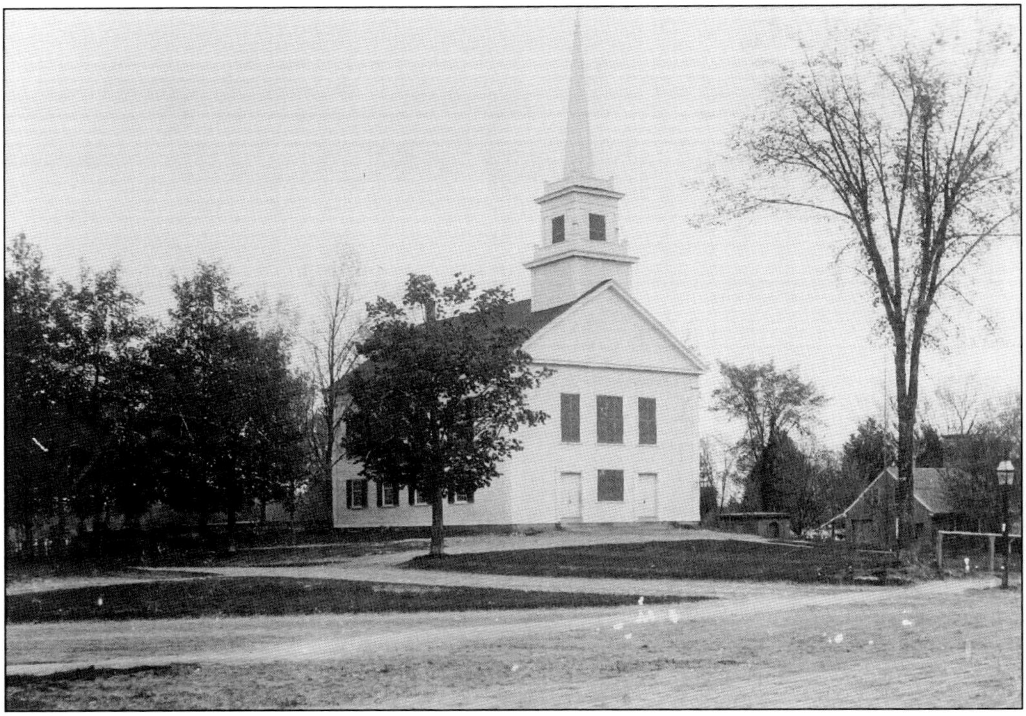

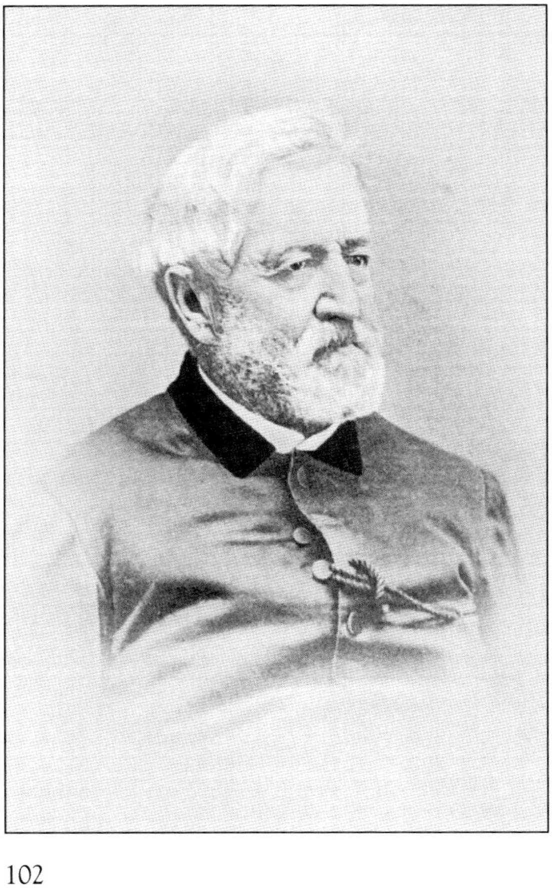

After much dissension between the townspeople, Pepperell's first church was built just behind the common at the corner of Main and Park Streets. It was dedicated in 1745 as the First Church of Christ, later called the First Parish Unitarian Church. In 1769 a new and better church was erected at the same location fronting on Park Street. That building was later turned around to face Main Street, where it remained until destroyed by fire in 1917.

After a split in the congregation effected the beginning of the Evangelical Congregational Society, Reverend Charles Babbidge became minister of the Unitarian Church, remaining there for fifty-three years. He was known as a "hard-hitting preacher with a flair for the dramatic" who seldom missed an opportunity to point out the iniquities of the rival church. However, he was well respected by the townspeople, held an honorary degree from Harvard, and was the first chaplain to enlist in the Civil War.

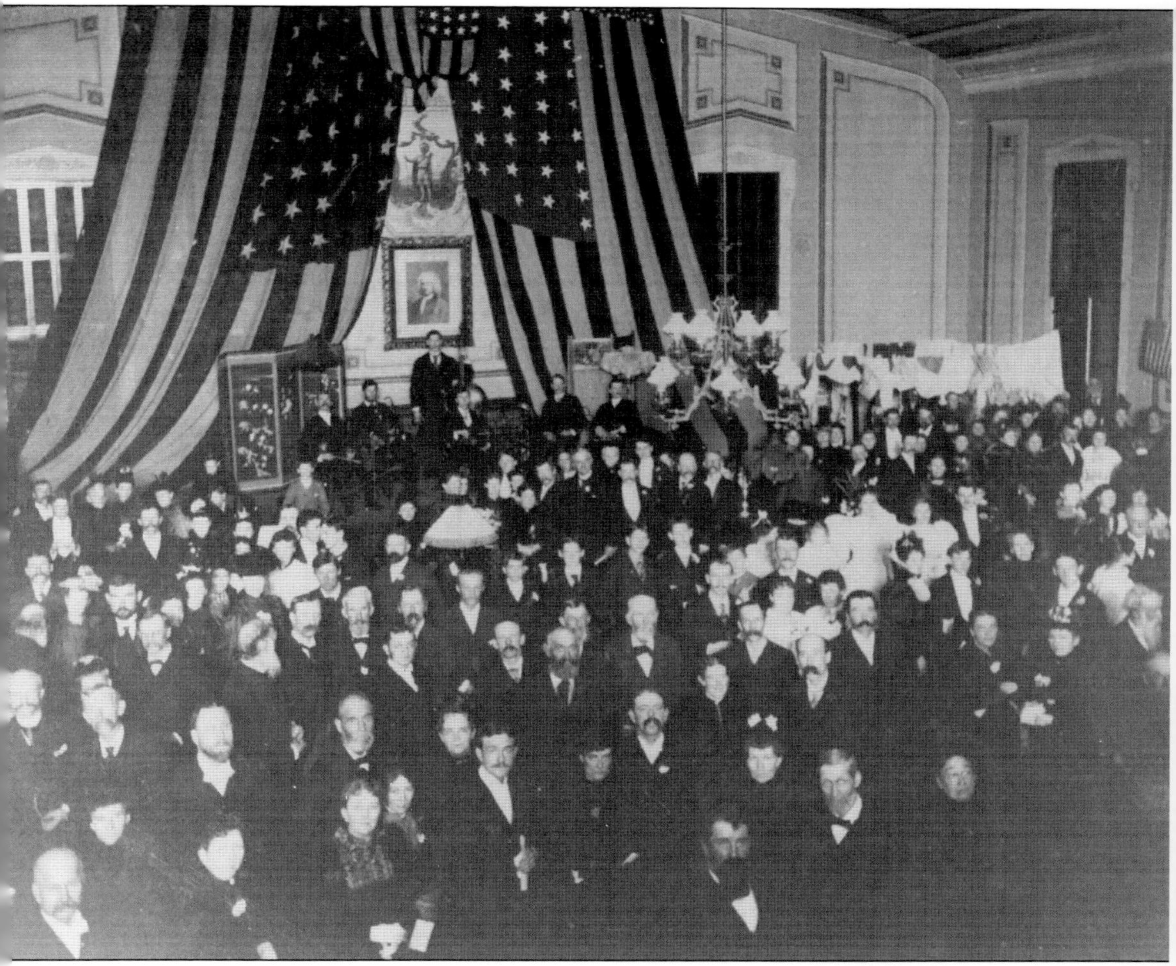

The hall of the Unitarian church is draped for a patriotic holiday as people gather for a *c.* 1889 celebration and dance.

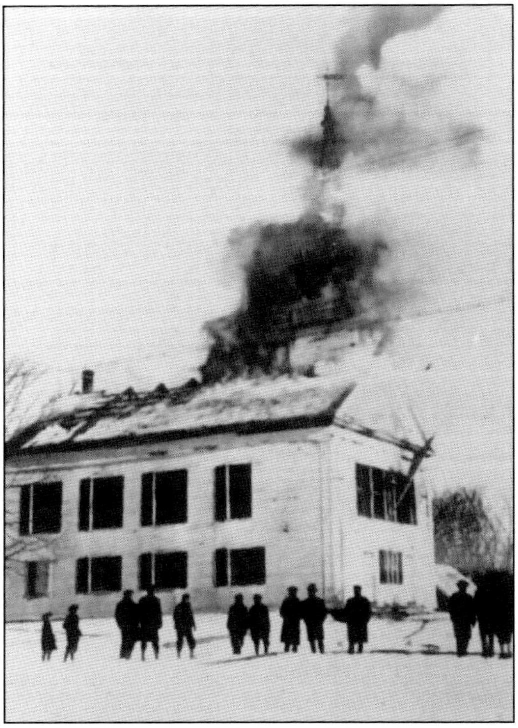

Fire destroyed the First Parish Unitarian Church on the morning of December 30, 1917. In this picture firemen are working at getting the blaze, which began at 12:15 am, under control. Because of the smoke it is difficult to tell if the steeple is still in place. It was only after this fire that the Congregational and Unitarian churches were able to put an end to their difficulties and merge into one congregation.

The fire report states the cause of the fire as a defective flue and also shows that an inadequate amount of insurance was carried on the building and its contents, as was often the case.

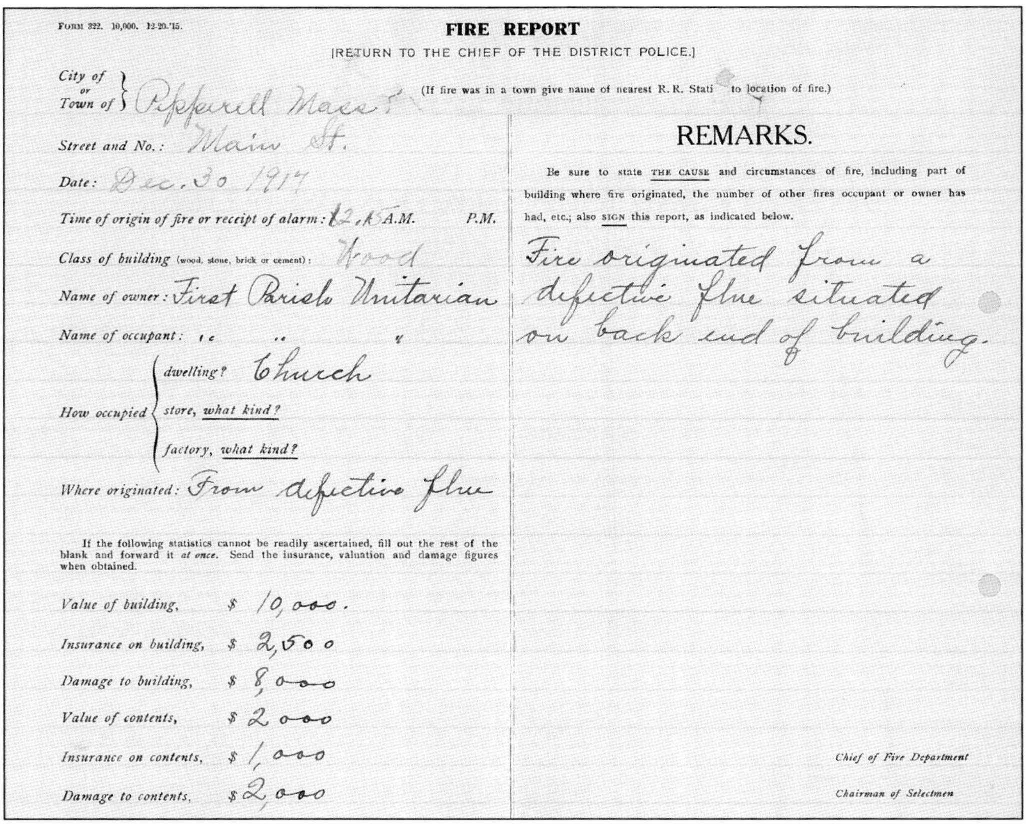

FORM 322. 10,000. 12-20-'15.

FIRE REPORT

[RETURN TO THE CHIEF OF THE DISTRICT POLICE.]

City of or Town of: Pepperell Mass.

(If fire was in a town give name of nearest R. R. Stati to location of fire.)

Street and No.: Main St.

Date: Dec. 30 1917

Time of origin of fire or receipt of alarm: 12.15 A.M. P.M.

Class of building (wood, stone, brick or cement): Wood

Name of owner: First Parish Unitarian

Name of occupant: " " "

How occupied
- dwelling? Church
- store, what kind?
- factory, what kind?

Where originated: From defective flue

If the following statistics cannot be readily ascertained, fill out the rest of the blank and forward it *at once*. Send the insurance, valuation and damage figures when obtained.

Value of building, $ 10,000.

Insurance on building, $ 2,500

Damage to building, $ 8,000

Value of contents, $ 2,000

Insurance on contents, $ 1,000

Damage to contents, $ 2,000

REMARKS.

Be sure to state THE CAUSE and circumstances of fire, including part of building where fire originated, the number of other fires occupant or owner has had, etc.; also SIGN this report, as indicated below.

Fire originated from a defective flue situated on back end of building.

Chief of Fire Department

Chairman of Selectmen

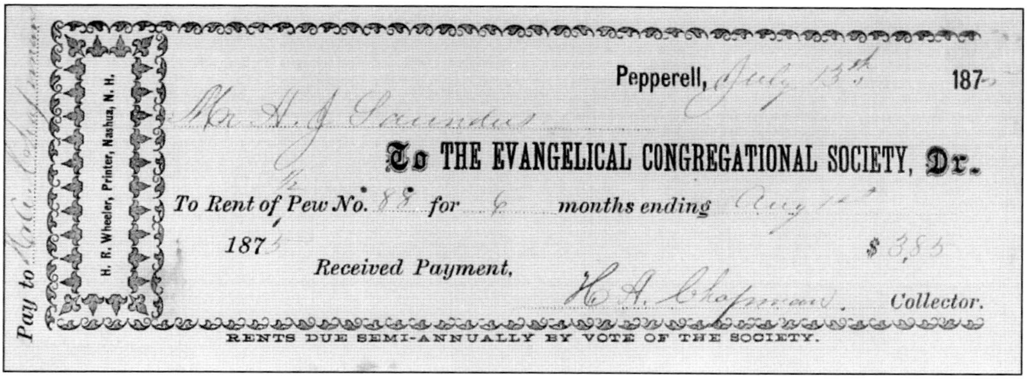

H. R. Wheeler, Printer, Nashua, N. H.

Pepperell, July 13th 1875

Mr. H. J. Saunders

To THE EVANGELICAL CONGREGATIONAL SOCIETY, Dr.

To Rent of ½ Pew No. 88 for 6 months ending Aug 1st 1875

$ 3.85

Received Payment, H. A. Chapman, Collector.

Pay to

RENTS DUE SEMI-ANNUALLY BY VOTE OF THE SOCIETY.

This is a receipt for payment of $3.85 for six months' rent on Pew No. 88 at the Evangelical Congregational Society, later the Community Church.

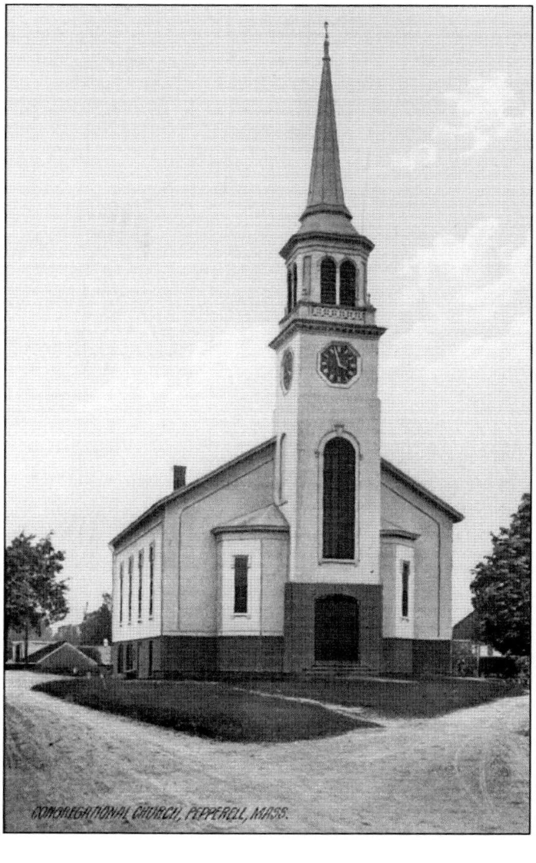

The Evangelical Congregational Society built their first church in 1832 across the street from the Unitarian church, where Squire Lemuel Parker's Tavern once stood. This burned in 1859 and another was built on the same site in 1859–60, which is the present Community Church. Shown is a postcard picture of the Congregational/Community Church as it appeared when the bottom section was painted to look like stone.

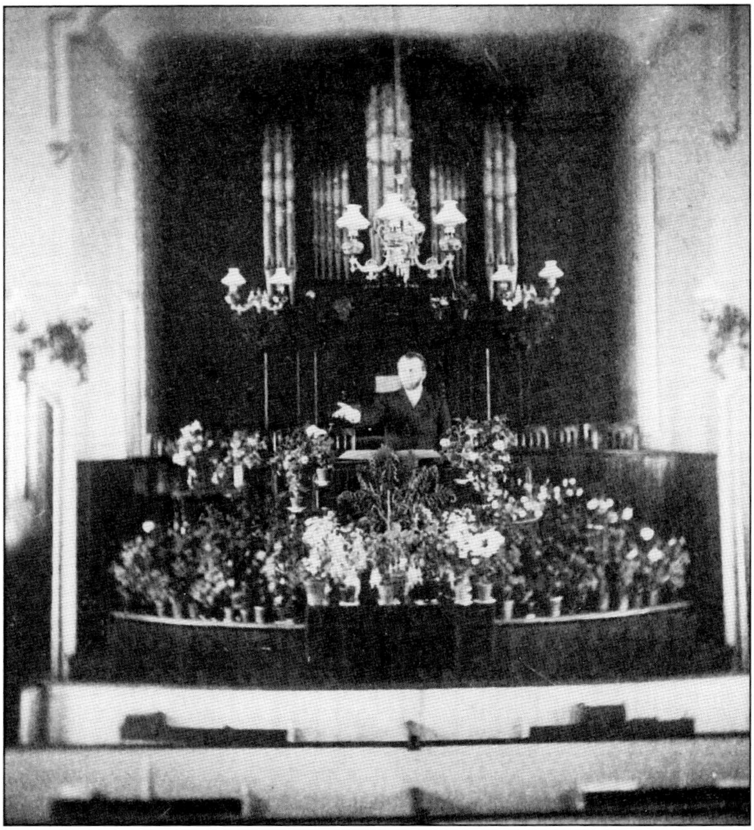

An early stereoscopic photograph of the interior of the Congregational church shows many flowers on the altar, perhaps for Easter. Unfortunately, the name of the minister is unknown.

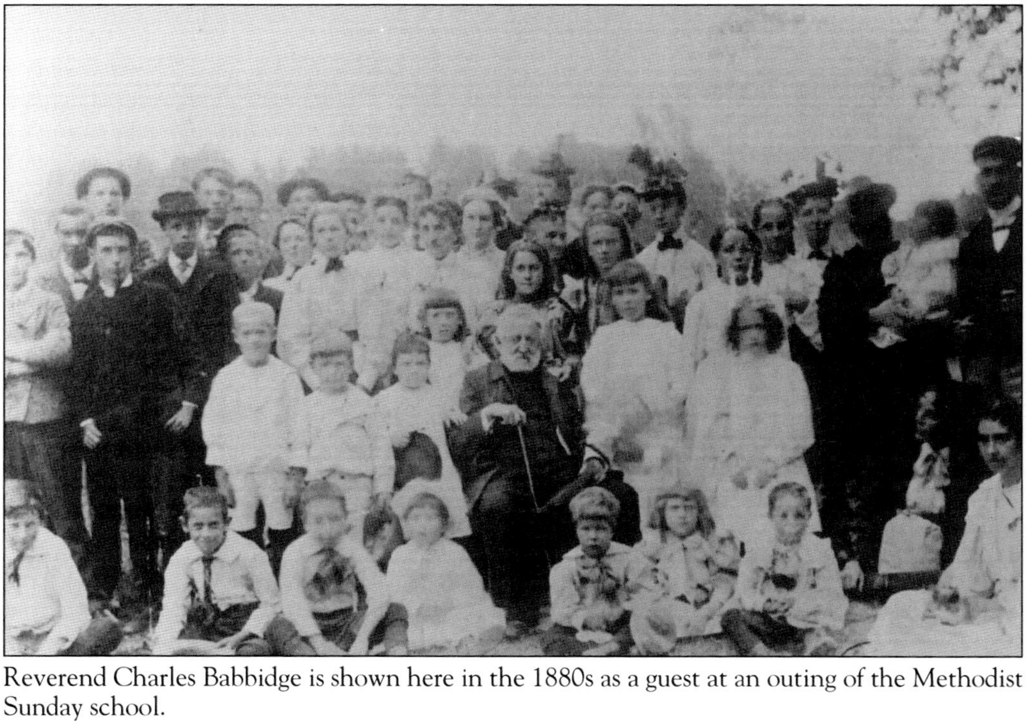

Reverend Charles Babbidge is shown here in the 1880s as a guest at an outing of the Methodist Sunday school.

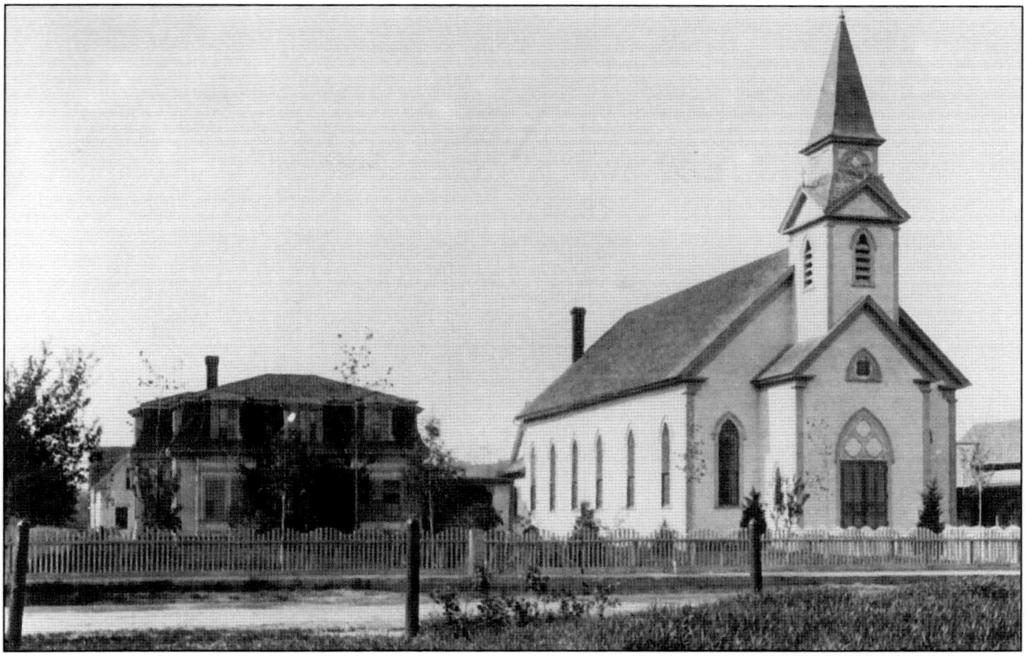

Saint Joseph's was first started in 1870 as a Catholic mission of Saint Mary's Church in Ayer. Prior to that, Catholic families traveled to Nashua or Ayer or North Chelmsford to attend church, some riding in their own wagons and others hiring a carriage from the livery stable. In 1881 the small chapel on Tarbell Street was enlarged and made into a new and attractive church. The parish census in 1895 showed one Italian, 175 French, 200 Canadian, and 309 Irish families.

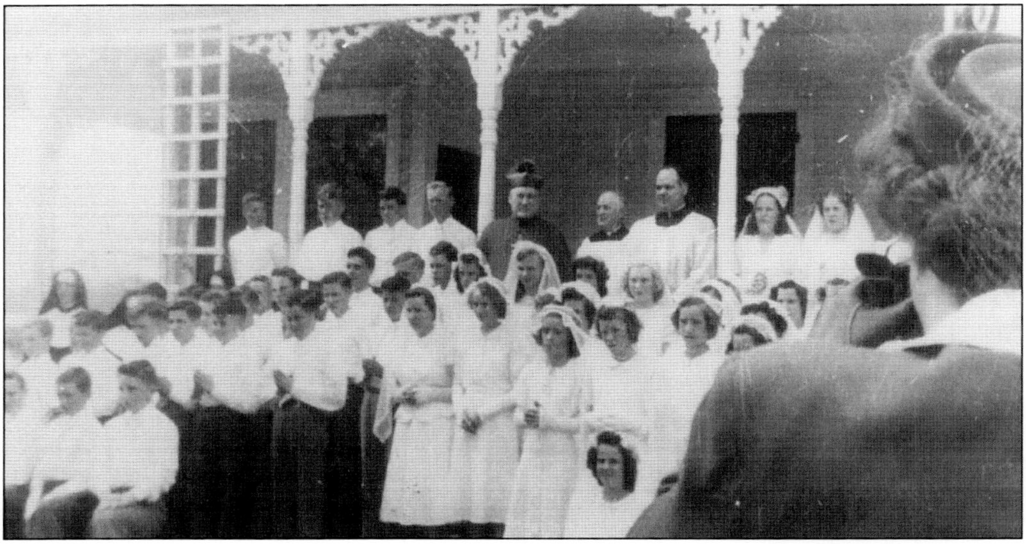

Standing on the steps of the parish rectory, the Confirmation class of 1947 has a special guest in their midst. Cardinal Cushing can be seen in the middle of the back row. Included in the group of teenagers making their Confirmation are: Maureen Leary, Joan Flagg, Maryjane Markham, Frances Markham, Marybeth Foley, Nancy Chase, Betty Herbert, Jean Herbert, Charlene Mayou, Wanda Tierney, Judy Tierney, Larry Foley, "Rabbit" Pillsbury, Roger Dorion, and Arthur Glow.

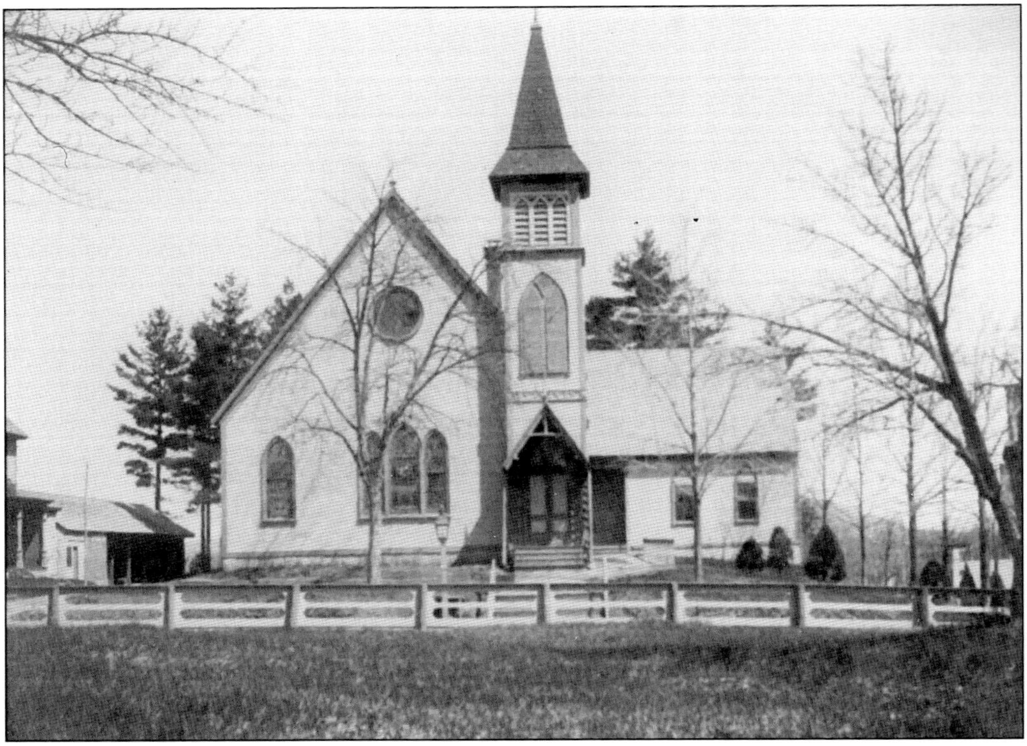

The first Methodist church was organized in Pepperell in May of 1866 at a prayer meeting under the leadership of a Methodist layman from Boston. The church met in different locations around town until December of 1873, when the Gothic Revival-style church was finished. This building was renovated and enlarged over the next few decades.

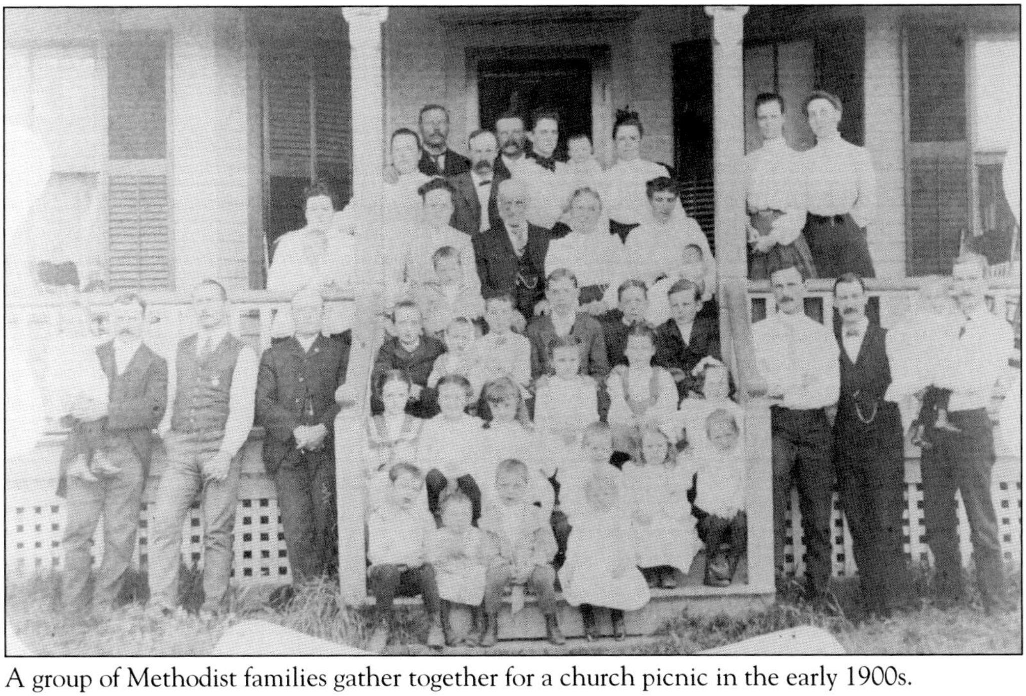

A group of Methodist families gather together for a church picnic in the early 1900s.

Eight

Hometown Folk

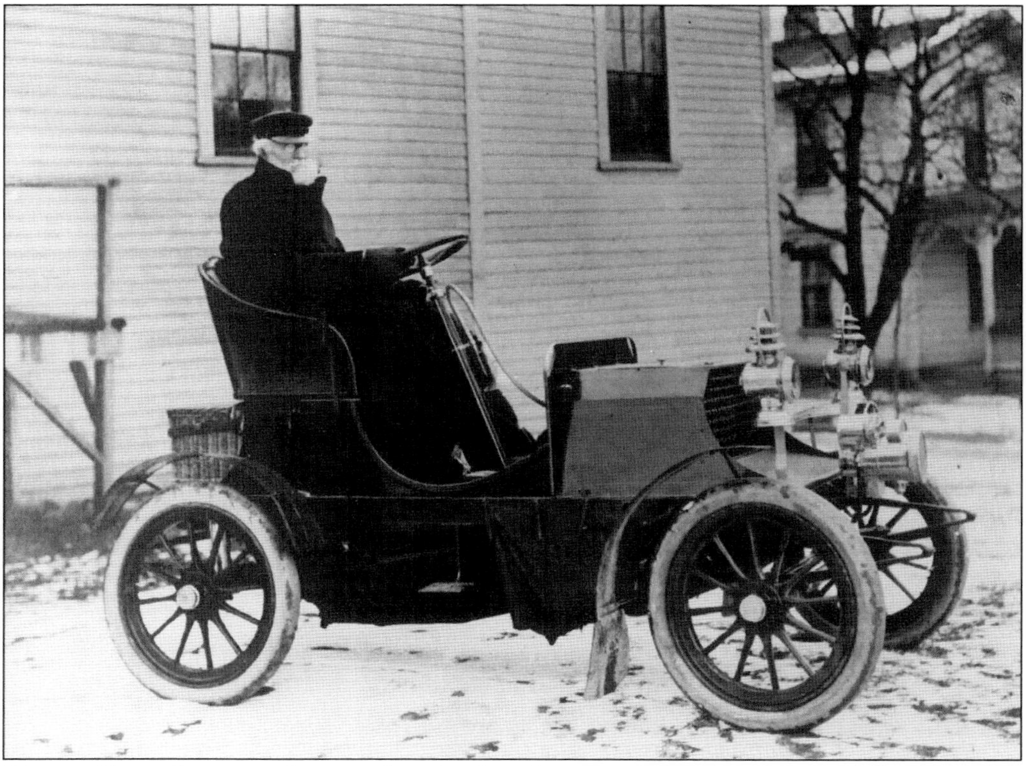

Chester Shattuck is out to have a ride in his brand new car, but stops to show it off and have his picture taken. Reportedly his was the very first car in town.

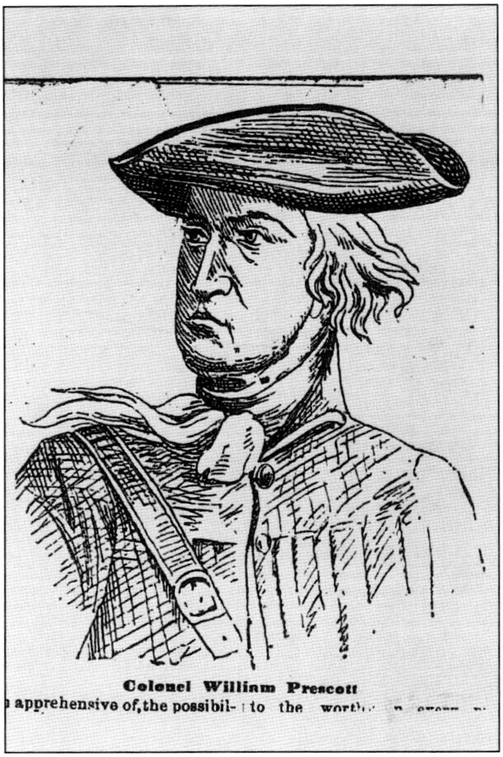

Pepperell's Revolutionary War hero, Colonel William Prescott, is remembered by many as the leader of a regiment of local minutemen who marched to Cambridge on April 19, 1775. Many also recall the colonel's famous command, given during the Battle of Bunker Hill, of "Don't shoot until you see the white of their eyes." This copy of an etching of Colonel William Prescott depicts the quiet resoluteness with which he faced the advancing British forces at Bunker Hill.

Several years after arriving in Pepperell, Edward Franc Jones attained captaincy of the Prescott Guards and later was made colonel of the 6th Massachusetts Volunteer Militia in the Civil War. In April 1861, Colonel Jones and the 6th MVM were greeted in Washington by President Lincoln, who expressed thankfulness that they had arrived in time to save the Capital from rebel invasion. The colonel later organized and fought with the 26th Massachusetts Volunteer Regiment at the Battle of New Orleans.

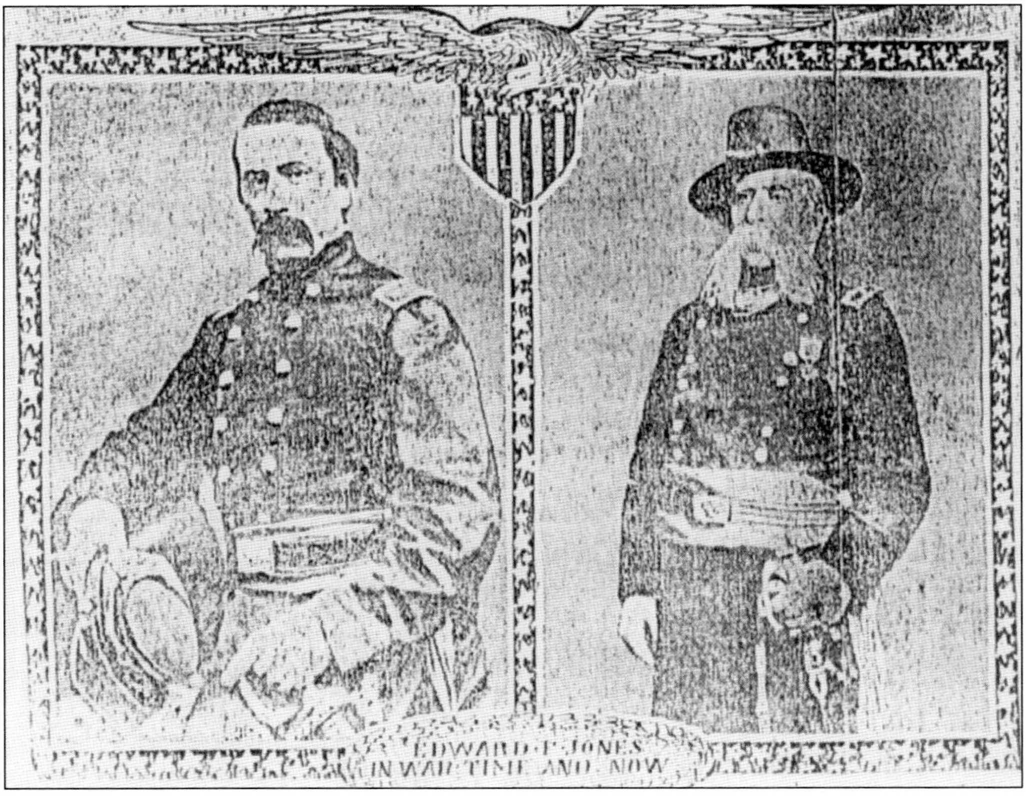

William Hickley Prescott, grandson of Colonel William Prescott, was a well-known author and historian. He had homes in Lynn and Nahant, Massachusetts, but spent many of his summers at the family home in Pepperell working on his writing. Mr. Prescott had been blinded in one eye as a youth but made adjustments to continue with his work. This photograph is from a copy of an early tintype taken in the 1840s.

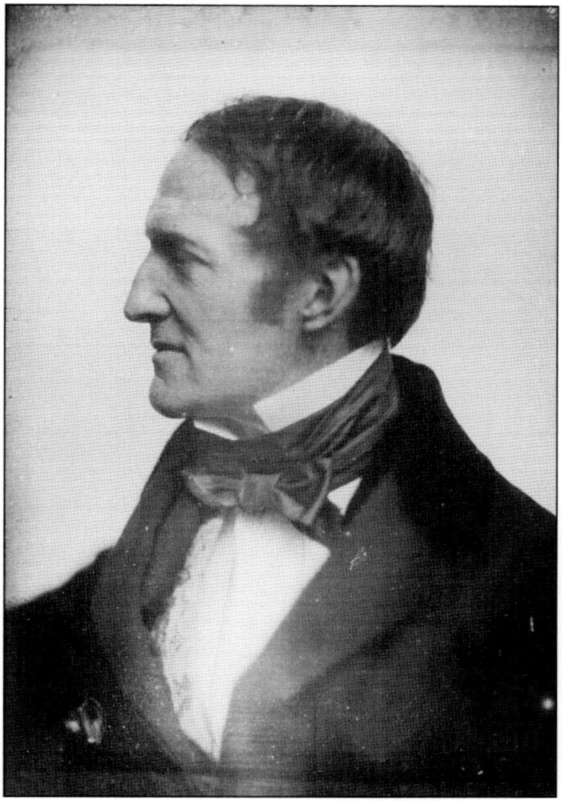

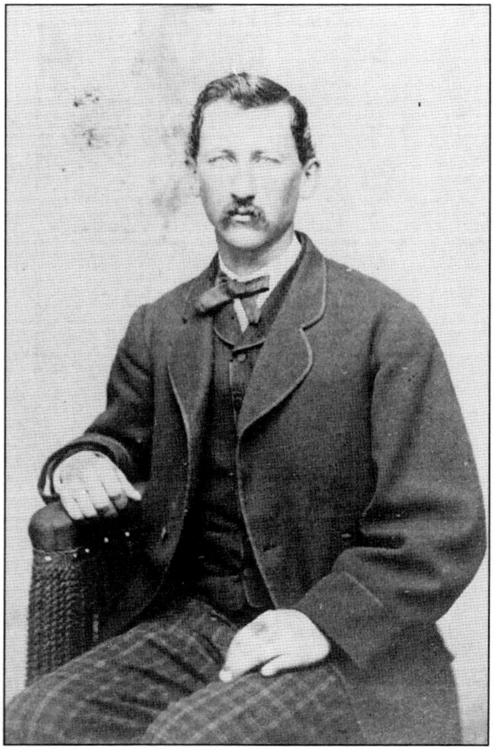

Christopher Capelle was one of the patriotic men from Pepperell who fought in the Civil War, serving with Colonel Edward F. Jones in the 26th Massachusetts Volunteer Militia. He later transferred to the 5th Light Artillery, and the next year transferred to the Navy, where he remained until the end of the war. Returning from the war, he worked at the Fairchild Paper Company, and was associated with the fire department and the police force.

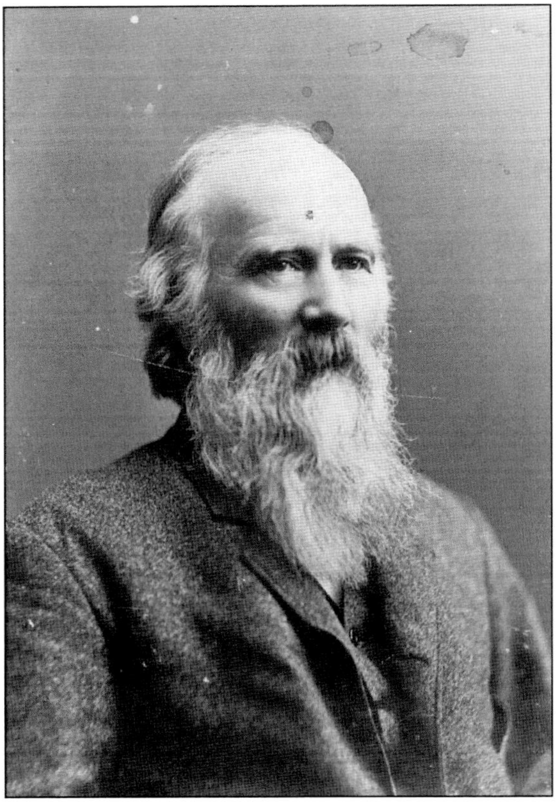

Samuel W. Fletcher was one of Pepperell's most respected and beloved doctors. He graduated from Harvard in 1858 and carried on a practice in Pepperell until entering the army in 1863. As a surgeon with the 32nd Massachusetts Regiment, Dr. Fletcher was present at the bloody battles of the Wilderness, Cold Harbor, Mine Run, and Appomattox. He returned to his practice in Pepperell, remaining active in a number of medical societies, and contributing a number of useful inventions to science.

A "wonderful" clambake was enjoyed by all at the Riverside Trotting Park in 1910. Those enjoying the day were: (front row) William Sliney, Kirk Gilman, Al Tabor, John Fredericks, Mr. Aldrich, Frank Ward, Elmer Weston, and the dog; (back row) Frank Goff, Silas Nokes, Jerry Annis, Bert Morrill, George Herrig, Amos Boulia, Lincoln Johson, and William Kemp.

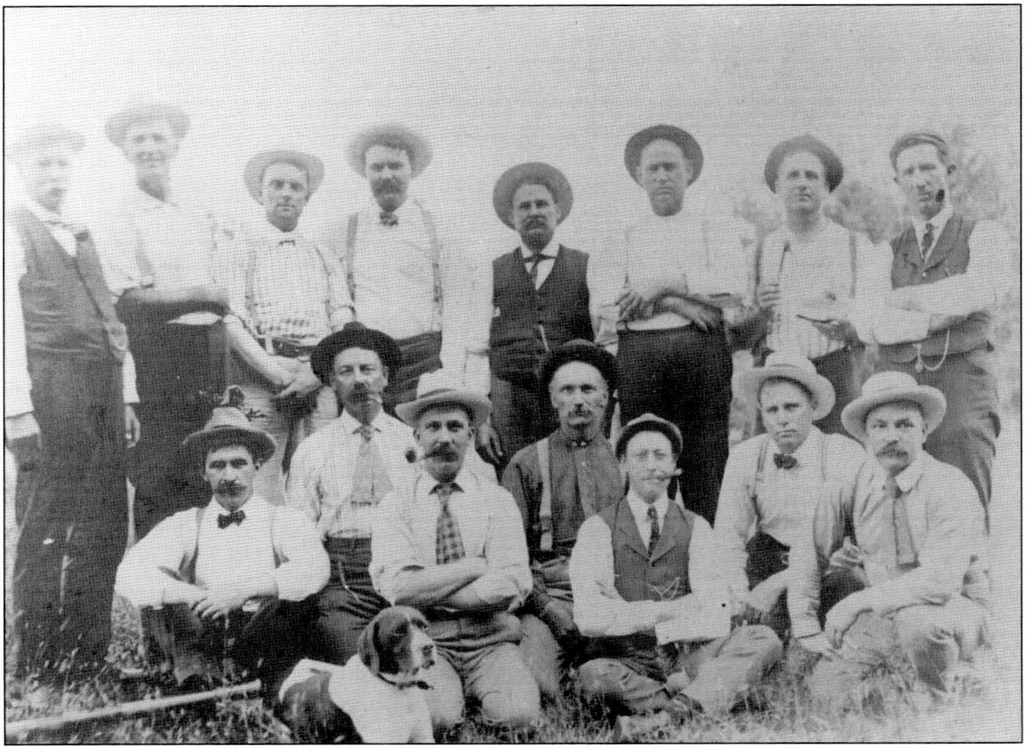

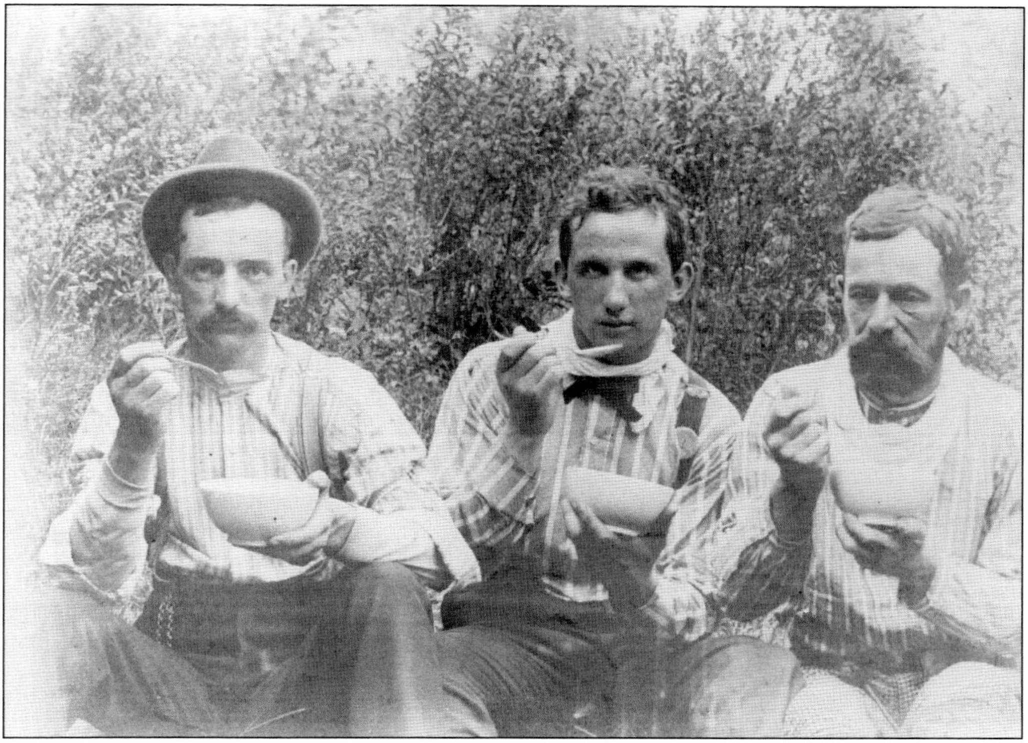

These three men are caught in the middle of their meal, perhaps eating clam chowder at the same clambake at Riverside Park. Unfortunately, their names are not available; we can only speculate that the man on the right is George Rice's father.

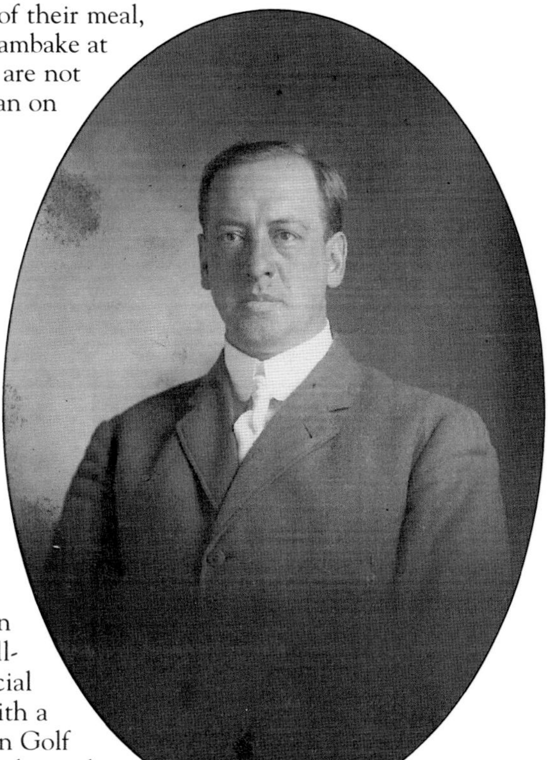

Dr. Charles G. Heald followed his father in the practice of medicine and became a well-known figure, taking part in many town social activities. He was also an avid golfer and with a partner won the 1934 New Hampshire Open Golf Tournament held in Nashua. His office was located in the East Pepperell business district.

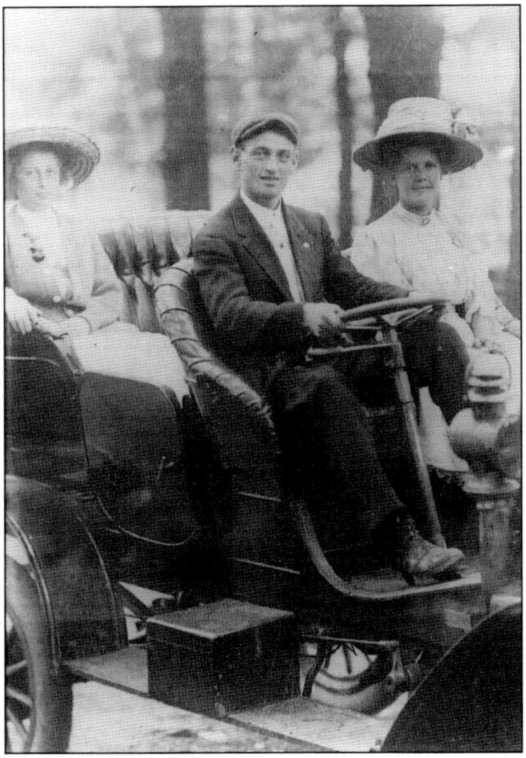

All dressed up and riding in style on a trip to Whalom Park on July 4, 1921, are Chester Shattuck, Emma Stone, and Bernice Holmes (sitting in the back seat).

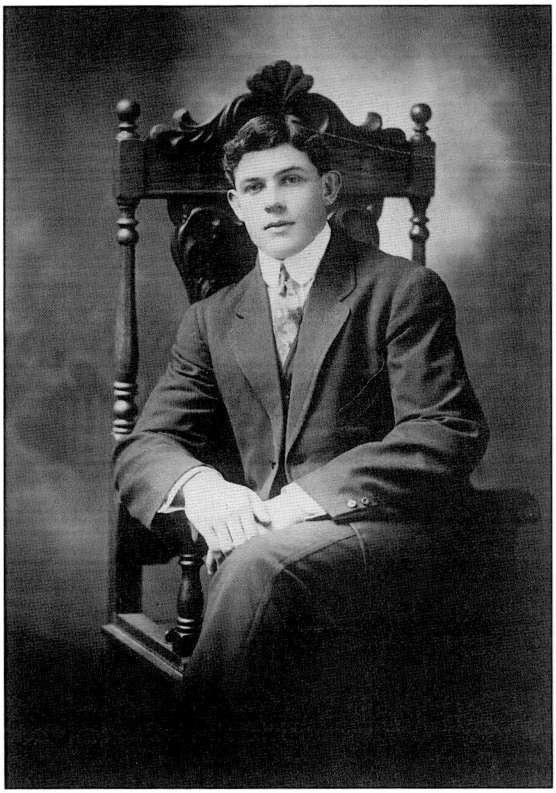

This handsome well-dressed young man is Leo Russell, father of Bob Russell. He lived on Pleasant Street and was a member of the Odd Fellows. This photograph was taken around 1920.

Lena Lillis and Cecile Tarbell keep warm in their beaver coats while viewing the fire damage in Railroad Square. The location is the corner of Main and Groton Streets and the damaged building behind them was then the Dupaw Pharmacy. Currently this is the site of the Pepperell Spa, a popular eatery run by the Bozicas family since 1941.

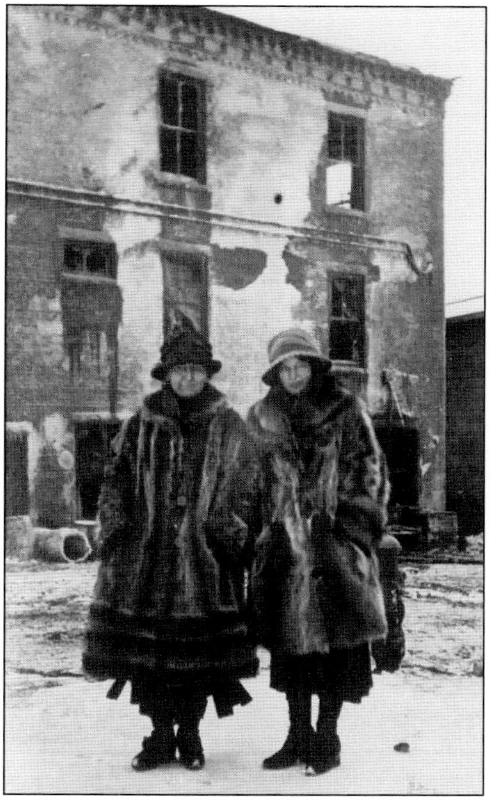

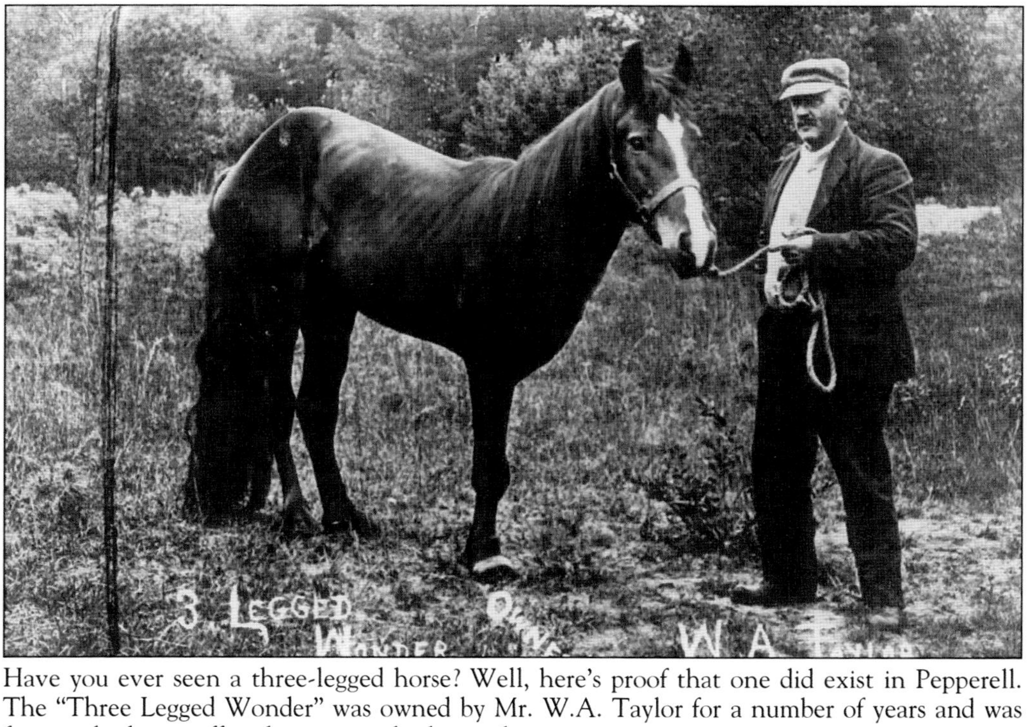

Have you ever seen a three-legged horse? Well, here's proof that one did exist in Pepperell. The "Three Legged Wonder" was owned by Mr. W.A. Taylor for a number of years and was frequently shown off at the races and other gatherings.

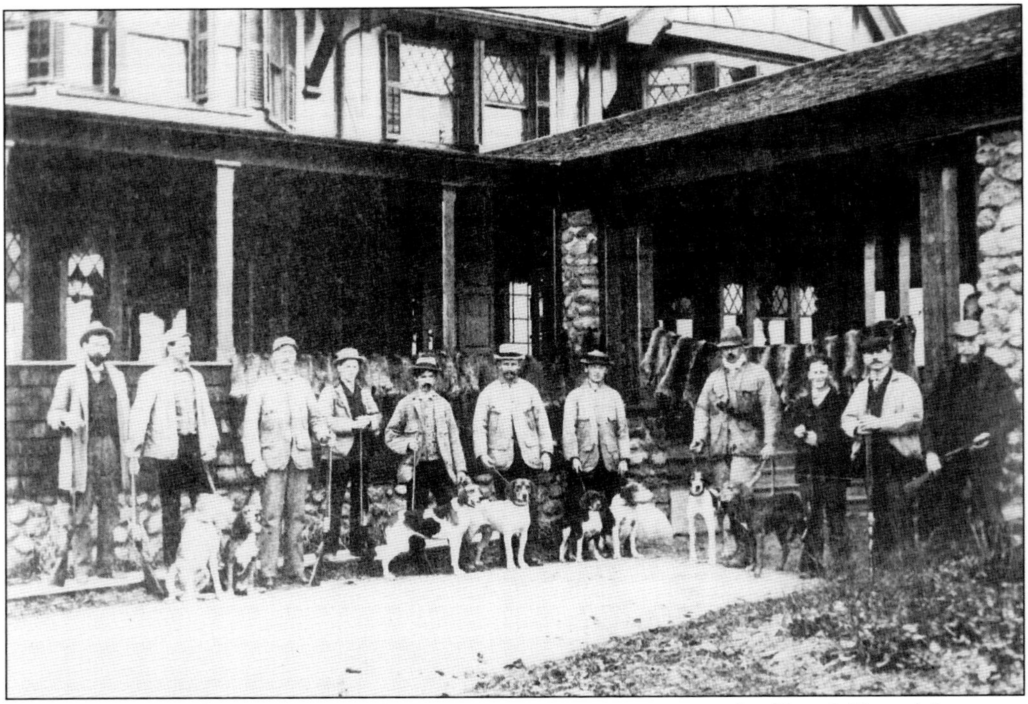

The New England Fox Hunters' Association met once a year at the Broad View Manor on Mount Lebanon Street until it fell victim to fire around 1930. Membership was made up mostly of professional people, doctors, and lawyers. Frank Tierney and Harry Hutchinson were two who belonged to the association.

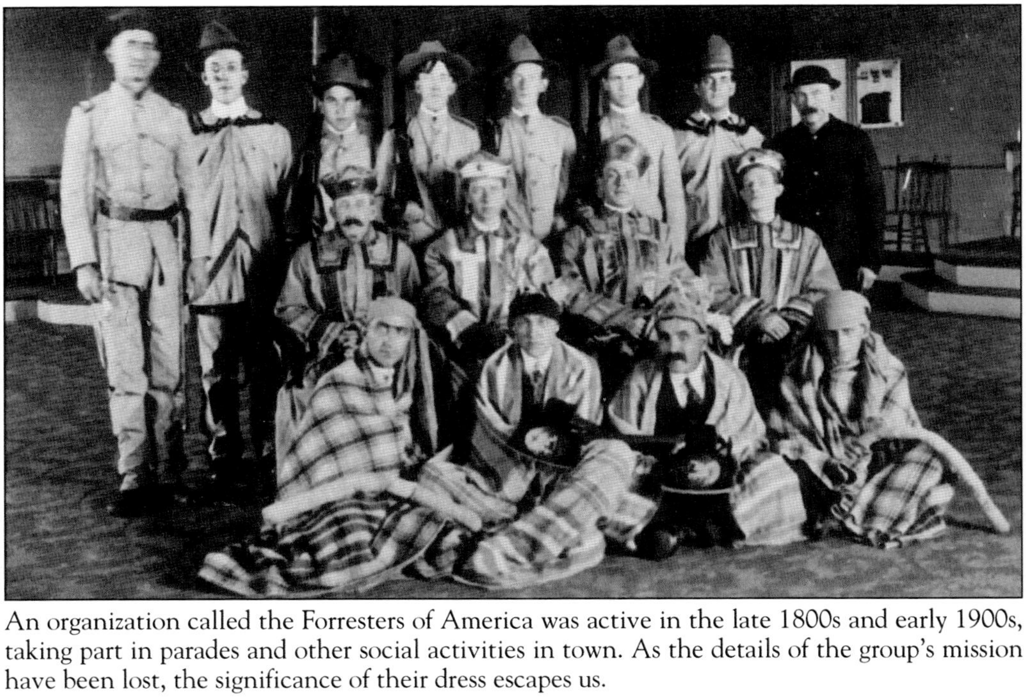

An organization called the Forresters of America was active in the late 1800s and early 1900s, taking part in parades and other social activities in town. As the details of the group's mission have been lost, the significance of their dress escapes us.

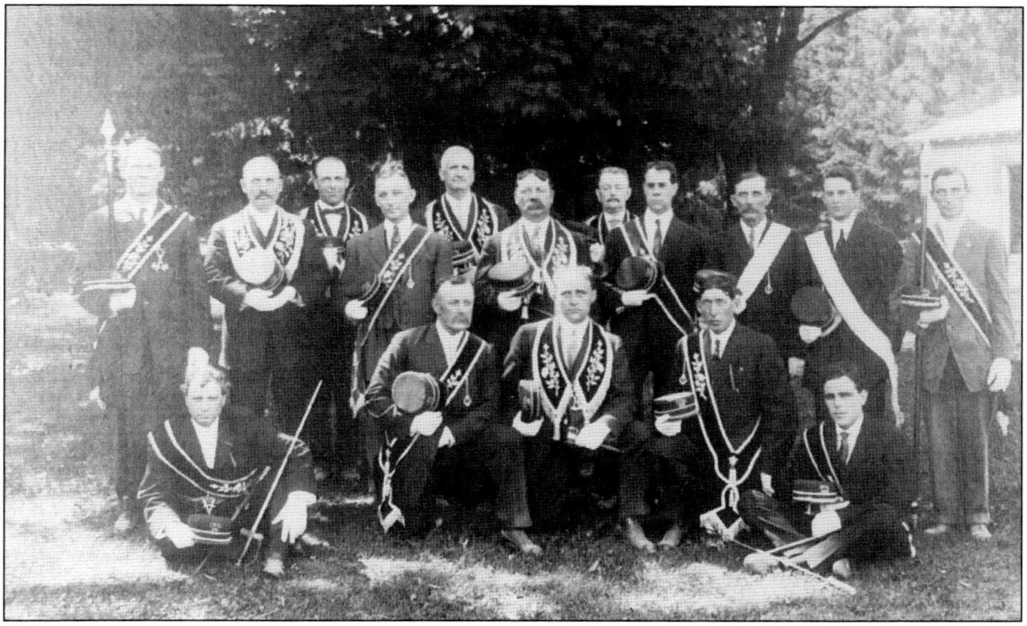

A group of the Pepperell Odd Fellows, dressed in their finery, poses for a picture. From left to right are: (front row) Neil McWilliams, Frank Conant, Don Rivers, Wallace Willey, and William Withrow; (back row) W.E. Chapman, L.P. Shattuck, J.G. Willey, Silas Shaw, Lincoln Johnson, Kirk Gilman, Luther G. Robbins, John Fiske, Put Shattuck, unknown, and Chester Shattuck.

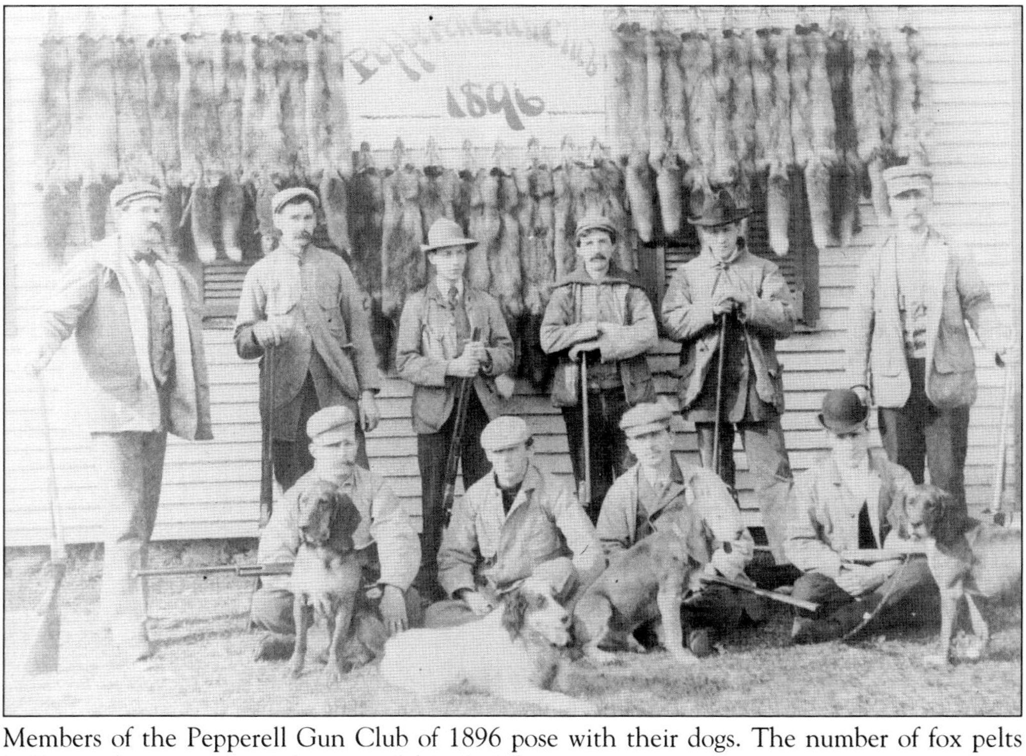

Members of the Pepperell Gun Club of 1896 pose with their dogs. The number of fox pelts indicates they were certainly successful in their hunt.

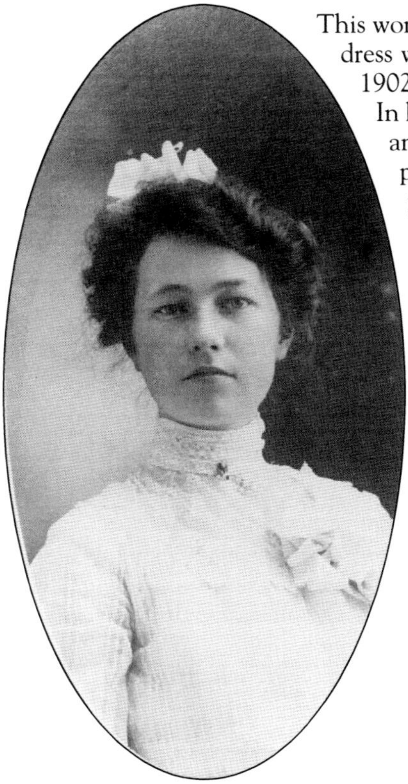

This wonderful old picture shows Helen Robbins in a fancy white dress with a bow in her hair. The photograph was taken about 1902 and was perhaps Helen's high school graduation picture. In later years Helen collected town memorabilia, kept books, and was cashier for some of the town businessmen. Her penmanship was a joy to behold, a fact which must have put her in great demand.

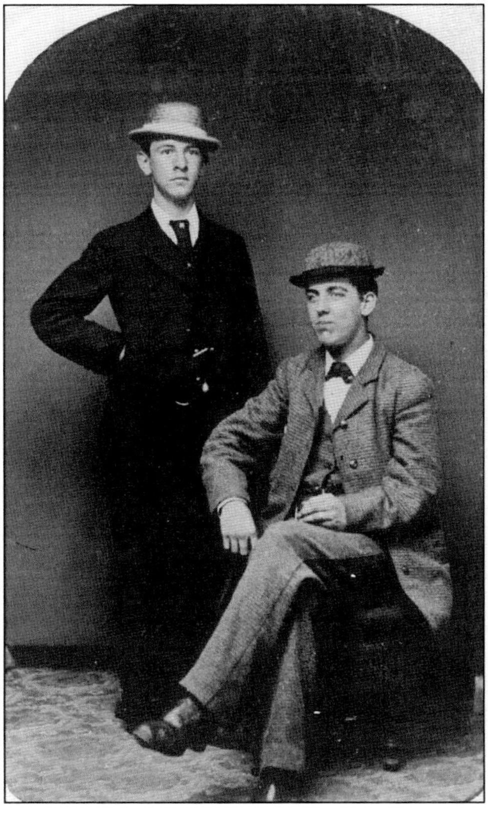

Two young dandies, Luther Tarbell and Joseph Saunders, got all dressed up in their three-piece suits to have a picture made. This photograph was copied from a tintype done in the mid-1880s.

Arthur Grenier was one of Pepperell's barbers; he was in business for some time in the late 1800s and early 1900s. He ran his barbershop at several different locations on Main Street and was the first to reopen his shop after the fire of 1903.

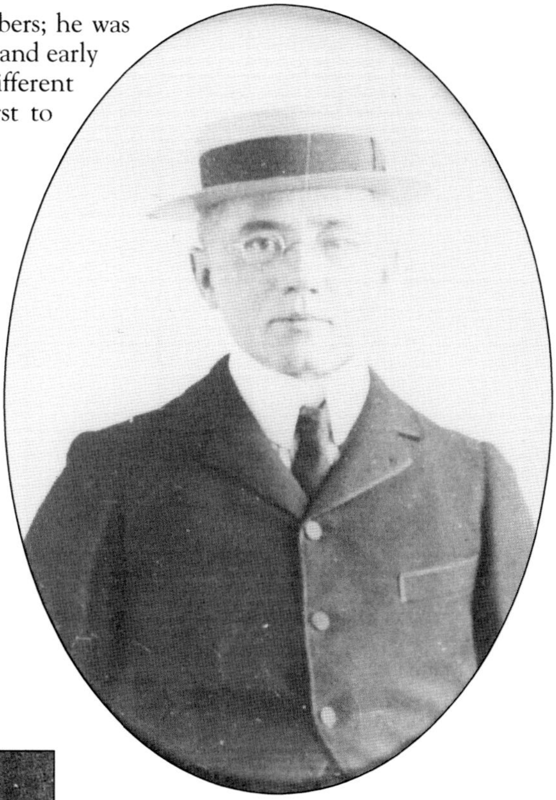

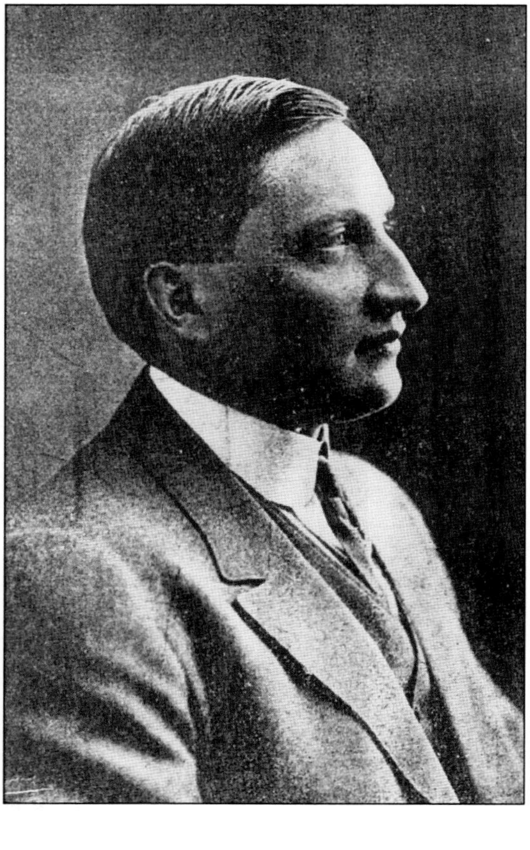

Rainsford Deware was known to the townspeople as a generous and active person. He was president of Pepperell Card and Paper and had an impressive home on Chase Hill just above the high school. In addition to his business duties, Mr. Deware found time to join the fire department and take part in many other social activities in town. He was host to employees and friends at an outing held every year at the Babbatassett Driving Park.

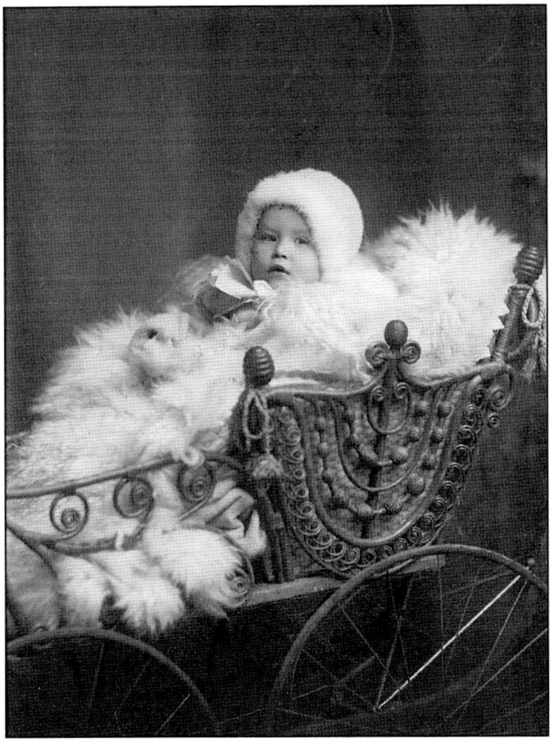

Babies and children were often photographed in fancy dress and settings years ago. Clarence Rivers is the baby surrounded by the white carriage robe and sitting in the elegant wicker carriage so typical at the turn of the century.

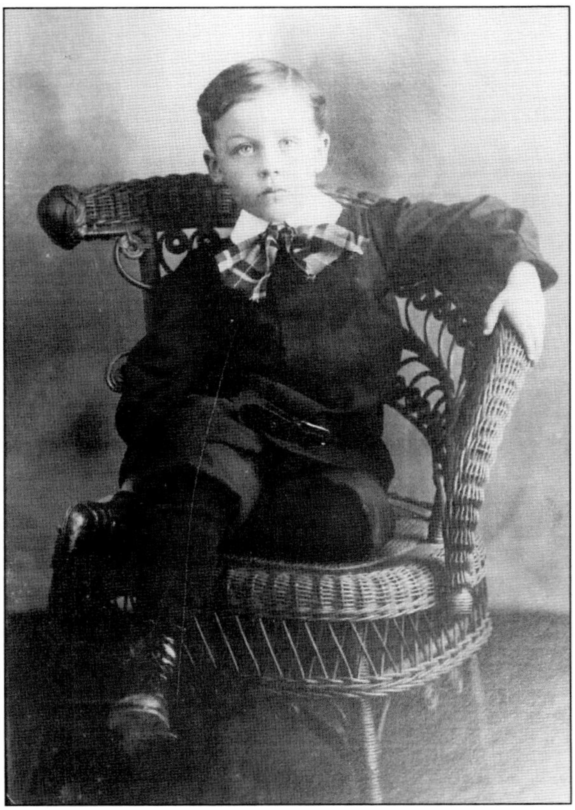

This 1907 photograph shows Amos J. Saunders, age six, looking quite bored and unhappy at having his picture taken.

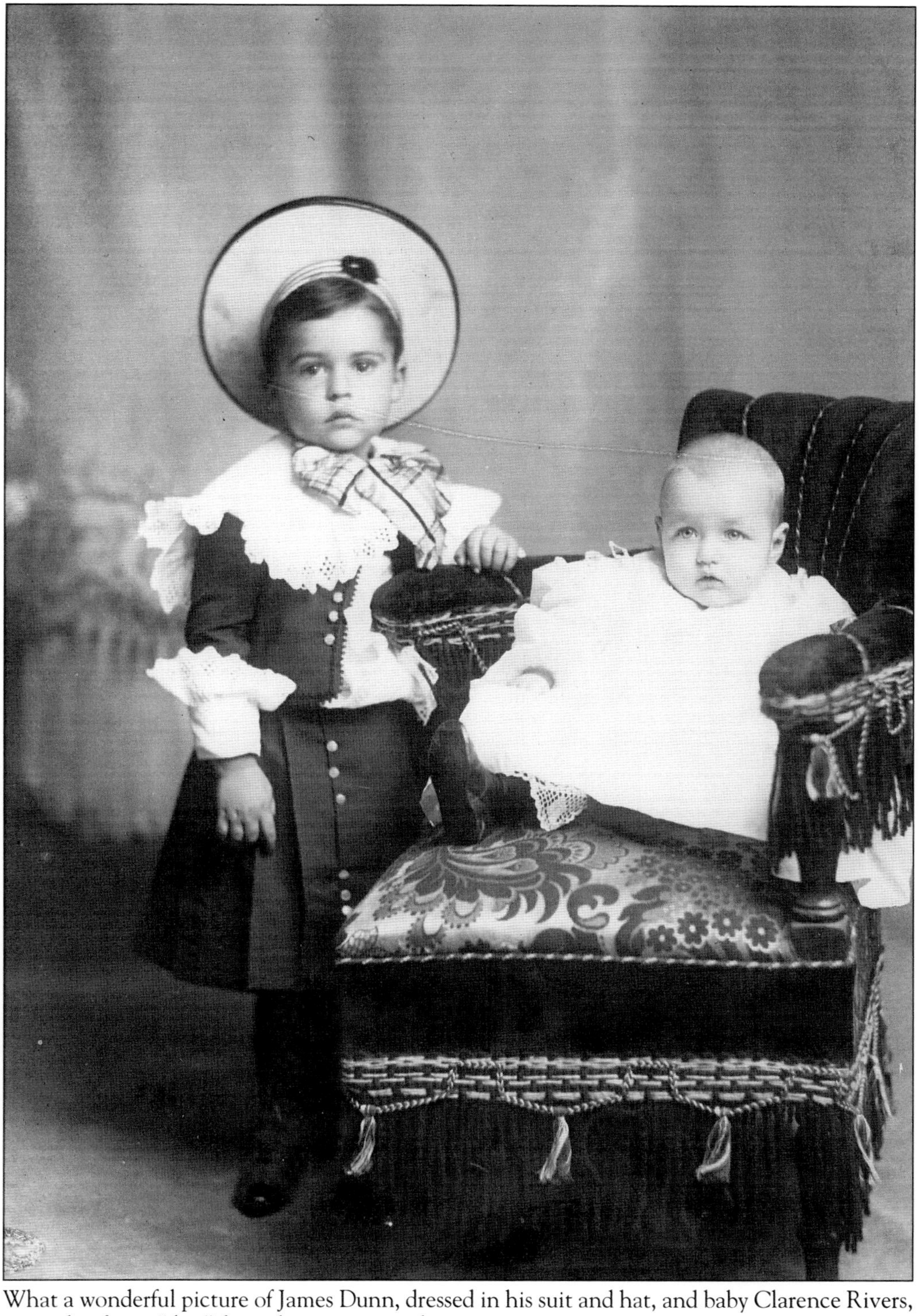

What a wonderful picture of James Dunn, dressed in his suit and hat, and baby Clarence Rivers, minus his fancy "digs" from the picture on the previous page.

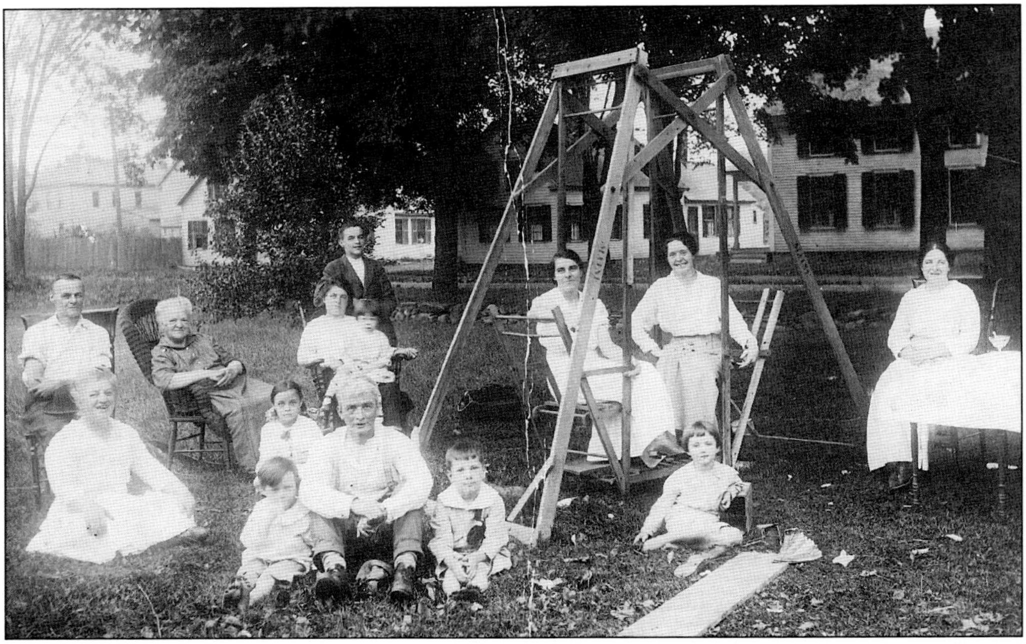

The Fitzpatrick family is shown here on the lawn of their homestead on Cottage Street. Seated on the ground are Elizabeth (Fitzpatrick) Markham and her husband, Michael Markham. The children surrounding him are: (front row) James Markham, Anna Drumm, Francis Markham, and Cletus Murphy (by the swing); (back row) Mike Drumm, Mary (Baker) Fitzpatrick, Mary "Mame" Drumm (with Marjorie and Francis), Alice and Theresa Fitzpatrick (on the swing), and Katherine F. Murphy (to the right).

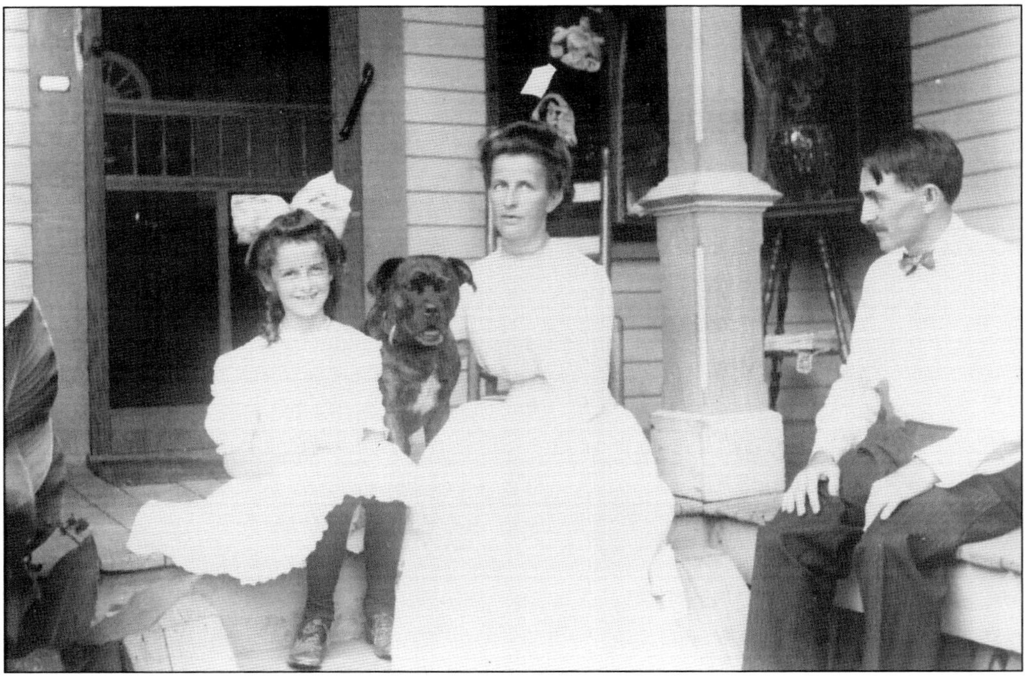

Sitting on the porch, the little girl with the big bow in her hair poses quite happily while her parents seem somewhat concerned about the family dog.

The Toomey children gathered around the photographer's pony *c.* 1925 to have their picture taken. From left to right are: Eileen, Dennis, Glenys, Norman, and Mary (Nellie).

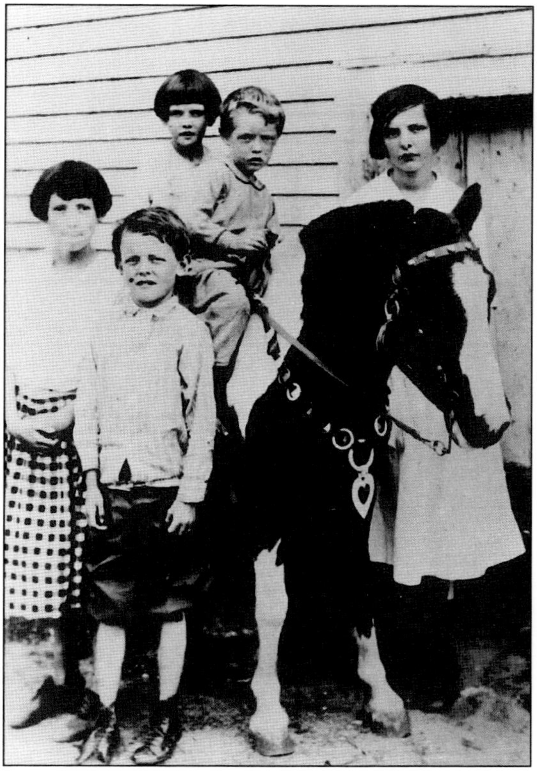

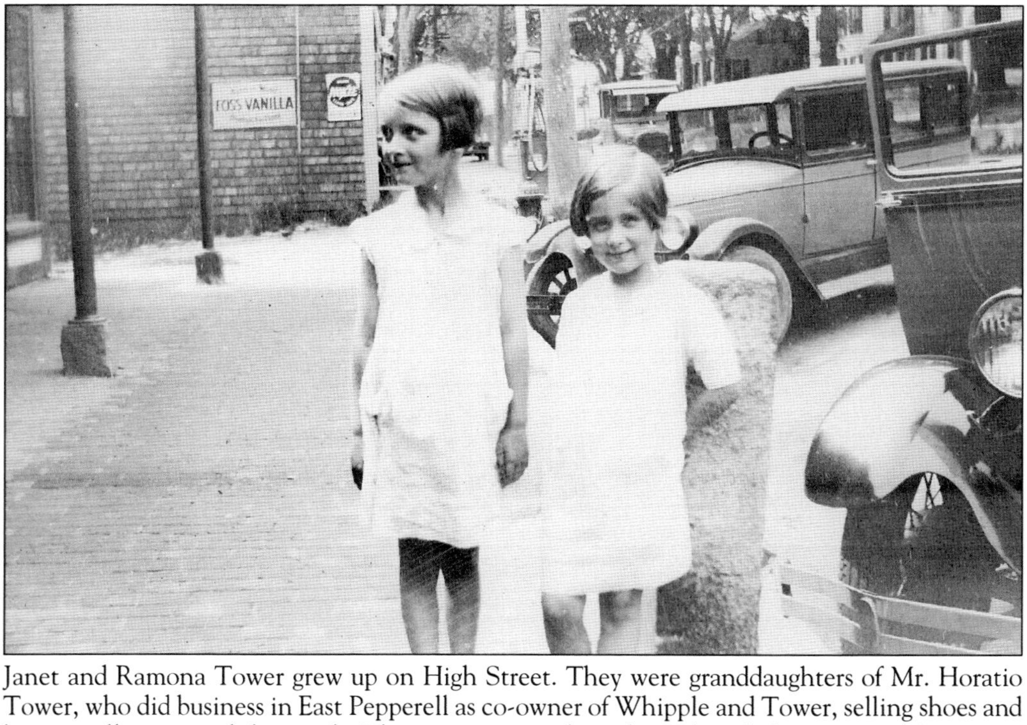

Janet and Ramona Tower grew up on High Street. They were granddaughters of Mr. Horatio Tower, who did business in East Pepperell as co-owner of Whipple and Tower, selling shoes and boots, wallpaper, and dry goods. This writer remembers the girls as babysitters and Janet as a Girl Scout leader.

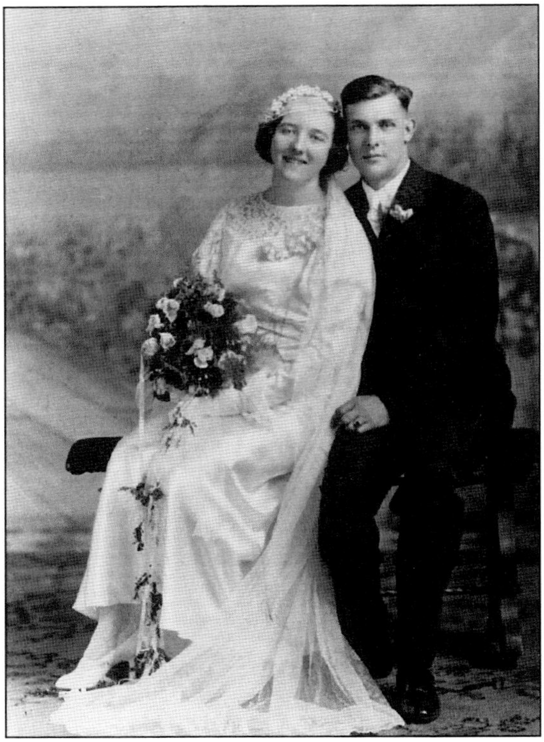

This is Mae and Donald Toomey's wedding picture, taken in the early 1930s.

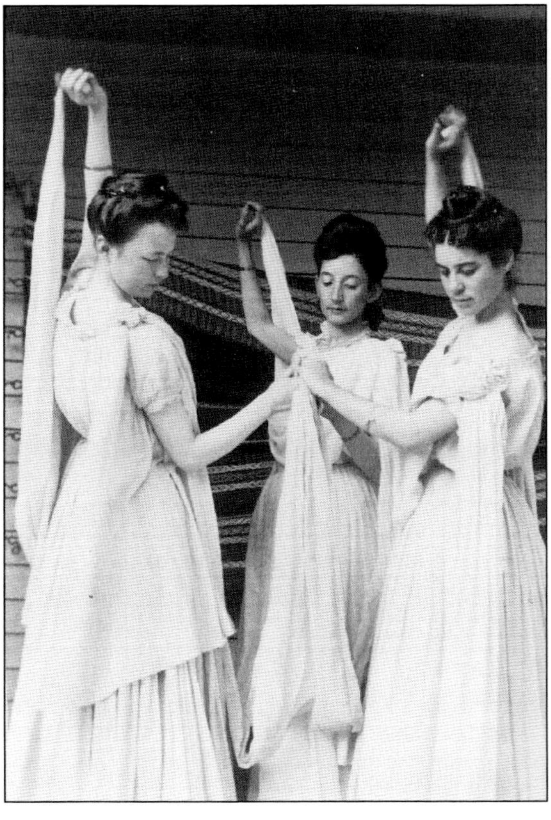

These young ladies with their flowing dresses and veils were part of an acting production that took place about 1900. The young lady in the center of the photograph is Lena Gagnon.

These flappers from the 1920s—Florence (Cotton) Crowley and Frances (Hamilton) Gagnon—pose on the roadside holding their cigarettes.

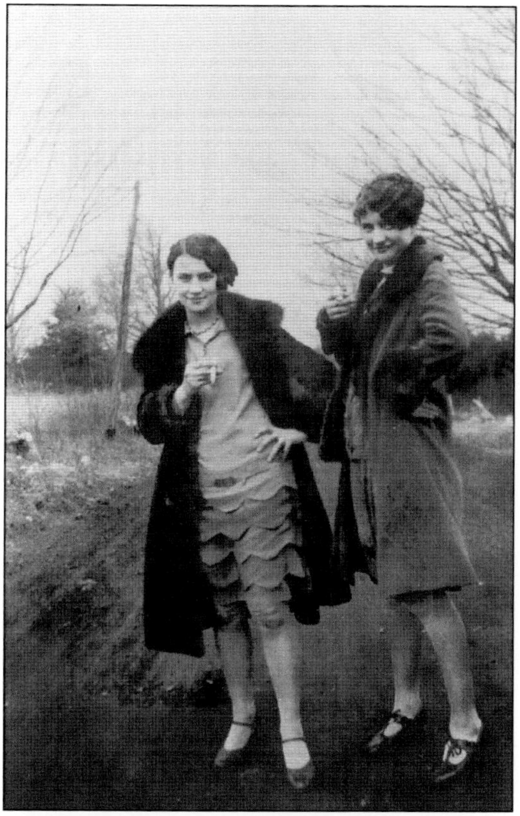

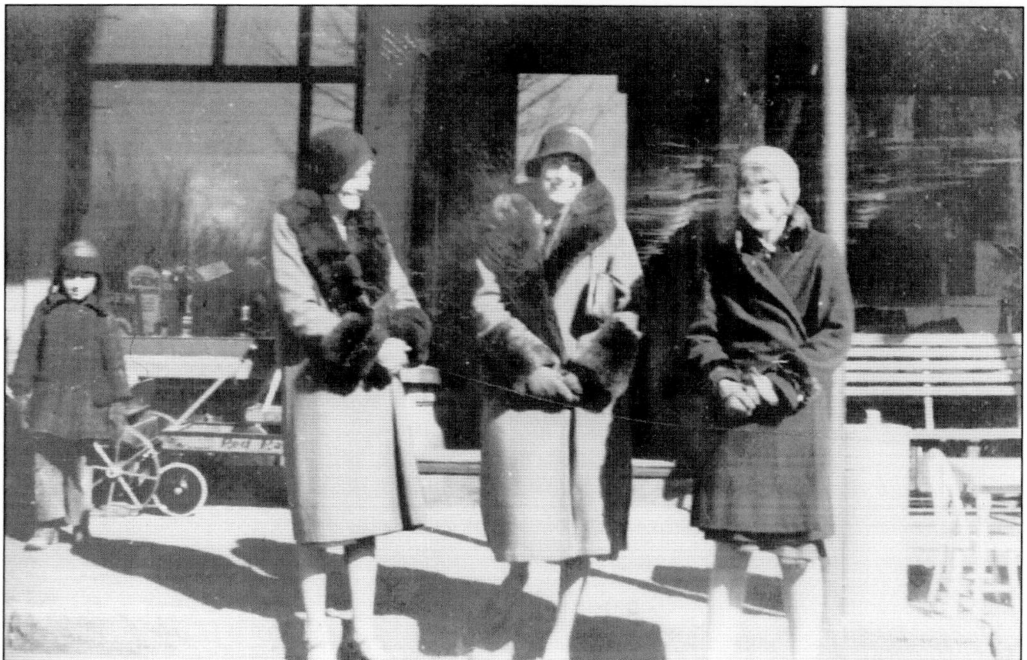

All smiles as they stop for a photograph in front of Saunders store are Laura Saunders, Lena Kimball, and June Kimball. The date is about 1930.

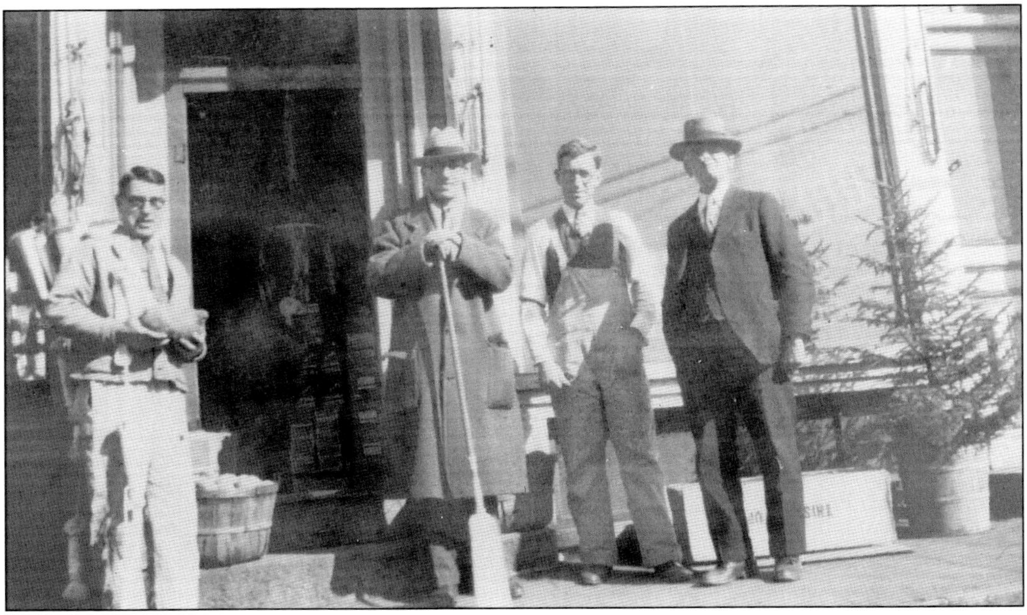

Standing outside the Attridge Brothers grocery store in the early 1930s are John Attridge, Amos Saunders, Jim Attridge, and Joseph Saunders. The Attridge Brothers store was located on Main Street at the corner of Mill Street, and across from the Odd Fellows Building.

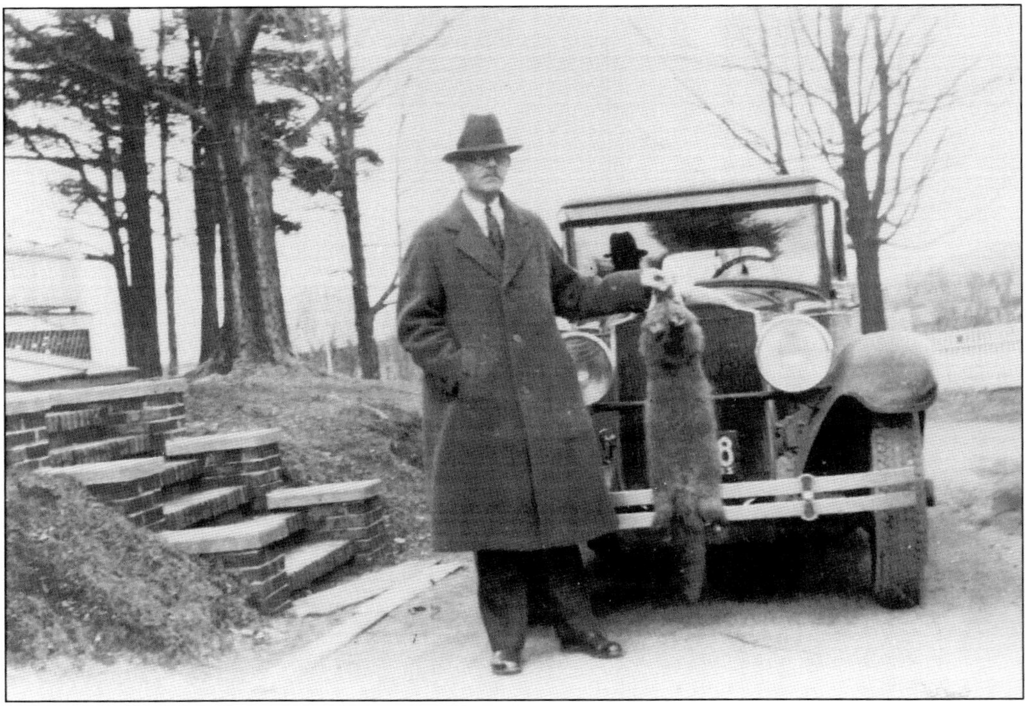

The Kimballs lived near the end of High Street on a hill that had a scenic view of the Nashua River. Mr. Kimball owned a mill in Gilmanton, New Hampshire, but in his spare time enjoyed fox hunting. Standing at his back steps he proudly displays his catch.

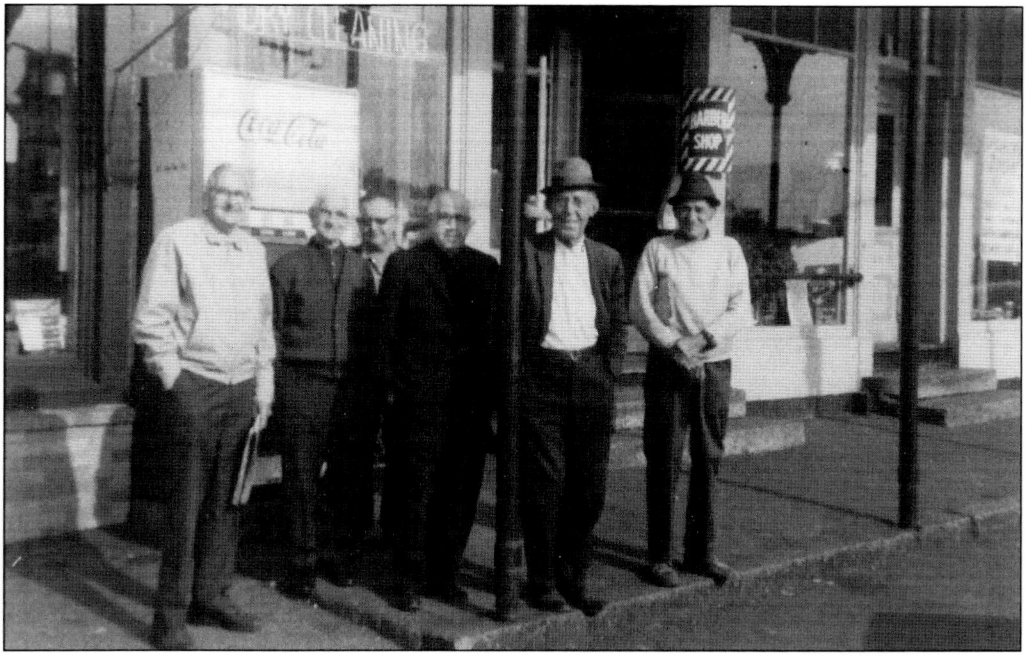

The "boys" met every day outside the paper store in East Pepperell to discuss town news and world affairs. This picture was taken in 1968 of, from left to right, Ted Gagnon, Ed Gagnon, Pat Walsh, Father Flynn, Mike Morrissey, and James Dunn.

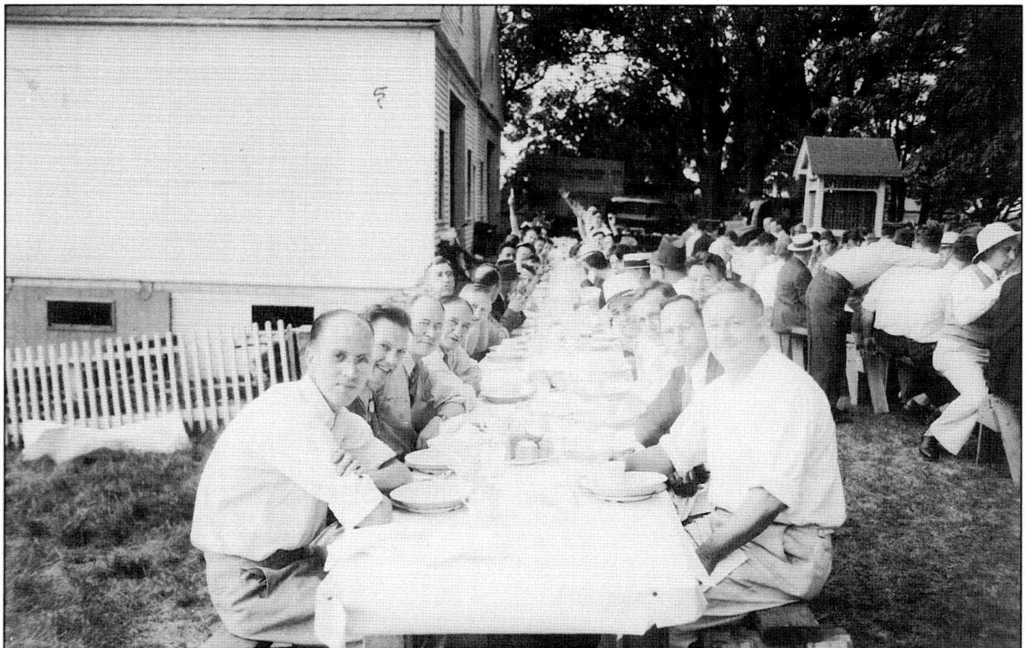

The Pepperell Town Club hosted a catered outdoor party *c.* 1940 at the large barn on Oak Hill now owned by Jim Dunn. On the left, second from the front is Fred Cobb, fourth from the front is James Dunn, fifth from the front is George Shultz, and behind them is Jim Attridge. First on the right is Ralph Buck; fourth back on the right is Bob Yuetter.

ACKNOWLEDGMENTS

I want to extend my heartfelt thanks to the many people who have helped this book come together by sharing their pictures, family histories, maps, and stories, and by filling in those empty spots in my memory. Particular thanks go to Chet Babineau for sharing his great collection, to Evelyn Hamilton for her help with mill history, to Patrick McNabb for his maps, and also to Jerrilyn and Paul Bozicas, Bob Trotter, Peter Smith, Frank Dunn, Dan Nelson, and Sarah Bosley for their pictures and postcards.

Two wonderful collections of pictures and memorabilia that went into this book have come from historians who are no longer here, but have left behind an inspiring legacy of the past. Lyman Robbin's collection of pictures and many historical articles, now stored in the genealogy room of the Lawrence Library, offers an invaluable look at what life was like in earlier days. Many thanks are in order to Jeanne Palmer and everyone at the library for all their help and for putting up with my endless questions and requests.

The second archive of early history was compiled by my grandfather, Joseph A. Saunders, who fortunately for me was an inveterate collector and left behind a treasure trove of town and family memorabilia. Over the years I have had a fascinating look at the past through his eyes.

A very special thanks goes to Maryjane and Jim Dunn for all the time they spent reminiscing and not only sharing photographs of family and friends, but also opening their home to me, feeding me, and giving lots of support and encouragement.